Benjamin S. Heath

Labor and Finance Revolution

Benjamin S. Heath

Labor and Finance Revolution

ISBN/EAN: 9783743320659

Manufactured in Europe, USA, Canada, Australia, Japa

Cover: Foto ©ninafisch / pixelio.de

Manufactured and distributed by brebook publishing software (www.brebook.com)

Benjamin S. Heath

Labor and Finance Revolution

INTRODUCTION.

To Liberty and Labor this volume is respectfully dedicated. In presenting it to the public the author is not unmindful of the responsibility resting upon him, and he has therefore, with scrupulous care and conscientious regard for the best interests of his fellow countrymen, endeavored to treat fairly, honorably, truthfully, but fearlessly the various subjects discussed.

In this country, where the government, the laws, the political, social, financial and educational institutions are just what the majority choose to make them, it is of the most vital importance that this majority be properly educated, so that these institutions may promote the general welfare.

Humanity is groaning and dying upon the rack of false and pernicious theories—theories based upon the serfdom and degradation of the masses.

From time immemorial, a law-favored and a law-making aristocratic few, have rolled in idle luxury at the expense of the toiling many.

They have devised, promulgated, and confirmed in the human mind, political as well as religious dogmas, both degrading and enslaving, which have become so deeply and firmly rooted that it is next to impossible to eradicate them.

God in His wisdom and benevolence placed the whole human family upon the stream of time, and furnished all with the necessary means and facilities for a safe and prosperous voyage.

He provided ample resources to gratify every normal desire, hope and aspiration of man; and had not avarice, selfishness and ambition confiscated the patrimony of unborn generations, the world to-day might have been an Eden, and men, knowing neither want nor misery, would have been at peace with one another, and in harmony with every department of nature.

The mission of the age is to restore to humanity its confiscated patrimony, to eradicate false and pernicious theories, and to establish society upon the rock of Eternal Truth, Justice and Equality. To do this, old errors must be exposed, their dangers and evil tendencies clearly demonstrated, and truth so plainly illustrated that he who runs may read and understand.

Every man of mature age has seen and experienced " good times " and " hard times."

Many remember the prosperous days of 1855 and '56, and many a financial wreck to-day dates its misfortunes to the crash of '57.

In 1865 there were but 530 business failures in the United States, with liabilities but a trifle over $8,000,-000. In 1875 there were 7,044 business failures, with a loss of over $200,000,000.

Why this change in ten years?

Why were all departments of trade and all kinds of labor active and prosperous in 1855 and 1865, and why the reverse in the years that immediately succeeded?

The resources of nature had not dried up.

The earth had not refused her annual abundance.

The sun continued to shine, the rains to fall, and the seasons to come and go.

The energies of man had not abated or his wants diminished.

The cattle on a thousand hills, the fish of the sea, the birds of the air, and the beasts of the forest, as well as their aboriginal competitor, fared as sumptuously, and were supplied as abundantly during the periods of embarrassed, bankrupted, starving and demoralized civilization, as ever.

Hard times, then, as well as the bankruptcies, enforced idleness, starvation, and the crime, misery and moral degradation growing out of conditions like the present, being unnatural, not in accordance with, or the result of any natural law, must be attributed to that kind of unwise and pernicious legislation which history proves to have produced similar results in all ages of the world.

It is the mission of the age to correct these errors in human legislation, to adopt and establish policies and systems, in accord with, rather than in opposition to divine law.

The aim of government should be to protect man in his natural rights, "to insure domestic tranquility," "to promote the general welfare," and to insure the blessings of liberty.

No one will deny but these objects have been shamefully neglected.

The rights to sin, starve and suffer, are about the only ones vouchsafed to American toilers to-day.

The times aggravate and provoke discord and violence, and threaten anarchy rather than peace and tranquility.

The finance legislation of the past few years has been disastrous to the general welfare; it has deprived the masses of the blessings of liberty, and if allowed to remain in force, that blessed boon must sooner or later become erased from our inventory of inheritance, and the sons of Revolutionary sires consigned to that doom to which the same system has subjected the toilers of the Old World.

Should this volume aid in convincing any number of my fellow countrymen of the correctness of the principles and policy it advocates, it will vindicate the judgment of those who induced me to prepare it for publication; and should it be the means of enlisting any number of recruits for the little army now being organized to revolutionize the social, political, and financial institutions of the age, so as to emancipate labor, and establish society upon the basis of Justice, Equity and Human Rights, it will gratify the most ardent wish of

THE AUTHOR.

CHICAGO, ILL., 1880.

CONTENTS.

INTRODUCTION 3
DECLARATION OF INDEPENDENCE 11
CONSTITUTION OF THE UNITED STATES 13

CHAPTER I.
THE COMING REVOLUTION 27

CHAPTER II.
OUR RESOURCES 41

CHAPTER III.
CAUSE OF THE DARK AGES 44
    Effects of Currency Contraction 49

CHAPTER IV.
NATURE AND FUNCTIONS OF MONEY 54
    Material of Money 58
    Antiquity of the Greenback System 60
    Power to Create Money 64
    Value 69
    Price 73

CHAPTER V.
COLONIAL MONEY 75

CHAPTER VI.
CONTINENTAL MONEY 79
    The first United States Bank 88
    The second United States Bank 91
    State Banks 94

CHAPTER VII.
BANK OF VENICE 98

CHAPTER VIII.

METALLIC MONEY..104
   Not a Standard of Value..................................106
   Digest of Coinage Acts...................................112
   Coin in the United States................................112
   The World's Annual Production of Gold and Silver.........123
   Annual Consumption in the Arts...........................124
   Gold, Silver and Base Metal in Europe....................124
   Annual Production from American Mines....................125
   Amount of Coin and Bullion in Bank of England............126
   Amount Held by the Bank of France........................126
   Silver Standard Countries................................127
   Double Standard Countries................................127
   Gold Standard Countries..................................128
   Average Gold Value of Greenbacks from 1864 to 1878.......128
   Why and How Silver was Demonetized.......................128

CHAPTER IX.

NATIONAL BANKS...133
   Legal Tender of Bank Notes...............................134
   National Bank Circulation................................134
   Security of Bank Notes...................................137
   Amount Outstanding.......................................137
   Circulation of Bank of France............................137
   Number of Banks, Capital, Surplus, and Profits...........138
   Imperial Bank of Germany.................................138
   Bank Taxation..139
   Origin of Bank Notes.....................................140
   Constitutionality of Bank Notes..........................143

CHAPTER X.

LEGAL TENDER PAPER MONEY.......................................147
   Amount of Legal Tender Paper Money in the World..........147
   The Greenback..148
   Constitutionality of the Legal Tender Act—Decision of the
      Supreme Court...153

CHAPTER XI.

THE PUBLIC DEBT..158
    Of France, England and America compared................162

CHAPTER XII.

DIGEST OF FINANCE LEGISLATION SINCE 1860....................168

CHAPTER XIII.

THE BOND AGE..183

CHAPTER XIV.

TABLES..188
    What the Bonds Cost......................................188
    Foreign Coins..189
    Monthly Range of Gold, 1862 to 1868......................190
    Amount of Paper Currency, 1854 to 1879...................191
    Refunding..192
    Bonds to Mature 1880 and 1881............................192
    Exports and Imports......................................193
    Agricultural Products....................................193
    Money in the Country.....................................193
    Debts, Revenues, etc., of Nations........................194
    Public Debt of the United States from 1791 to 1879.......195
    Population, Capitals, and Areas of Nations...............196
    Table of Prices for Fifty Years..........................197
    Compound Interest Table..................................199
    Value of Farm Products, 1878, 1879.......................200
    Importation of Specie....................................201
    Power of Interest to Rob.................................201
    The Increasing Value of Money............................202
    Salaries of Public Officers..............................203
    Supreme Court of the United States.......................204
    Business Failures..205
    Circulation and Specie of State Banks....................206
    Popular Vote of 1856.....................................207
        "   " of 1876..................................208

PART SECOND.

CHAPTER I.
THE RIGHTS OF MAN..209

CHAPTER II.
THE LAND QUESTION.......................................214

CHAPTER III.
DEBT AND USURY..224

CHAPTER IV.
NATIONAL CONVENTIONS....................................233

CHAPTER V.
GREENBACK LABOR PLATFORM................................239
   Jefferson's Political Maxims.........................241

CHAPTER VI
WHAT CONGRESS HAS DONE FOR SHYLOCK......................242

CHAPTER VII.
OUR FLAT-HEAD POLICY....................................246

CHAPTER VIII.
THE GREAT NATIONAL BEAR.................................249

CHAPTER IX.
ENGLAND'S AMERICAN POLICY...............................252

CHAPTER X.
THE ARROGANCE OF CAPITAL................................258

CHAPTER XI.
A FARMERS' REPUBLIC.....................................264

CHAPTER XII.
CONCLUSION..277
THE DEMON TASK MASTER (POEM)............................282

APPENDIX.
NOTES, QUESTIONS AND ANSWERS........................284–302

THE DECLARATION OF INDEPENDENCE.

When, in the course of human events, it becomes necessary for one people to dissolve the political bands which have connected them with another, and to assume among the powers of the earth, the separate and equal station to which the laws of nature and of nature's God entitles them, a decent respect to the opinions of mankind requires that they should declare the causes which impel them to the separation.

We hold these truths to be self-evident, that all men are created equal; that they are endowed by their Creator with certain inalienable rights; that among these are life, liberty and the pursuit of happiness. That to secure these rights, governments are instituted among men, deriving their just powers from the consent of the governed; that, whenever any form of government becomes destructive of these ends, it is the right of the people to alter or to abolish it, and to institute a new government, laying its foundations on such principles, and organizing its powers in such form, as to them shall seem most likely to effect their safety and happiness. Prudence, indeed, will dictate that governments long established should not be changed for light and transient causes; and, accordingly, all experience hath shown that mankind are more disposed to suffer, while evils are sufferable, than to right them by abolishing the forms to which they are accustomed. But when a long train of abuses and usurpations, pursuing invariably the same object, evinces a design to reduce them under absolute despotism, it is their right, it is their duty to throw off such government, and to provide new guards for their future security. Such has been the patient sufferance of these colonies, and such is now the necessity which constrains them to alter their former systems of government. The history of the present King of Great Britain is a history of repeated injuries and usurpations, all having in direct object the establishment of an absolute tyranny over these States. To prove this let facts be submitted to a candid world:

He has refused his assent to laws the most wholesome and necessary for the public good.

He has forbidden his Governors to pass laws of immediate and pressing importance, unless suspended in their operation till his assent should be obtained; and when so suspended, he has utterly neglected to attend to them.

He has refused to pass other laws for the accommodation of large districts of people, unless those people would relinquish the right of representation in the legislature; a right inestimable to them, and formidable to tyrants only.

He has called together legislative bodies at places unusual, uncomfortable, and distant from the depository of their public records, for the sole measure of fatiguing them into compliance with his measures.

He has dissolved representative houses repeatedly for opposing, with manly firmness, his invasions on the rights of the people.

He has refused, for a long time after such dissolution, to cause others to be elected; whereby the legislative powers, incapable of annihilation, have returned to the people at large for their exercise; the State remaining in the meantime exposed to all the danger of invasion from without, and convulsions within.

He has endeavored to prevent the population of these States; for that purpose, obstructing the laws for naturalization of foreigners; refusing to pass others to encourage their migration hither, and raising the conditions of new appropriations of lands.

He has obstructed the administration of justice, by refusing his assent to laws for establishing judiciary powers.

He has made judges dependent on his will alone, for the tenure of their offices, and the amount and payment of their salaries.

He has erected a multitude of new offices, and sent hither swarms of officers to harass our people, and eat out their substance.

He has kept among us in times of peace, standing armies, without the consent of our legislature.

He has affected to render the military independent of, and superior to, the civil power.

He has combined with others, to subject us to a jurisdiction foreign to our constitution, and unacknowledged by our laws; giving his assent to their acts of pretended legislation.

For quartering large bodies of armed troops among us:

For protecting them, by a mock trial, from punishment for any murders which they should commit on the inhabitants of these States:

For cutting off our trade with all parts of the world:

For imposing taxes on us without our consent:

For depriving us, in many cases, of the benefits of trial by jury:

For transporting us beyond the seas to be tried for pretended offenses:

For abolishing the free system of English laws in a neighboring province, establishing therein an arbitrary government, and enlarging its boundaries, so as to render it at once an example and fit instrument for introducing the same absolute rule into these colonies:

For taking away our charters, abolishing our most valuable laws, and altering fundamentally, the powers of our government:

For suspending our own legislatures, and declaring themselves invested with power to legislate for us in all cases whatsoever.

He has abdicated government here, by declaring us out of his protection, and waging war against us.

He has plundered our seas, ravaged our coasts, burnt our towns, and destroyed the lives of our people.

He is, at this time, transporting large armies of foreign mercenaries to complete the work of death, desolation, and tyranny, already begun, with circumstances of cruelty and perfidy scarcely paralleled in the most barbarous ages, and totally unworthy the head of a civilized nation.

He has constrained our fellow-citizens, taken captive on the high seas, to bear arms against their country, to become the executioners of their friends and brethren, or to fall themselves by their hands.

He has excited domestic insurrections amongst us, and has endeavored to bring on the inhabitants of our frontiers, the merciless Indian savages, whose known rule of warfare is an undistinguished destruction of all ages, sexes and conditions.

In every stage of these oppressions, we have petitioned for redress, in the most humble terms; our repeated petitions have been answered only by repeated injury. A prince, whose character is thus marked by every act which may define a tyrant, is unfit to be the ruler of a free people.

Nor have we been wanting in attention to our British brethren. We have warned them from time to time, of attempts made by their Legislature to extend an unwarrantable jurisdiction over us. We have reminded them of the circumstances of our emigration and settlement here. We have appealed to their native justice and magnanimity, and we have conjured them, by the ties of our common kindred, to disavow these usurpations, which would inevitably interrupt our connections and correspondence. They, too, have been deaf to the voice of justice and consanguinity. We must, therefore, acquiesce in the necessity which denounces our separation, and hold them, as we hold the rest of mankind, enemies in war, in peace, friends.

We, therefore, the representatives of the UNITED STATES OF AMERICA, in GENERAL CONGRESS assembled, appealing to the Supreme Judge of the World for the rectitude of our intentions, do, in the name, and by the authority of the good people of these colonies, solemnly publish and declare: That these United Colonies are, and of right ought to be FREE AND INDEPENDENT STATES; that they are absolved from all allegiance to the British crown, and that political connection between them and the State of Great Britain is, and ought to be totally dissolved; and that, as FREE AND INDEPENDENT STATES, they have full power to levy war, conclude peace, contract alliances, establish commerce, and do all other acts and things which INDEPENDENT STATES may of right do. And, for the support of this declaration, and in a firm reliance upon the protection of DIVINE PROVIDENCE, we mutually pledge to each other our lives, our fortunes, and our sacred honor.

CONSTITUTION OF THE UNITED STATES OF AMERICA.

We the People of the United States, in order to form a more perfect Union, establish justice, insure domestic tranquility, provide for the common defense, promote the general welfare, and secure the blessings of liberty to ourselves and our posterity, do ordain and establish this Constitution for the United States of America.

ARTICLE I.

SECTION I.—All legislative powers herein granted shall be vested in a Congress of the United States, which shall consist of a Senate and House of Representatives.

SEC. II.—1. The House of Representatives shall be composed of members chosen every second year by the people of the several States, and electors in each State shall have the qualifications requisite for electors of the most numerous branch of the State legislature.

2. No person shall be a representative who shall not have attained to the age of twenty-five years, and been seven years a citizen of the United States, and who shall not, when elected, be an inhabitant of that State in which he shall be chosen.

3. Representatives and direct taxes shall be apportioned among the several States which may be included within this Union, according to their respective numbers, which shall be determined by adding to the whole number of free persons, including those bound to service for a term of years, and excluding Indians not taxed, three-fifths of all other persons. The actual enumeration shall be made within three years after the first meeting of the Congress of the United States, and within every subsequent term of ten years, in such manner as they shall by law direct. The number of representatives shall not exceed one for every thirty thousand, but each State shall have at least one representative; and until such enumeration shall be made the State of New Hampshire shall be entitled to choose three; Massachusetts, eight; Rhode Island and Providence Plantations, one; Connecticut, five; New York, six; New Jersey, four; Pennsylvania, eight; Delaware, one; Maryland, six; Virginia, ten; North Carolina, five; South Carolina, five, and Georgia, three.

4. When vacancies happen in the representation from any State, the executive authority thereof shall issue writs of election to fill such vacancies.

5. The House of Representatives shall choose their speaker and other officers; and shall have the sole power of impeachment.

SEC. III.—1. The Senate of the United States shall be composed of two senators from each State, chosen by the legislature thereof, for six years; and each senator shall have one vote.

2. Immediately after they shall be assembled in consequence of the first election, they shall be divided as equally as may be into three classes. The seats of the senators of the first class shall be vacated at the expiration of the second year, the second class at the expiration of the fourth year, and of the third class at the expiration of the sixth year, so that one-third may be chosen every second year; and if vacancies happen by resignation, or otherwise, during the recess of the legislature of any State, the executive thereof may make temporary appointments until the next meeting of the legislature, which shall then fill such vacancies.

3. No person shall be a senator who shall not have attained the age of thirty years, and been nine years a citizen of the United States, and who shall not, when elected, be an inhabitant of that State for which he shall be chosen.

4. The Vice President of the United States shall be President of the Senate, but shall have no vote, unless they be equally divided.

5. The Senate shall choose their other officers, and also a President *pro tempore*, in the absence of the Vice President, or when he shall exercise the office of President of the United States.

6. The Senate shall have the sole power to try all impeachments,

When sitting for that purpose they shall be on oath or affirmation. When the President of the United States is tried, the Chief Justice shall preside; and no person shall be convicted without the concurrence of two-thirds of the members present.

7. Judgment in cases of impeachment shall not extend further than to removal from office, and disqualification to hold and enjoy any office of honor, trust or profit under the United States; but the party convicted shall nevertheless be liable and subject to indictment, trial, judgment and punishment, according to law.

Sec. IV.--1. The times, places and manner of holding elections for senators and representatives, shall be prescribed in the State by the legislature thereof; but the Congress may at any time by law make or alter such regulations, except as to the places of choosing senators.

2. The Congress shall assemble at least once in every year, and such meeting shall be on the first Monday in December, unless they shall by law appoint a different day.

Sec. V.--1. Each house shall be judge of the elections, returns and qualifications of its own members, and a majority of each shall constitute a quorum to do business; but a smaller number may adjourn from day to day, and may be authorized to compel the attendance of absent members, in such manner, and under such penalties as each house may provide.

2. Each house may determine the rules of its proceedings, punish its members for disorderly behavior, and, with the concurrence of two-thirds, expel a member.

3. Each house shall keep a journal of its proceedings, and from time to time publish the same, excepting such parts as may in their judgment require secrecy; and the yeas and nays of the members of either house on any question shall, at the desire of one-fifth of those present, be entered on the journal.

4. Neither house, during the session of Congress, shall, without the consent of the other, adjourn for more than three days, nor to any other place than that in which the two houses shall be sitting.

Sec. VI.--1. The senators and representatives shall receive a compensation for their services, to be ascertained by law, and paid out of the Treasury of the United States. They shall in all cases, except treason, felony, and breach of the peace, be privileged from arrest during their attendance at the session of their respective houses, and going to and returning from the same; and for any speech or debate in either house, they shall not be questioned in any other place.

2. No senator or representative shall, during the time for which he was elected, be appointed to any civil office under the authority of the United States, which shall have been created, or the emoluments whereof shall have been increased during such time; and no person holding any office under the United States, shall be a member of either house during his continuance in office.

Sec. VII.--1. All bills for raising revenue shall originate in the House of Representatives; but the Senate may propose or concur with amendments as on other bills.

2. Every bill which shall have passed the House of Representatives and the Senate, shall, before it become a law, be presented to the President of the United States; if he approve he shall sign it; but if

not he shall return it, with his objections, to that house in which it shall have originated, who shall enter the objections at large on their journal, and proceed to reconsider it. If after such reconsideration two-thirds of that house shall agree to pass the bill, it shall be sent, together with the objections, to the other house, by which it shall likewise be reconsidered, and if approved by two-thirds of that house, it shall become a law. But in all such cases the votes of both houses shall be determined by yeas and nays, and the names of the persons voting for and against the bill shall be entered on the journal of each house respectively. If any bill shall not be returned by the President within ten days (Sunday excepted) after it shall have been presented to him, the same shall be a law, in like manner as if he had signed it, unless the Congress by their adjournment prevent its return, in which case it shall not be a law.

3. Every order, resolution, or vote to which the concurrence of the Senate and House of Representatives may be necessary (except on a question of adjournment) shall be presented to the President of the United States; and before the same shall take effect, shall be approved by him, or being disapproved by him, shall be re-passed by two-thirds of the Senate and House of Representatives, according to the rules and limitations prescribed in the case of a bill.

SEC. VIII.—The Congress shall have power—

1. To lay and collect taxes, duties, imposts and excises, to pay the debts and provide for the common defense and general welfare of the United States; but all duties, imposts and excises shall be uniform throughout the United States.

2. To borrow money on the credit of the United States.

3. To regulate commerce with foreign nations, and among the several States, and with the Indian tribes.

4. To establish an uniform rule of naturalization, and uniform laws on the subject of bankruptcies throughout the United States.

5. To coin money, regulate the value thereof, and of foreign coin, and fix the standard of weights and measures.

6. To provide for the punishment of counterfeiting the securities and current coin of the United States.

7. To establish post offices and post roads.

8. To promote the progress of science and useful arts, by securing for limited times to authors and inventors the exclusive right to their respective writings and discoveries.

9. To constitute tribunals inferior to the Supreme Court.

10. To define and punish piracies and felonies committed on the high seas, and offenses against the law of nations.

11. To declare war, grant letters of marque and reprisal, and make rules concerning captures on land and water.

12. To raise and support armies, but no appropriation of money to that use shall be for a longer term than two years.

13. To provide and maintain a navy.

14. To make rules for the government and regulation of the land and naval forces.

15. To provide for calling forth the militia to execute the laws of the Union, suppress insurrections and repel invasions.

16. To provide for organizing, arming, and disciplining the militia,

and for governing such part of them as may be employed in the service of the United States, reserving to the States respectively, the appointment of the officers, and the authority of training the militia according to the discipline prescribed by Congress.

17. To exercise exclusive legislation in all cases whatsoever, over such district (not exceeding ten miles square) as may, by cession of particular States, and the acceptance of Congress, become the seat of the government of the United States, and to exercise like authority over all places purchased by the consent of the legislature of the State in which the same shall be, for the erection of forts, magazines, arsenals, dock-yards, and other needful buildings; and

18. To make all laws which shall be necessary and proper for carrying into execution the foregoing powers, and other powers vested by this Constitution in the government of the United States, or in any department or officer thereof.

SEC. IX.—1. The migration or importation of such persons as any of the States now existing shall think proper to admit, shall not be prohibited by the Congress prior to the year one thousand, eight hundred and eight, but a tax or duty may be imposed on such importation, not exceeding ten dollars for each person.

2. The privilege of the writ of *habeas corpus* shall not be suspended, unless when in cases of rebellion or invasion the public safety may require it.

3. No bill of attainder or *ex post facto* law shall be passed.

4. No capitation, or other direct, tax shall be laid, unless in proportion to the census or enumeration hereinbefore directed to be taken.

5. No tax or duty shall be laid on articles exported from any State.

6. No preference shall be given by any regulation of commerce or revenue to the ports of one State over those of another; nor shall vessels bound to, or from, one State, be obliged to enter, clear, or pay duties in another.

7. No money shall be drawn from the treasury, but in consequence of appropriations made by law; and a regular statement and account of the receipts and expenditures of all public money shall be published from time to time.

8. No title of nobility shall be granted by the United States; and no person holding any office of profit and trust under them, shall, without the consent of the Congress, accept any present, emolument, office, or title, of any kind whatever, from any king, prince, or foreign State.

SEC. X.—1. No State shall enter into any treaty, alliance, or confederation; grant letters of marque and reprisal; coin money; emit bills of credit; make anything but gold and silver coin a tender in payment of debts; pass any bill of attainder, *ex post facto* law, or impairing the obligation of contracts, or grant any title of nobility.

2. No State shall, without the consent of the Congress, lay any imposts or duties on imports or exports, except what may be absolutely necessary for executing its inspection law; and the net produce of all duties and imposts, laid by any State on imports or exports, shall be for the use of the Treasury of the United States; and all such laws shall be subject to the revision and control of the Congress.

3. No State shall, without the consent of Congress, lay any duty of

tonnage, keep troops, or ships of war in time of peace, enter into any agreement or compact with another State, or with a foreign power, or engage in war, unless actually invaded, or in such imminent danger as will not admit of delay.

ARTICLE II.

SECTION I.--1. The executive power shall be vested in a President of the United States of America. He shall hold his office during the term of four years, and, together with the Vice President, chosen for the same term, be elected as follows:

2. Each State shall appoint, in such manner as the legislature thereof may direct, a number of electors, equal to the whole number of senators and representatives to which the State may be entitled in the Congress; but no senator or representative, or person holding an office of trust or profit under the United States, shall be appointed an elector.

Annulled. See Amendments, Article XII.

3. The electors shall meet in their respective States, and vote by ballot for two persons, of whom one at least shall not be an inhabitant of the same State with themselves. And they shall make a list of all the persons voted for, and of the number of votes for each; which list they shall sign and certify, and transmit sealed to the seat of government of the United States, directed to the President of the Senate. The President of the Senate shall, in the presence of the Senate and House of Representatives, open all the certificates, and the votes shall then be counted. The person having the greatest number of votes shall be the President, if such number be a majority of the whole number of electors appointed; and if there be more than one who have such majority, and have an equal number of votes, then the House of Representatives shall immediately choose by ballot one of them for President; and if no person shall have a majority, then from the five highest on the list the said House shall in like manner choose the President. But in choosing the President the votes shall be taken by States, the representation from each State having one vote; a quorum for this purpose shall consist of a member or members from two-thirds of the States, and a majority of all the States shall be necessary to a choice. In every case, after the choice of the President, the person having the greatest number of votes of the electors shall be the Vice President. But if there should remain two or more who have equal votes, the Senate shall choose from them the Vice President.

4. The Congress may determine the time of choosing the electors, and the day on which they shall give their votes; which day shall be the same throughout the United States.

5. No person except a natural-born citizen, or a citizen of the United States, at the time of the adoption of this Constitution, shall be eligible to the office of President; neither shall any person be eligible to that office who shall not have attained to the age of thirty-five years, and been fourteen years a resident within the United States.

6. In case of the removal of the President from office, or of his death, resignation or inability to discharge the powers and duties of

the said office, the same shall devolve upon the Vice President, and the Congress may by law provide for the case of removal, death, resignation or inability, both of the President and Vice President, declaring what officer shall then act as President, and such officer shall act accordingly, until the disability be removed, or a President shall be elected.

7. The President shall, at stated times, receive for his services, a compensation, which shall neither be increased nor diminished during the period for which he shall have been elected, and he shall not receive within that period any other emolument from the United States, or any of them.

8. Before he enter on the execution of his office, he shall take the following oath or affirmation:

" I do solemnly swear (or affirm) that I will faithfully execute the office of President of the United States, and will to the best of my ability, preserve, protect and defend the Constitution of the United States."

Sec. II.—1. The President shall be the Commander-in-Chief of the Army and Navy of the United States, and of the militia of the several States, when called into the actual service of the United States; he may require the opinion, in writing, of the principal officer in each of the executive departments, upon any subject relating to the duties of their respective offices, and he shall have power to grant reprieves and pardons for offenses against the United States, except in cases of impeachment.

2. He shall have power, by and with the advice and consent of the Senate, to make treaties, provided two-thirds of the Senate present concur; and he shall nominate, and by and with the advice and consent of the Senate, shall appoint ambassadors, and other public ministers and consuls, Judges of the Supreme Court, and all other officers of the United States, whose appointments herein are not otherwise provided for, and which shall be established by law; but the Congress may by law vest the appointment of such inferior officers, as they may think proper, in the President alone, in the courts of law, or in the heads of departments.

3. The President shall have power to fill up all vacancies that may happen during the recess of the Senate, by granting commissions which shall expire at the end of their next session.

Sec. III.—He shall from time to time give to the Congress information of the state of the Union, and recommend to their consideration such measures as he shall judge necessary and expedient; he may, on extraordinary occasions, convene both houses, or either of them, and, in case of disagreement between them, with respect to the time of adjournment, he may adjourn them to such time as he shall think proper; he shall receive ambassadors and other public ministers; he shall take care that the laws be faithfully executed, and shall commission all the officers of the United States.

Sec. IV.—The President, Vice President and all civil officers of the United States, shall be removed from office on impeachment for, and conviction of, treason, bribery, or other high crimes and misdemeanors.

Article III.

Section I.—The judicial power of the United States shall be vested in one Supreme Court, and in such inferior courts as the Congress may from time to time ordain and establish. The judges, both of the Supreme and inferior courts, shall hold their offices during good behavior, and shall, at stated times, receive for their services, a compensation, which shall not be diminished during their continuance in office.

Sec. II.—1. The judicial power shall extend to all cases, in law and equity, arising under this Constitution, the laws of the United States, and treaties made, or which shall be made, under their authority; to all cases affecting ambassadors, other public ministers and consuls; to all cases of admiralty and maritime jurisdiction; to controversies to which the United States shall be a party; to controversies between two or more States; between a State and citizens of another State; between citizens of different States; between citizens of the same State, claiming lands under grants of different States; and between a State, or the citizens thereof, and foreign States, citizens or subjects.

2. In all cases affecting ambassadors, other public ministers and consuls, and those in which a State shall be party, the Supreme Court shall have original jurisdiction. In all the other cases before mentioned, the Supreme Court shall have appellate jurisdiction, both as to law and fact, with such exceptions, and under such regulations as the Congress shall make.

3. The trial of all crimes, except in cases of impeachment, shall be by jury; and such trial shall be held in the State where the said crimes shall have been committed; but when not committed within any State, the trial shall be at such place or places as the Congress may by law have directed.

Sec. III.—1. Treason against the United States, shall consist only in levying war against them, or in adhering to their enemies, giving them aid and comfort. No person shall be convicted of treason unless on the testimony of two witnesses to the same overt act, or on confession in open court.

2. The Congress shall have power to declare the punishment of treason, but no attainder of treason shall work corruption of blood, or forfeiture except during the life of the person attained.

Article IV.

Section I.—Full faith and credit shall be given in each State to the public acts, records and judicial proceedings of every other State. And the Congress may by general laws prescribe the manner in which such acts, records and proceedings shall be proved, and the effect thereof.

Sec. II.—1. The citizens of each State shall be entitled to all privileges and immunities of citizens in the several States.

2. A person charged in any State with treason, felony, or other crime, who shall flee from justice, and be found in another State,

shall on demand of the executive authority of the State from which he fled, be delivered up to be removed to the State having jurisdiction of the crime.

3. No person held to service or labor in one State, under the laws thereof, escaping into another, shall, in consequence of any law or regulation therein, be discharged from such service or labor, but shall be delivered up on claim of the party to whom such service or labor may be due.

SEC. III.—1. New States may be admitted by the Congress into this Union; but no new State shall be formed or erected within the jurisdiction of any other State; nor any State be formed by the junction of two or more States, or parts of States, without the consent of the legislatures of the States concerned as well as of the Congress.

2. The Congress shall have power to dispose of and make all needful rules and regulations respecting the territory or other property belonging to the United States; and nothing in this Constitution shall be so construed as to prejudice any claims of the United States, or any particular State.

SEC. IV.—The United States shall guarantee to every State in this Union a republican form of government, and shall protect each of them against invasion; and, on application of the legislature, or of the executive (when the legislature can not be convened) against domestic violence.

ARTICLE V.

The Congress, whenever two-thirds of both houses shall deem it necessary, shall propose amendments to this Constitution, or, on the application of the legislatures of two-thirds of the several States, shall call a convention for proposing amendments, which, in either case, shall be valid to all intents and purposes, as part of this Constitution, when ratified by the legislatures of three-fourths of the several States, or by conventions in three-fourths thereof, as the one or the other mode of ratification may be proposed by the Congress; provided that no amendment which may be made prior to the year one thousand eight hundred and eight shall in any manner affect the first and fourth clauses in the ninth section of the first article; and that no State, without its consent, shall be deprived of its equal suffrage in the Senate.

ARTICLE VI.

1. All debts contracted and engagements entered into, before the adoption of this Constitution, shall be as valid against the United States under this Constitution, as under the Confederation.

2. This Constitution, and the laws of the United States which shall be made in pursuance thereof; and all treaties made, or which shall be made, under the authority of the United States, shall be the supreme law of the land; and the judges in every State shall be bound thereby, any thing in the Constitution or laws of any State to the contrary notwithstanding.

3. The senators and representatives before mentioned, and the members of the several State legislatures, and all executive and judicial officers, both of the United States and of the several States shall be bound by oath or affirmation, to support the Constitution; but no religious test shall ever be required as a qualification to any office or public trust under the United States.

Article VII.

The ratification of the conventions of nine States shall be sufficient for the establishment of this Constitution between the States so ratifying the same.

Done in convention by the unanimous consent of the States present the seventh day of September in the year of our Lord one thousand, seven hundred and eighty-seven, and of the Independence of the United States of America the twelfth. In witness whereof, we have hereunto subscribed our names,

G°: WASHINGTON,
President, and Deputy from Virginia.

The Constitution was adopted by the Convention on the 17th of September, 1787, appointed in pursuance of the Resolution of the Confederation of the 21st of February, 1787, and ratified by the Conventions of the several States, as follows:

Delaware, December 7th, 1787, unanimously.
Pennsylvania, December 12th, 1787, by a vote of 46 to 23.
New Jersey, December 18th, 1787, unanimously.
Georgia, January 2d, 1788, unanimously.
Connecticut, January 9th, 1788, by a vote of 128 to 40.
Massachusetts, February 6th, 1788, by a vote of 187 to 168.
Maryland, April 28th, 1788, by a vote of 63 to 12.
South Carolina, May 23d, 1788, by a vote of 149 to 73.
New Hampshire, June 21st, 1788, by a vote of 57 to 47.
Virginia, June 25th, 1788, by a vote of 89 to 79.
New York, July 26th, 1788, by a vote of 30 to 25.
North Carolina, November 21st, 1789, by a vote of 193 to 75.
Rhode Island, May 29th, 1790, by a majority of 2.
Vermont, January 10th, 1791, by a vote of 105 to 4.

Declared ratified by resolution of the Congress, September 13th, 1788.

The first Congress under its provisions was to have met in New York, March 4th, 1789, but on that day no quorum was present in either House. The House of Representatives organized on the 1st of April, and the Senate secured a quorum on the 6th of April, 1789.

AMENDMENTS TO THE CONSTITUTION.

Article I.

Congress shall make no law respecting an establishment of religion, or prohibiting the free exercise thereof; or abridging the freedom of speech or of the press; or the right of the people peaceably to assemble, and to petition the government for a redress of grievances.

Article II.

A well-regulated militia being necessary to the security of a free state, the right of the people to keep and bear arms shall not be infringed.

Article III.

No soldier shall, in time of peace, be quartered in any house, without the consent of the owner, nor in time of war, but in a manner to be prescribed by law.

Article IV.

The right of the people to be secure in their persons, houses, papers, and effects, against unreasonable searches and seizures, shall not be violated, and no warrants shall issue but upon probable cause, supported by oath or affirmation, and particularly describing the place to be searched, and the persons or things to be seized.

Article V.

No person shall be held to answer for a capital, or otherwise infamous crime, unless on a presentment or indictment of a grand jury, except in cases arising in the land or naval forces, or in the militia, when in actual service in time of war or public danger; nor shall any person be subject for the same offense to be twice put in jeopardy of life or limb; nor shall be compelled in any criminal case to be a witness against himself; nor be deprived of life, liberty or property, without due process of law; nor shall public property be taken for public use, without just compensation.

Article VI.

In all criminal prosecutions, the accused shall enjoy the right to a speedy and public trial, by an impartial jury of the State and district wherein the crime shall have been committed, which district shall have been previously ascertained by law, and to be informed of the nature and cause of the accusation; to be confronted with the witnesses against him; to have compulsory process for obtaining witnesses in his favor, and to have the assistance of counsel for his defense.

Article VII.

In suits at common law, where the value in controversy shall exceed twenty dollars, the right of trial by jury shall be preserved, and no fact tried by a jury shall be otherwise re-examined in any court of the United States, than according to the rules of the common law.

Article VIII.

Excessive bail shall not be required, nor excessive fines imposed, nor cruel and unusual punishments inflicted.

Article IX.

The enumeration in the Constitution of certain rights, shall not be construed to deny or disparage others retained by the people.

Article X.

The powers not delegated to the United States by the Constitution, nor prohibited by it to the States, are reserved to the States respectively, or to the people.

Article XI.

[Proposed by Congress March 5th, 1794, and declared in force January 8, 1798.]

The judicial power of the United States shall not be construed to extend to any suit in law or equity, commenced or prosecuted against one of the United States by citizens of another State, or by citizens or subjects of any foreign state.

Article XII.

[Proposed December 12th, 1803, in the first session of the Eighth Congress, and declared in force September 25th, 1804.]

The electors shall meet in their respective States, and vote by ballot for President and Vice President, one of whom, at least, shall not be an inhabitant of the same State with themselves; they shall name in their ballots the person voted for as President, and in distinct ballots the person voted for as Vice President, and they shall make distinct lists of all persons voted for as President, and of all persons voted for as Vice President, and of the number of votes for each, which lists they shall sign and certify, and transmit sealed to the seat of the government of the United States, directed to the President of the Senate;--The President of the Senate shall, in the presence of the Senate and House of Representatives, open all the certificates and the votes shall then be counted;--the person having the greatest number of votes for President, shall be President, if such number be a majority of the whole number of electors appointed; and if no person have such majority, then from the persons having the highest numbers not exceeding three on the list of those voted for as President, the House of Representatives shall choose immediately, by ballot, the President. But in choosing the President, the votes shall be taken by States, the representation from each State having one vote; a quorum for this purpose shall consist of a member or members from two-thirds of the States, and a majority of all the States shall be necessary to a choice. And if the House of Representatives shall not choose a President whenever the right of choice shall devolve upon them, before the fourth day of March next following, then the Vice President shall act as President, as in the case of the death or other constitutional disability of the President. The person having the greatest number of votes as Vice President, shall be the Vice President, if such number be a majority of the whole number of electors appointed, and if no person have a majority, then from the two highest members on the list the Senate shall choose the Vice President; a quorum for the purpose shall consist of two-thirds of the whole number of senators, and a majority of the whole number shall be necessary to a choice. But no person constitutionally ineligible to the office of President shall be eligible to that of President of the United States.

Article XIII.

[Proposed by Congress February 1st, 1865, and declared in force December 18th, 1865.

Ratified by Arkansas, California, Connecticut, Florida, Georgia, Illinois Indiana, Iowa, Kansas, Louisiana, Maine, Maryland, Massachusetts, Michigan, Minnesota, Missouri, Nevada, New Hampshire, New Jersey, New York, North Carolina, Ohio, Oregon, Pennsylvania, Rhode Island, South Carolina, Tennessee, Vermont, Virginia, West Virginia, and Wisconsin—32 States out of 36. Ratified conditionally by Alabama and Mississippi. Rejected by Delaware and Kentucky —2. Not acted upon by Texas.]

Section 1. Neither slavery nor involuntary servitude, except as a punishment for crime whereof the party shall have been duly convicted, shall exist within the United States, or any place subject to their jurisdiction.

Sec. 2. Congress shall have power to enforce this Article by appropriate legislation.

Article XIV.

[Proposed by Congress June 16th, 1866, and declared in force July, 1868.

Ratified by Alabama, Arkansas, Connecticut, Florida, Georgia, Illinois, Indiana, Iowa, Kansas, Louisiana, Maine, Massachusetts, Michigan, Minnesota, Mississippi, Missouri, Nebraska, Nevada, New Hampshire, New Jersey, New York, North Carolina, Ohio, Oregon, Pennsylvania, Rhode Island, South Carolina, Tennessee, Texas, Vermont, Virginia, West Virginia and Wisconsin—33 States out of 37.

Of the above, Arkansas, Florida, Georgia, Louisiana, Mississippi, North Carolina, South Carolina, Texas and Virginia (9) first rejected the amendment, but finally ratified it. New Jersey and Ohio (2) rescinded their ratification.

Rejected by Delaware, Kentucky and Maryland—3.

No final action was taken by California—1.]

Section I. All persons born or naturalized in the United States, and subject to the jurisdiction thereof, are citizens of the United States, and of the State wherein they reside. No State shall make or enforce any law which shall abridge the privileges or immunities of citizens of the United States; nor shall any State deprive any person of life, liberty, or property, without due process of law; nor deny to any person within its jurisdiction the equal protection of the laws.

Sec. 2. Representatives shall be apportioned among the several States according to their respective numbers, counting the whole number of persons in each State, excluding Indians not taxed. But when the right to vote at any election for the choice of electors for President and Vice President of the United States, representatives in Congress, the executive and judicial officers of a State, or the members of the legislature thereof, is denied to any of the male inhabitants of such State, being twenty-one years of age, and citizens of the United States, or in any way abridged, except for participation in rebellion, or other crime, the basis of representation therein shall be reduced in the proportion which the number of such male citizens shall bear to the whole number of male citizens twenty-one years of age in such State.

SEC. 3. No person shall be a senator or representative in Congress, or elector of President and Vice President, or hold any office, civil or military, under the United States, or under any State, who, having previously taken an oath as a member of Congress, or as an officer of the United States, or as a member of any State legislature, or as an executive or judicial officer of any State, to support the Constitution of the United States, shall have engaged in insurrection or rebellion against the same, or given aid or comfort to the enemies thereof. But Congress may, by a two-thirds vote of each house remove such disability.

SEC. 4. The validity of the public debt of the United States, authorized by law, including debts incurred for payment of pensions and bounties for services in suppressing insurrection or rebellion, shall not be questioned. But neither the United States nor any State shall assume or pay any debt or obligation incurred in aid of insurrection or rebellion against the United States, or any claim for the loss or emancipation of any slave; but all such debts, obligations and claims shall be held illegal and void.

SEC. 5. The Congress shall have power to enforce, by appropriate legislation, the provisions of this Article.

ARTICLE XV.

[Proposed by Congress February 26th, 1869, and declared in force March 30th, 1870.

Ratified by Alabama, Arkansas, Connecticut, Florida, Georgia, Illinois, Indiana, Iowa, Kansas, Louisiana, Maine, Massachusetts, Michigan, Minnesota, Mississippi, Missouri, Nebraska, Nevada, New Hampshire, New York, North Carolina, Ohio, Pennsylvania, Rhode Island, South Carolina, Texas, Vermont, Virginia, West Virginia, and Wisconsin—30 States out of 37.

Of the above, Georgia and Ohio at first rejected but finally ratified. New York rescinded its ratification.

Rejected by California, Delaware, Kentucky, Maryland, New Jersey, and Oregon—6.

No final action was taken by Tennessee—1.]

SECTION 1. The right of citizens of the United States to vote shall not be denied or abridged by the United States or by any State on account of race, color, or previous condition of servitude.

SEC. 2. The Congress shall have power to enforce this article by appropriate legislation.

NOTE.—Another proposed amendment, styled Article XIII., was proposed by Congress to the State legislatures at the second session of the 36th Congress, March 2d, 1861:

"ART. XIII.—No amendment shall be made to the Constitution which will authorize or give to Congress the power to abolish or interfere within any State with the domestic institutions thereof, including that of persons held to labor or service by the laws of said State."

It was not acted upon by a majority of the States.

LABOR AND FINANCE REVOLUTION.

CHAPTER I.

THE COMING REVOLUTION.

The world has always contained two classes of people, one that lived by honest labor and the other that lived *off* of honest labor.

In early times the former had fixed habitations, occupied their time in tilling the soil and raising flocks and herds. They provided for their own wants; they had few incentives to crime and violence.

They were governed more by their natural instincts of justice, and respect and attachment for one another, than by arbitrary rules, hence their government was simple, democratic and inexpensive.

The other class consisted of roving bandits, who banded together under chiefs or leaders, and subsisted by swooping down upon and plundering the peaceful herders.

After years of marauding, a band, strong enough, would select a certain territory, rich in products and producers, overcome and subdue the people and then divide the spoils between themselves according to rank.

Each brigand had his portion of the territory set off to himself, and each was invested with a title to nobility according to rank, and possessions, and clothed with authority to exact from each of his serfs, or tenants, such contributions as the robber chief and his council might determine.

The chief became "monarch," his brigands "nobility," and thus was royalty and aristocracy established. That aristocracy might be limited to the royal few, and not be lost and diffused among the plebian masses, the law of primogeniture was established, entailing upon the eldest son of each noble, the exclusive right to inherit the estates and title of the father.

The throne of England was established by the chief of a Norman banditti, her titles of nobility inherited from freebooters, and her soil wrenched from its rightful owners whom they reduced to serfdom, as the curfew bell proclaimed the "Divine right" of robber rule.

Thus did bands of ruffians parcel out the world, divide it into dominions, and establish thrones on an assumption of power, for their own personal aggrandizement.

They considered the conquered not as prisoners, or citizens, but as property whose toil and products belonged to them and not to the conquered.

As civilization advanced, and robbery became obnoxious to the more sensitive and refined intelligence of the age, as royalty became ashamed of its ancestry, its successors have attempted to obliterate the history of its beginning by assuming new relations to the balance of humanity, and new appearances to cut off the entail of its disgrace, while its principles and its objects remain the same.

What was originally plunder, has assumed the softer names of *revenue* and *rent*, and the powers which royalty usurped, it affects to inherit.

Thus was monarchy in Europe established, the divine

right to rule inherited, and the titles of nobility originated.

The same two classes exist to-day, as of old, both in Europe and America. We have the toiling, tax-paying producers, and the idle, non-taxed, who absorb the fat of the land without labor.

The valleys of this grand republic, with their unparalleled resources, and their millions of industrious, intelligent toilers, afford tempting inducements to the avarice of civilized brigandage. But instead of collecting their horsemen, they collect lobbies, and marshal them against state and national legislatures. Instead of captains, they select lawyers. Instead of mail and spear they use statutes. Instead of scooping up the wealth of the valleys and leaving the peasants free, modern brigandage demands the increase for the next century, and has set guards of law to enforce its delivery. They craved fifteen hundred millions of interest spoil, and drew it with the war debt, which need not have been a debt.

Their greed grows with their wealth, and their avarice intensifies with their success, and craving three thousand millions more, they have saddled the levy upon labor by their damnable funding scheme. Not yet satisfied, but fearing to create alarm and revolt among their dupes, they have doubled the levy by depreciating values and doubling the purchasing power of the levy.

The English brigands practice a slightly different method of robbery. There are thousands of them, but we will give a few as examples. Their system is that of pensions and annuities. Under the pretense of loaning to the government, a boss robber, for some trivial consideration, is allowed a perpetual annual income for himself and his heirs for all time to come, which labor and its posterity are compelled to pay, thus establishing two classes, the nobility who feast and fatten off of labor through their annuities, and the serf, or toiler, who is compelled to clothe himself in rags that the noble robber may dress in purple.

There is another class whose nobility is based upon their pensions. These pensions are hereditary, and many of them date back to the reign of Charles II. Very few people in England have any idea of the extent of the pension list in that country. A pension of £4,000 a year was allowed by Charles II. to Sir L. Charges and his heirs. This pension has been held for over two hundred years, and is annually paid to the heirs. The yearly pensions of a few of the nobility are as follows:

Earl Nelson, per annum	$17,000
Lord Rodney	5,000
Duke of Wellington	20,000
Viscount Eversby	20,000
Lord Pagent	6,000
W. G. Romaine	5,000
C. V. Villien	6,000
S. H. Walpole	10,000

Viscount Exmouth has held a pension of $10,000 per annum for sixty-four years. Viscount St. Vincent was allowed a pension of $15,000 in 1606. In the duke of Marlborough's name stands a pension of $22,000 per annum, granted in 1710, which has cost England $2,360,000. The heirs of the duke of Schomberg have been drawing a pension of $20,000 a year ever since 1695. This was granted for no service or consideration to the government or the people of England who are now taxed to pay it, but simply because Schomberg was a personal friend of King William III.

Thus did the brigands of the past seize sovereign

power, and parcel out to one another and their heirs and assigns forever, royal pensions to be collected from the toil and blood of the peasantry.

Every title of nobility in England has a pension behind it, conferred upon some ancestor as a share of the spoils, when ancient brigandism declared itself the nobility and pensioned their posterity upon the toil of unborn generations of plebians and serfs. The English system of high-toned robbery varies slightly from the one being inaugurated in America, but the principle, the object, and the results are identical. The object of both is to establish an idle, untaxed aristocracy of wealth, accumulated through incomes not earned by those who receive them, but filched from labor without consideration.

That which was called robbery and plunder in old times, is called usury and taxation to-day. The robber castles have given away to banking houses and boards of trade. While the brigand has assumed the title of financier, and exchanged his battle ax for bonds, and his shield and armor for special legislation.

The depredations of civilized brigandry are as destructive to the peace and happiness of society as were those of their barbarous predecessors. Death by the bludgeon and the lance of the freebooters was no more deadly than is that produced by want, starvation and suicide; while the colossal fortunes amassed by usury, rents, the contraction and appreciation of money, are no less the results of robbery, than were the accumulation of the ancient banditti by plunder. It matters but little by what process the few untaxed idlers manage to get possession of the wealth products of the toilers it is the result that constitutes the crime, and not the name given to the process.

During the last twelve years a hundred thousand men and firms have been ruined financially, and over sixteen hundred million of dollars wrenched from them by bankruptcy and the shrinkage of values, while those who have been able to stand under the pressure, find the value of their possessions dwindled to one-third their real worth, that the swallowing process may be made easy, when confidence in resumption shall enable the money sharks to open their bank inflation throats to gulp down what remains. Governments, whether monarchial or representative, are but faro tables for gamblers, and the people are the dupes of the games, and it will be so until the masses become more intelligent in public matters, less partisan in their prejudices, and command their servants in high places, instead of being controlled and blindly led by them.

Our pilgrim fathers fled from the religious intolerance and persecutions of Old England, and bore patiently the dangers and privations of the wilderness, to enjoy the liberty of hanging witches, banishing Baptists and whipping Quakers in New England.

Our patriotic fathers of '76 fought seven long years to defend and establish the equal, inalienable rights of all men to life, liberty and the pursuits of happiness; then celebrated their success, and sealed their blood-bought victories by riveting the chains of bondage on the limbs and souls of millions of their battle-scarred companions.

A century passed away before the law recognized the patriotic professions of its makers, and even this concession was wrung out of the blood-stained garments of thousands who fell at the feet of the bondsmen in their efforts to include them also in the inventory of "all men."

In this country revolutions have consisted in bloody struggles to establish in practice, and in fact, such measures and principles as a previous revolution had declared in theory to be right and just.

To-day we are living under laws, and are governed by systems, social, political and financial, as much at variance with the essence and spirit of the constitution, under which they were enacted, as was the institution of slavery with the spirit of the Declaration of Independence.

The preamble to the constitution which was designed as a brief interpretation of its spirit, declares that it was ordained and established "*For the purpose of transmitting to posterity the blessings of liberty, to establish justice, to insure domestic tranquility, and to promote the general welfare!*"

To secure the benefits of these pledges, and to enjoy, in fact, the privileges and rights thus declared to be man's inheritance, are the important and just demands which will precipitate the pending revolution.

Whether this revolution shall be characterized by the blood stains and heart aches which mark the pathway of its predecessors, depends upon the means used by avarice, greed, ambition and selfishness, to deprive the present generation of their inalienable rights, and posterity of its patrimony.

What is that liberty which the present policy of our law makers has in store for posterity?

The soil, the parent of humanity, from whose breast all substance must come—the green earth, which God filled with goodness and gave to all His children as an inheritance jointly and in common, has been usurped by avarice and greed, whose heirs will hold it to purchase the toil of unborn generations as effectually as the title to the mother carried with it the services and life-long toil of every dark son and daughter of the South.

This is not all. Posterity has not only been robbed of its rights to the soil, compelling it to enter the world a pauper and a trespasser in law, but a burden is being prepared to hang about its neck in the form of an immortalized public debt, whose interest-fetters will bind its limbs and forever deprive it of the liberty our fathers enjoined upon us to transmit to those who should come after us.

The present generation has an undoubted right to contract debts of its own, and to clothe the law with power to collect them, if it chooses to do so; but what unborn soul has authorized, or by what right do we authorize Congress to control and take away the freedom of posterity, and impose upon coming generations conditions and burdens who were not here to give or withhold their consent?

The coming revolution will break every fetter forged for posterity, and transmit to it the blessing of liberty as required by the constitution and the laws of God.

"To establish justice," is another object that will be contended for by the coming revolution. Uniform taxation, every person and interest to pay for the support of the government just in proportion to the amount of protection required, and benefits conferred.

The abolition of all laws creating monopolies, and granting special privileges, and the establishment of such as will insure to labor and enterprise the full benefit and enjoyment of the fruits of their toil.

Usury will be shorn of its power to rob, and usurers pass into history as the law-protected brigands of a darker age.

Then, when the medium of commercial exchanges shall be wrested from the control of the usurer, and restored to its legitimate service as a hand-maid, and not a robber of labor—and when, by the establishment of justice, the wealth products of labor shall be equitably distributed among their producers, domestic tranquility will then, and not till then, be insured.

All of which will tend "*to promote the general welfare.*"

That this revolution will come, and that these ends will be accomplished, is as certain as that they were recognized by our fathers as *right*, and bequeathed to this generation under the blood seal of the revolution of 1776, as a joint inheritance.

That it is at our doors, is evident from the numbers and earnestness of those demanding it, represented by the million votes cast at the recent elections.

May it be bloodless, and wrought by a substitution of ballots for the bullets of its predecessors. But let it come.

Nothing short of a radical and absolute financial revolution will meet the demands of the age. The day of patch-work reform, and relief measures under a system based on robbery and oppression, has passed. The financial and monarchical systems of Christendom are twin-sisters, each dependent upon the other for existence; in fact, each is but part of a perfect whole, which, when united, constitute tyranny in the most absolute and oppressive form. Without the "money of the world," the monarchies of the world could not endure for a generation, and that republic which adopts the monarchical financial system can remain such only in name. It may have the form of a republic, but it will possess the soul of a tyrant.

The revolution of '76 is not yet completed. The true republic is not yet born. The efforts of our fathers, like those of too many of the present day, were for reform, simply. They appealed for a redress of grievances. The blood that flowed at Lexington, Concord and Bunker Hill was not for liberty and independence, but for temporary relief. The war of the revolution was not at first waged against the system of monarchy, but against the severity of the monarch.

It was not to break or remove the yoke of the king, but to lighten its pressure, and not until they found that all their efforts were futile did the most venturesome mind dare to strike at the root of the evil, and declare for a government by the people. Those were times that not only tried men's souls, but tested their wisdom, their patriotism, and their statesmanship. They traced the cause of their sufferings back of parliament, to the crown. They traced it to a system of government based upon injustice, and supported by oppression. They saw that redress and relief, under such a system, would be but temporary patch-work. They resolved to strike at what they deemed the great tap root of the evil, and emancipate themselves from the rule of hereditary tyrants, for throughout the world they saw misery and monarchy marching hand in hand, and inspired by a nobler spirit than had before animated a people they cried aloud: "O, ye that love mankind! Ye that dare oppose, not only the tyranny but the TYRANT, stand forth! Every spot of the old world is overrun with oppression. Freedom hath been hunted round the globe. Asia and Africa have long since expelled her, and Europe regards her an alien and a stranger. Let America receive the fugitive, and prepare in time an asylum for the oppressed of earth."

When told that reconciliation and relief under the protection of the crown was the wisest policy, they cited the cruelties and the inhumanities inflicted upon them by the crown. The writer of the crisis said:

"Hath your house been burnt?

"Hath your property been destroyed before your face?

"Are your wife and children destitute of a bed to lie on, or bread to live on?

"Have you lost a parent or a child by the tyrant's hand, and you the wretched ruined survivor?

"If you have not, then you are not a judge of those who have. But if you have, and can still shake hands with the murderers, then are you unworthy of the name of husband, father, brother or lover, and whatever may be your rank or title in life, you have the heart of a coward, and the spirit of a sycophant."

Another inconsistency of a government by the people was the long-cherished custom of centralizing or materializing sovereignty in some one individual to be exercised for the masses. It was tauntingly asked: "What will be your king in the Republic?" and the answer was:

"I'll tell you, friend, he reigns above, and doth not make havoc of mankind like the royal brute of Britain, yet that we may not appear defective even in earthly honors, let a day be solemnly set apart for proclaiming the charter; let it be brought forth, placed on the divine law—the Word of God; let a crown be placed thereon, by which the world may know that so far as we approve of a monarch in America *the law is king.*"

Our fathers supposed that when they had thrown off the yoke of King George, they had, as far as they were concerned, dethroned the tyrant. They looked over the world, and saw misery, poverty and degredation among the tax-burdened and royally oppressed people, and naturally attributed man's hard lot to the tyranny of monarchs, and the lack of self-government among the masses.

But the light of a century has disclosed the fact that away back of the monarch, in his gilded den, sits the real tyrant, Avarice. That monarchical governments, the tyranny of kings, and the hereditary succession of power, are simply outgrowths of an underlying system of robbery so old that it is revered, and so popular that at the communion table of Christendom it is given the seat of honor. Gold for money, that usury may rob, is the corner stone of every throne in Europe, and the foundation of the political rings which rule, oppress, and rob the industries of the republic. When our fathers cast off the British yoke, they kept the yoke-maker, and set him up in business. Specie basis, and the inevitable debt system for usury, is the arch tyrant which is oppressing and crushing humanity to-day. This is the monster which must be dethroned, and his scepter broken. With our fathers let us say: " O, ye that love mankind, ye that dare oppose, not only the tyranny, but the tyrant, stand forth! Every spot in the old world is overrun with the oppressions of specie basis and usury. It has driven freedom from the habitations of civilization, and Christianity from Christendom. Let us receive these fugitives, and with an exchange medium of intelligence, and a nobler civilization, that which struck the manacles from the limbs of African slavery, prepare an asylum for the oppressed of all nations; and when the worshipers of the golden tyrant tauntingly ask, "What's your fiat basis?" tell them it is intelligence and popular sovereignty, with

God's green earth, and the fullness thereof as collaterals.

And when unlimited coinage and silver bill compromises are claimed to be ample panaceas for the ills we have been and are suffering, put the questions which patriotism put to Toryism in 1776.

Have you lost your home?

Has your property been sacrificed before your face, under the sheriff's hammer?

Has your fortune been swept away by the shrinkage of values?

Has your business been ruined, and your children made beggars?

Are your wife and children destitute of bed to lie on or bread to live on?

Have you lost a parent or child by suicide, from want or despair?

Have disease and death entered your unthatched roof, and carried off your idols, and you the wretched, ruined survivors?

Are you out of employment, tramping up and down the earth for sustenance, or eking out a prison life, in preference to starvation?

Are you one of the millions who have been bankrupted, robbed and ruined for life, with hopes blasted, prospects blighted, a living wreck, that the usurer might lay in his harvest of gold, dress in fine linen, and fare sumptuously every day? If you have suffered none of these things, you are not a judge of those who have. But if you have, knowing them to be the fruits of specie basis and usury, and still shake hands with those who advocate the murderous system, then you are unworthy the name of freemen, and whatever may be your rank or title in life, you have "the heart of a coward, and the spirit of a sycophant."

With the exception of the incidents and results of the revolution of '76, national affairs and national politics never presented questions of such momentous importance to the American people as stand to-day foremost on the calendar of public discussion. Circumstances seem to be culminating to precipitate a struggle which may, and probably will, result in another revolution of greater importance to the world than any which has preceded it. The revolution of a century ago was the triumph of democracy over monarchy, the ballot over the scepter. The struggle now pending, is between the same spirit that won the victories of the revolution, and demonstrated the possibility of political liberty, and that power behind the throne, stronger and more despotic than he who sat upon it. As vigilance is the price of liberty, every patriot is called upon to contribute his share.

CHAPTER II.

OUR RESOURCES.

Probably no territory on earth of the same area is more richly endowed with natural resources and the elements of wealth and prosperity, than that embraced within the United States. It possesses every variety of climate, soil and production, with unmeasured and unimagined mineral deposits of every conceivable variety, magnificent forests of timber, with ocean-bound coasts on the east and west, on the north, a chain of inland seas, and the land-locked gulf on the south, while a net work of the grandest rivers in the world afford natural highways, and cheap and easy transportation and distribution of the products of labor, and the bountiful supplies of nature's store houses. Whence came these generous supplies, and for whom were they designed? After God had created the earth and the fullness thereof, He created man, the crown and coronation of His work, and gave the earth into his possession, with instructions to multiply and replenish. He said to man, " Behold, I have given to you every herb bearing seed, to you it shall be for meat. Have dominion over the fish of the sea, and over the fowls of the air, and over the cattle, *and over all the earth*, and over every creeping thing that creepeth upon the earth."

All of these are the free gifts of God to man. Each man inherits, in common with the universal brotherhood of man, these blessings. We are all heirs of God, and joint and equal heirs of these, His gifts. There is enough for all the needs and luxuries of the human race, and an abundance to spare for the beasts of the field, the fish of the sea, and the fowls of the air.

Every soul is born into the world naked and helpless, but anticipating its advent and wants, a benevolent Creator has from the morning of creation supplied an abundance to satisfy all the needs and luxuries of His creatures, and if any child of God is not in the full enjoyment of all that is necessary for his bodily wants and soul's development, it is because he has been deprived of his just inheritance by the hand of legalized robbery.

In the United States there is yet sufficient unclaimed and unoccupied soil to give every man a farm. Sufficient unowned and unpossessed timber, stone, brick, paint, nail, and glass material to construct for every family a palace. Ample unclaimed and unappropriated facilities for raising cotton, woolen, silk, and fur fabrics to construct royal robes for every man, woman and child in America. Abundance of material going to waste to fashion into form elegant furniture, carpets, bedding, and ornamentation for every palace and home in the land. There are millions of acres of uncultivated soil pregnant and groaning with the elements of food for every hungry family.

There is no lack of skill and labor to raise, fashion, and produce from natural resources an abundance to supply every want and gratify every desire, taste, hope, and holy aspiration of man. Nature's storehouse is full of unclaimed raw material, requiring only the magic touch of labor to bring forth that which will satisfy every want of man.

Millions of laborers stand idle in the market places, offering their services and begging to be employed.

Millions of women and children go hungry and half clad through the streets begging for bread and clothing.

Famine stalks abroad at noon-day, while the vaults of nature are bursting with the fullness of food.

Able bodied and skillful laborers are tramping the streets for a beggar's subsistence, and moulding themselves into felons that they may be adapted to the conditions which surround them.

What is the matter?

No lack of resources. No lack of skill to fashion, or labor to produce. No lack of transportation to distribute and exchange the fruits of earth and the products of skill. But one thing for which the earth cries aloud, and for want of which humanity is rapidly going down-grade to perdition. "Without money, civilization could never have had a beginning. With an insufficient quantity of it, it will languish, and finally die."

With an abundant supply, our country can be made a paradise, and our generation inaugurate the millennium. It is not gold and silver we want, but the money that carried the nation through the war, fought our battles in the clouds, spanned the continent and bound the two oceans together with iron bands.

It will give us colleges in place of prisons, schools in place of courts, increase in place of ruinous taxation, teachers in place of sheriffs and policemen, refinement in place of demoralization, skilled artisans in place of tramps, wealth in place of poverty, justice in place of robbery, and peace on earth and good will toward one another in place of crime and violence.

Unlike other nations of earth, the people of America have the means in their own hands, and the power in their own sovereignty, to bring about these glorious results.

CHAPTER III.

CAUSE OF THE "DARK AGES."

FACTS GLEANED FROM THE REPORT OF THE MONETARY COMMISSION.

"At the Christian era, the metallic money of the Roman empire amounted to *one thousand, eight hundred million dollars.* By the end of the fifteenth century, it had shrunk to less than *two hundred million dollars.*

"During this period, the most extraordinary and baleful change took place in the condition of the world. Commerce, art, wealth and freedom disappeared. The people were reduced by poverty and misery to the most degraded condition of serfdom and slavery.

"Whether the cause or not, this period was coincident with the shrinkage in the volume of money which had no historic parallel.

"The crumbling of institutions kept even step with the shrinkage in the stock of money and the *failing of prices.*

"It is a suggestive coincidence, that the first glimmer of light only came with the invention of bills of exchange, and paper substitutes, through which the scanty stock of precious metals was increased in efficiency.

"It needed the heroic treatment of *rising prices* to enable society to re-unite its shattered links, to shake off the shackles of feudalism, to re-light and uplift the almost extinguished torch of civilization.

"That the disasters of the Dark Ages were caused by decreasing money and falling prices, and that the recovery therefrom and the comparative prosperity which followed the discovery of America, were due to an increasing supply of the precious metals and rising prices, will not seem surprising or unreasonable when the noble functions of money are considered.

"Money is the great instrument of association, the very fibre of social organism, the vitalizing force of industry, the protoplasm of civilization, and as essential to its existence as oxygen is to animal life.

"Without money civilization could not have had a beginning, *with a diminishing supply it must languish,* and, unless relieved, *finally perish.*

"Symptoms of disaster, similar to those which befell society during the dark ages, were observable on every hand during the first half of this century.

"In 1809 the revolutionary war between Spain and her American colonies broke out. These troubles resulted in a great diminution of the production of the precious metals, which was quickly indicated by a fall in general prices.

"The purchasing power of the precious metals increased between 1809 and 1848 fully 145 per cent., or, in other words, the general range of prices was 60 per cent. lower in 1848 than it was in 1809.

"During this time the volume of money did not materially decrease, but the supply was not sufficient to keep the stock up to the proper correspondence with the increasing demand of advancing civilization.

"The world has rarely passed through a more gloomy period than this one. Again do we find falling prices and misery and destitution inseparable companions.

"The poverty and distress of the industrial masses were intense and universal. In England the sufferings of the people found expression in demands upon Parliament, for relief, in bread riots. The military arm had to be strengthened to prevent the all-pervading discontent from ripening into open revolt. On the Continent the fires of revolution smoldered everywhere and blazed out at many points, threatening the overthrow of States and the subversion of social institutions.

"Wherever and whenever the mutterings of discontent were hushed by the fear of increased standing armies, the foundation of society were honeycombed by powerful secret political organizations.

"The cause at work to produce this state of things was so subtle, and its advances so silent, that the masses were entirely ignorant of its nature. They had come to regard money as an institution fixed and immovable in value, and when prices of property and wages of labor fell, they charged the fault not to the money, but to property and the employer.

"They were taught that the mischief was the result of *over-production*. Never having observed that over-production was complained of only when the money stock was decreasing, their prejudices were aroused against labor-saving machinery.

"They were angered at capital because it either declined altogether to embark in industrial enterprises, or would only embark in them upon the condition of employing labor at the most scanty remuneration.

"They forgot that falling prices compelled capital to avoid such enterprises on any other conditions, and, for the most part, to avoid them entirely. They did not comprehend that money in shrinking volume was the prolific parent of enforced idleness and poverty, and that falling prices divorced money, capital, and labor; but they none the less felt the paralyzing pressure of the shrinking metallic shroud that was closing around industry."

William Jacob, F. R. S., gives the following table, showing the progress of contraction to the year 806, when the lamp of civilization went out, and the night of the dark ages prevented him from continuing the report:

A. D. 14	$1,790,000,000
A. D. 230	909,000,000
A. D. 410	537,000,000
A. D. 662	256,000,000
A. D. 806	168,000,000

The first glimmer of light from the midnight of the gold and silver era, came on the wings of paper substitutes, the invention of bills of exchange.

EFFECTS OF CURRENCY CONTRACTION.

The effects of a decreasing volume of currency upon the business, prosperity, and people of a country are well stated in the following extracts:*

"While the volume of money is decreasing, even though very slowly, the value of each unit of money is increasing in a corresponding ratio, *and property and wages are decreasing.*

"Those who have contracted to pay money, find that it is constantly becoming more difficult to meet their engagements. The margin of securities melt rapidly, and their confiscation by the creditor becomes only a question of time.

"All productive enterprises are discouraged and stagnate, because the cost of producing commodities to-day will not be covered by the price obtainable for them to-

---
*Congressional Monetary Commission.

morrow. Exchanges become sluggish, because those who have money will not part with it for either property or service, for the obvious reason that money alone *is increasing in value*, while everything else is decreasing in price.

"This results in the withdrawal of money from the channels of circulation, and its deposit in great hordes where it can exert no influence on prices.

"Money in shrinking volume becomes the *paramount object of commerce*, instead of the beneficent instrument. Instead of mobilizing industry, it poisons and dries up its life currents.

"It is the fruitful source of *political and social disturbance*.

"It foments strife between labor and other forms of capital, while itself, hidden away, gorges on both.

"It rewards close-fisted lenders, and filches from, and bankrupts, enterprising producers."

The *American Review* (1876) says:

"Diminishing money and falling prices are not only oppressive upon debtors, but they cause stagnation in business, reduce production, and enforce idleness. Falling markets annihilate profits, and as it is only the expectation of gain that stimulates capital to invest in operations, inadequate employment is found for labor, and those who are employed can only be so on diminished wages."

Leon Fanchet (1843) says:

"If all the nations of Europe adopt the system of Great Britain, the price of gold would be raised beyond measure, and we should see produced a result lamentable enough."

David Hume, in Essays on Money, says:

"We find that in every kingdom into which money *begins to flow* in greater abundance than formerly, *everything takes a new face;* labor and industry gain life, the merchants become more enterprising, the manufacturers more diligent and skillful, and the farmer follows his plow with greater attention and alacrity. The good policy of the government consists of keeping it, if possible, *still increasing,* as long as there is an undeveloped resource or room for a new emigrant, because by that means there is kept alive a spirit of industry in the nation, which increases the *stock of labor, in which consists all real power and riches.*

"A nation whose money decreases, is actually weaker and more miserable than other nations, which possess less money, but are on the increasing hand."

Wm. H. Crawford, Secretary of the Treasury, in his report, Feb., 1820, says:

"All intelligent writers on currency agree that when it is decreasing in amount, poverty and misery must prevail."

The following table, compiled from official sources, shows the amount of our circulation, per capita, and its contraction from 1865 to 1877:

YEAR.	CURRENCY.	POP.	PER CAP.
1865	$1,651,282,373	34,819,531	$47.42
1866	1,803,702,726	35,537,148	50.76
1867	1,330,414.677	36,269,502	36.68
1868	817,199,773	37,016,949	22.08
1869	750,025,989	37,779,800	19.85
1870	710,039,179	38,558,371	19.19
1871	734,244,774	39,750,073	18.47
1872	736,349,912	40,978,607	17.97
1873	738,291,749	42,245,110	17.48
1874	779,031,589	43,550,756	17.84
1875	778,176,250	44,896,705	17.33
1876	735,358,832	46,284,344	15.89
1877	696,443,394	47,714,829	14.60

The component elements of the above volume of paper money in each year comprise the following items, according as these were in existence at the time: Demand, and one and two year treasury notes, (acts of Dec. 27, 1857; Dec. 17, 1860, and March 2, 1861); temporary ten day loans and one year certificates of indebtedness; treasury notes payable in two years and sixty days; seven-thirty three year notes; compound interest notes; three per cent. certificates; non-interest bearing demand and legal tender notes (acts of July 17, 1861; Feb. 25, 1862; July 11, 1872, and March 3, 1961); fractional currency; State bank notes; and national bank notes.

That business failures have resulted from, and kept even pace with, the contraction of the currency, there is no doubt, as the following table, prepared by Dunn, Barlow & Co., will show:

Hugh McCulloch was aware of the depressing and panicy influences of contraction when he said, in 1866:

"The process of contracting the circulation of the government notes *should go on just as rapidly as possible* WITHOUT PRODUCING A FINANCIAL CRASH."

McCulloch was wise enough to anticipate the results of contraction.

Hon. A. G. Spaulding, an eminent banker and member of congress from New York, wrote McCulloch, in 1866, then secretary, to "*contract slowly*, SO AS TO MAINTAIN A TOLERABLE EASY MONEY MARKET FOR AT LEAST A YEAR TO COME."

Sherman himself, then honest, stated in the senate that such contraction of the currency as was anticipated in the bill, "*would produce the most disastrous financial results that ever befell the nation.*"

Figures won't lie.

We all know that the panic and crash of 1857, during which year over 4,000 business failures took place, involving a loss of over $200,000,000 by bankruptcies, was wholly produced by the loss and contraction of the bank currency of the country, resulting from the exportation of coin from the United States to meet an extraordinary European demand.

The panic and crash of 1860, during which year over 6,000 business failures took place, was caused by the loss and contraction of nearly all our western currency by failure of banks based upon southern state stocks. After the greenback era of 1862, the number of failures diminished with the increasing of the currency, and when contraction commenced, in 1866, the failures commenced to increase and kept even pace with such contraction. Here are the figures, which are worth more than all the sophisms of demagogues.

Year.	Number.	Amount.
1857	4,932	$291,750,000
1858	4,225	95,749,000
1859	3,913	64,394,000
1860	3,673	79,807,000
1861	6,993	207,210,000
1862	1,652	23,049,300
1863	**485**	**6,864,700**
1864	**520**	**8,579,000**
1865	**530**	**17,625,000**
1866	**632**	**47,333,000**
1867	2,386	86,218,000
1868	6,608	63,774,000
1869	2,799	75,054,000
1870	3,551	88,242,000
1871	2,915	85,252,000
1872	4,069	121,056,000
1873	5,183	228,499,000
1874	5,830	155,239,000
1875	7,740	201,060,353
1876	9,092	191,117,786
1877	8,872	190,669,936
1878	10,478	234,383,132
1879 (six months)	4,058	65,779,398

If the number of failures for the first six months of the year 1879 were less than the number for the corresponding time the previous year, it is no evidence that the cause was being removed, but like the apparent improved condition of a scourge-cursed Memphis, there were fewer cases because there were fewer victims to destroy.

Secretary Sherman denies that resumption had any hand in the catastrophe, because the collapse occurred fourteen months before the act was passed. He failed to state that the object of contraction was to appreciate the remaining greenbacks to an equivalency with gold, and the act simply specified the day when the money sharks anticipated that they would, through contraction, reach that point. But notwithstanding the great appreciation of gold itself, it being some 34 per cent. from 1873 to 1879, contractions had been so rapid and disastrous to general values that the remaining greenbacks caught up with gold before the day appointed. It is true the congressional act providing for resumption on January 1, 1879, did not produce the panic, but preparing our national finances to enable congress to safely predict, and set a day when such a result could be legalized, did the work.

As the true causes Secretary Sherman ascribes "*the waste of war,*" "*over-production,*" "*wild speculation,*" "*inflated prices,*" *etc.* How an over-production of products could possibly co-exist with the wastes of war, and how the two could combine to result in a panic and widespread bankruptcy *nine years after the war terminated*, the learned demagogue left the public to cypher out.

"Inflated prices" and "over production" are equally inconsistent coincidents. Inflated prices generally have the effect to deplete stocks. It is generally the low priced stocks that move slow and accumulate.

The chief cause ascribed by Mr. Sherman was our *"irredeemable paper currency that varied in value from day to day."* Let an insulted public pause one moment, and consider if there ever was a day, while gold was bobbing between 100 and 285, but every dollar of this irredeemable paper money would pay a dollar of debts. The $2,000,000,000 of losses were not the result of irredeemable paper money, for with that money—as bad as it was, every debt could have been paid. It was for the want of it that disaster came. When the currency was poorest, relatively to gold, our prosperity was greatest, and our financial disasters fewest, nor was there a symptom or an indication of financial prostration until contraction had forced an undue inflation of credits.

CHAPTER IV.

THE NATURE AND FUNCTIONS OF MONEY.

"Money is the national medium of exchange for property and products. It must be instituted, and its value must be fixed by the laws of the nation, in order to make it a public tender in payment of debts. No debt can be paid with property or with individual notes, except by consent of the creditor; but when *money* is tendered, all creditors are compelled to receive it in full satisfaction of debts. The aim of legislation in regulating the value of money is to insure to all individuals, in making exchanges of their property for money, the full value of their products or property. Debts are postponements of the time of payment for the property or products received; and loans of money, and all rents of property, are mere rents of the use of certain amounts of legal or actual value, which use is to be paid for at the expiration of a specified period. Money is the legal tender, and must be offered and received in payment for all these debts.

"Certain properties are by law given to some substance, which bears the name and performs the functions of money. The term *money*, then, signifies a legal, public medium of exchange, which possesses all the qualifications necessary to effect a just exchange of property. In the discussion of the nature of money, it will appear that its properties are, in truth, the creation of law, and entirely different from the properties of the things which it exchanges.

"Money has four properties or powers, viz.: *power to represent value, power to measure value, power to accumulate value by interest*, and *power to exchange value*. These properties are co-essential to a medium of exchange: it is impossible that any one of them should exist in such a medium independently of the others. The *material of money* is a *legalized agent*, employed to express these powers, and render them available in trade. The powers of money, which alone render it useful, are created by legislation, therefore money can possess none but legal value. All legal value depends upon the actual value that it represents.

"Some writers, instead of considering money as a medium of exchange, call it *capital seeking investment*. If money be capital, it is already invested; because the capital would consist in the inherent value of the material of the money, and not in the thing the money seeks to obtain. But, when money has found one investment, it is as much a seeker for a second and a third investment, as if it had not been invested at all. It is always seeking investment, without being invested. It is no more real capital than a very poor horse, of which the appearance is such that he will do very well to exchange off. But if he should finally fall into the hands of a person who had not the good fortune to exchange him again for something else, the owner would have to depend upon his few useful qualities. And if a currency were formed in the various nations independently of gold and silver, and coins should cease to be a tender in payment of debts, the value of coins would depend upon their inherent qualities, as metals, as much as the value of the horse when he could be no longer exchanged for more than his actual worth, would depend upon the little labor that he could perform, or upon his hide and bones. The price of the gold and of the horse would then depend upon their actual usefulness, and not upon any capabilities for exchange.

"Money is, then, a combination of legal powers, expressed upon metal, paper, or some other substance; its value is the standard, or determiner of the value of all other things, and it serves as a public medium of exchange for land, labor, and all commodities."—*Kellog.*

Scattered throughout the length and breadth of the land, are the millions of workers, engaged in producing those commodities demanded for the needs and luxuries of man. These productions alone constitute wealth. Commerce consists in the modes and methods of distributing the various products of skill, so that each producer may enjoy the benefit of the product of every other man.

To accomplish this, with the least possible expense to both producer and consumer, is the mission of true political economy. An universally accepted and recognized medium of exchange is as essential as safe and cheap transportation.

One exchanges ownership, the other location.

Hence, cheap and abundant money is as essential to the prosperity of both producer and consumer, as abundant and cheap transportation.

If the medium of transportation is limited, or inadequate to effect the necessary change of location, consumption must be limited, and people in every part of the country must go destitute, and perhaps suffer for the want of many things which are produced in abundance but cannot be distributed. With such limited transportation, those who monopolize it can command any portion of the surplus of a country's production they choose, for transporting the balance. The result would be, low prices and an overstock at every point of production, and destitution and high prices, at every point of consumption. The same principle will hold good in regard to the medium of exchange. As it takes a certain number of cars to move the surplus products of the country from the places of production to the places of consumption, so it takes a certain number of dollars to effect the exchanges of ownership. If cars are too scarce, products accumulate, prices fall, and labor is thrown out of employment. If dollars are too few, exchanges cannot be made, products accumulate on the hands of producers, prices decline, and labor is thrown out of employment.

If railroads ramify all parts of the country, and rolling stock is abundant, the location of commodities can be changed at cost, and a fair recompense for use of the means invested. So if dollars are abundant, and not controlled by monopoly, exchanges of ownership may be so readily and cheaply effected as to provide every laborer and producer with a ready market, full employment, ample reward, and an abundance to supply all necessary wants and to gratify all proper desires. As an abundance of railroads lessens the profits of the railroad kings, and prevents them from fleecing the public, so an abundance of money lessens the banker's profits, and prevents him from robbing the producers of wealth. An expansion of either would bless the masses; a contraction of either would enrich their owners. As well style a single railroad track across the continent, and the exorbitant profits it could make on the amount invested, "honest transportation," and call such limited facilities, a "sound policy," as limit money to a safe gold basis and depress prices to the gold standard, and call it "honest money," and a "sound policy."

Nothing is honest that robs, and no policy is sound that deprives society of its natural wants, and tends to demoralize, rather than to elevate the human race. Before the wealth producers and toilers of this country can be free, and enjoy the fruits of their own labor, both money and transportation must be wrested from the hands of monopoly, and, controlled by wise legislation, made the servants and not the masters of labor.

MATERIAL OF MONEY.

Mr. Madden, author of coins of the Jews, states that in the West Indies and South America, pins, a slice of bread, a pinch of snuff, a dram of whisky, soap, chocolate and eggs were current money.

The aboriginal inhabitants of America used wampum, and cocoanuts. As late as 1635, wampum was made a legal tender in Massachusetts among the colonists.

Silver being demonetized in Great Britain, Thomas Baring says that in 1847 it was impossible to raise any money whatever on £60,000 of silver.

During a similar crisis in Calcutta in 1864, it was equally impossible to raise a single rupee on £20,000 of gold, that metal being demonetized in India.

In Britain at an early time a double standard was used, called "living money" and "dead money," or slaves and cattle, and land and metal.

In the twelfth century, gold and silver coins were redeemable in leather legal tenders in Sicily, under William I.

In the fourteenth century, the Chinese used a money coined from the inner bark of the mulberry tree.

The inhabitants of the coast of Africa use an "ideal" money—a sign of value, without money.

In the South Sea Islands beads and tools of iron were long used as money.

Salt is the current money of Abyssinia, codfish of Iceland and Newfoundland.

At an early day, deer and coon skins were legal tender in the State of Illinois.

In 1574, large amounts of pasteboard money were coined in Holland.

Rome used both wooden and leather money about 700 B. C.

Tin money was coined by Dionysius I, tyrant of Syracuse.

Platinum was coined in Russia from 1828 to 1845.

The Spaniards used leather money as late as 1574.

Under the Cæsars, lands were made money.

The Carthagenians had leather money.

France used leather money in 1360.

Sir John Mandeville, who traveled among the Asiatic nations in the 14th century, gives an account of an ancient fiat money used by the great Chan of Persia and Tartary, which is given by Jevon, in his "Money and Mechanism of Exchange," as follows:

"This Emperour may dispenden als moche as he wile, withouten estymacioun. For he despendeth not, he maketh no money, but of Lether emprented, or of Papyre. And of that money, is some of gretter prys, and som of lasse prys, aftre the dyvesiteer of his Statutes. And when that Money hathe ronne so longe that it begynneth to waste, then men beren it to the Emperoure's Tresorye; and than thei taken newe money for the olde And that money gothe thorghe out all the Contree and thorghe out all his Provynces.

"For there, and beyond hem, thei mak no Money nouther of Gold nor Sylver."

ANTIQUITY OF THE GREENBACK SYSTEM.

The hard money advocates characterize the popular uprising of the people in favor of a representative money as a "craze," a "financial epidemic," a political bubble, that will soon burst, and leave its followers stranded on the rocks of error and delusion.

These financial savans would do well to bear in mind that the so-called "fiat" or non-intrinsic money theory, is not new. It is as old as civilization.

It had its origin when men were honest, and only yielded to brute force in the hands of ambitious tyrants, who established a currency of intrinsic value—the easier to enslave and rob the masses.

Even after gold and silver were adopted, it was discovered that these metals did not increase proportionately with other commodities; and the wisdom of ancient legislators perceived that production must be arrested if no other distributive instrument than gold and silver were employed.

We quote from Jonathan Duncan: "One of the earliest plans adopted to surmount the difficulty was the *creation of a National Currency in each independent State, for internal trade;* and its distinctive characteristic was the *total absence of intrinsic value*, WHICH EFFECTUALLY PREVENTED ITS EXPORTATION.

"This invention greatly economized the use of the precious metals, allowing them to be *wholly employed in discharging the balance of foreign trade.*

"Thus the cities of Byzantium and Clazomenæ provided iron money for their own citizens, which circulated at home for the value impressed on it by public authority."

The monetary laws of Lycurgus were founded upon the same principle; who deprived his money of even the intrinsic value of iron, by first destroying its malleability, so it could not be converted even into implements of labor.

Seneca states that the Spartans used leather money, having a stamp to show what value it represented, and by whose authority it was issued.

Plato recommended a double currency in every nation: "A coin," he said, "for the purposes of domestic exchange and to pay wages to hired servants and settlers, for which purpose I affirm it must have value among the members of the State, *but no value to the rest of the world.*" For visiting, and using in other States, Plato proposed a coin of *intrinsic value*, which would pass current in foreign States.

Xenophon states that "most of the States of Greece have money which is not current except in their own territory."

Homer and Hesiod never speak of gold or silver money.

They express the value of things by saying they are worth so many oxen.

They estimated the riches of a man by the number of his flocks, and the wealth of a nation by the abundance of its pastures.

Homer values the golden armor of Glaucus at 100 oxen, and the brazen armor of Damocles at nine oxen. Cæsar had "tribute money," representing a tax to be paid, which was issued by the government, based upon taxes. It bought property, paid for labor, discharged debts, and was redeemed in taxes.

It bore inscriptions representing real money, which was cattle and property.

Thus, for greater cattle they were stamped with the figure of a horse or an ox; for less, with that of a hog; for corn fields, with an ear of corn; for a poll tax, with the head of a man.

"On these historical facts," says Duncan, "we have evidence that ALL THINGS OF VALUE, capable of being transferred from man to man, *were accounted* REAL MONEY, and they were all represented by symbols, or tokens, by which device they (the things of value) were rendered movable in the shape of currency representatives." The real money—the property of value, was the basis and security on which the tokens were issued, and whoever held a token, was admonished by it that he was a creditor to its amount on the real money of the country.

Money, in the strict sense of the term, is whatever the community consents to use as a medium of exchange. The constitution of the United States clothes congress with the power to "coin money and regulate the value thereof," but is silent in reference to the material upon which the money function shall be stamped. Money, in the strict sense of the term, does not possess intrinsic value more than a court judgment, or a statute of law. The value of gold and silver, which we call intrinsic, is not so, but is a value placed upon those metals by law.

Gold and silver are as abundant for the real uses of those metals as iron is for its real uses, and were the precious metals stripped of their artificial, legal or fiat value, their abundance for the real needs and uses of society would reduce their intrinsic value to that of iron or lead. The credit of the governments of the world, the faith of the people that these governments will receive their coins at their face and weight value, and that they will enforce the legal tender qualities of such coin are all that give them a value above their weight of iron. Of the commercial exchange of the world, Colwell and other standard authors estimate that they are made as follows:

With coin	50
Paper currency	2 50
Other credit devices	97 00
	100 00

The banking system the world over, supplies a currency of credit.

The Bank of England has long used about $75,000,000 of government debt as money, irredeemable. The banks grow rich by loaning their own credit, and that of their customers. They loan the credit of those who borrow credit of them. Through the machinery for swapping promises, called a clearing house, the banks are enabled to form a ring, and loan, also, each other's credits. The report of the comptroller shows that the banks are to-day loaning and drawing interest on three times as much credit as there is money in the country. It is the same in all the civilized world. Credit of one kind and another, constitutes the great bulk of the world's medium of exchange, while the precious metals constitute less than one-half of one per cent. As congress has the power, why then should it not coin the government credit, make it legal tender, and thus supply a more uniform medium of exchange, and one less expensive than that supplied by banks and capitalists?

There is but one objection, and that is, it would deprive the banks and money sharks of their rich interest harvests from loaning their own, and their customers credits for usury. Gold is not the money of the world, even restricting money to coin and bank paper, for the entire stock of Europe and America aggregates but a trifle over $1,900,000,000 against over $3,000,000,000 of government and bank issues.

The States are prohibited from making anything but gold and silver legal tender, but congress is not; for the first legal tender the government ever coined under the constitution was copper, which was a full legal tender for any and all amounts. No one disputes the right of the government to issue bills of credit, or treasury notes, and the supreme court has decided that this being conceded, "*the incidental power of giving such bills the quality of legal tender follows as a matter of course.*"

There is not sufficient gold and silver in the world to serve as a universal medium of exchange, hence it cannot be a money of the world. Bank and individual credit lack the necessary stability, safety and responsibility to constitute a money of the world, hence, they are not appropriate. The government credit alone, based upon the powers of its sovereignty and the combined credit, consent and mutual interest of society, can supply a safe, reliable, ample and uniform currency to effect all the necessary exchanges of commerce, and do away with that class of vampires, cormorants and middle-men, who now monopolize the supply, that they may reap the lion's share of labor's productions.

POWER TO CREATE MONEY.

The Constitution of the United States, Art. I, Sec. VIII, 5, declares congress shall have power to coin money, regulate the value thereof and of foreign coin, and fix a standard of weights and measures.

"To coin money," as used in the constitution does not

mean to shape, fashion, weigh, and stamp pieces of metal or paper. It simply means to determine what shall constitute the lawful money of the realm. This is a power inherent in sovereignty, and as sovereignty rests with the people in a republic, this prerogative was delegated to congress to be exercised for the people. A literal interpretation of the clause would be: "Congress shall have power to determine what shall constitute the exchange medium and lawful tender for debts in the United States." It certainly does not mean that congress shall perform the manual and mechanical labor of stamping coin or notes; if it does, then all of our mints are unconstitutional institutions. Congress has power to determine the material and style of the token or thing which shall represent the value of a dollar, when such value is agreed upon between the parties to an exchange; also the different denominations of such tokens, the functions they shall perform, and the extent and for what purposes they shall be lawful tender for debts.

The value of money is its purchasing power, which is governed by its volume, or the relation which the total volume sustains to the total volume of the exchangeable commodities of a country. The larger the money volume in proportion to the exchangeable commodity volume of a country, the less is the purchasing power of the former, and the higher are the prices of the latter. Hence, the value of money can be regulated only by regulating its volume, and as this sovereign power has been delegated to Congress in trust for the benefit of all the people, that body has no warrant in the constitution to delegate this important trust to individuals or corporations for their private benefit. Neither the people nor Congress have power to regulate the intrinsic value of money or anything else; it is only its exchange value that they can regulate. Whenever the intrinsic value of money rises above its exchange value, it ceases to serve the purposes of money, and goes to speculating on its commodity merits.

Jonathan Duncan says of money: "It may surprise some of our readers to be told that from the reign of Henry the First, down to the establishment of the Bank of England, *the legal tender money of England was fabricated out of wood.*

"Its intrinsic value was no more than the value of the wood of which it was fabricated, but its *representative value* denoted large sums.

"At this time Exchequer Tallies, the representatives of value, having no intrinsic value in themselves, *sustained trade;* but what happened when the tallies were extinguished, and the money prerogative of the crown was *transferred to the Bank of England?*"

The reader will bear in mind that the tally system of England was similar to our greenback legal-tender system. It supplied a home currency sufficient for the demands of commerce, which was not subject to the panics, pressures and financial disturbances which are always liable to occur from an exportable currency of intrinsic value.

The result upon the prosperity of the kingdom by the retirement of the legal-tender, and the introduction of the gold and silver basis system of the Bank of England, is given by Davenant, as follows:

"The government appeared like a distressed debtor, who was daily squeezed to death by the exorbitant greediness of the lender.

The citizens began to decline trade, and to turn usurers.

"Foreign commerce had infinite discouragements.

"We are going headlong to destruction with carrying on a losing trade with our neighbors; *and what has brought us to this low ebb?*

"When paper credit flourished, and tallies performed all the offices of money, the great payments for lands, or rich goods, were therefore easily made, the king's duties paid, and all kinds of business easily transacted."

Just as now, under our system, the usurious system of the Bank of England induced capital to leave the fields of production, and capitalists to invest for usury.

Interest was more profitable than production, and while the rich, through usury, grew richer; the poor, by production and excessive taxation to pay usury, grew poorer.

The legal tender system of America is not new.

It has cropped out all along the history of civilization, but like the frogs in the fable, it has been stoned back by Shylocks and usurers, and strangled by law-protected greed and selfishness.

It again came to the surface in England from 1797 till 1820, during which period that kingdom leaped with giant strides on the road of prosperity, but no sooner was the kingdom safe from the dangers of foreign foes, than it turned upon its own friends and defenders, and crushed their hopes and prosperity by a return to the damnable system of contraction, gold basis and usury.

The United States was compelled to adopt the rational legal-tender system during the War of the Rebellion, but no sooner had peace been restored when the old British system of bankruptcy, desolation and death was attempted to be saddled upon us again.

It is very hard to divorce the public mind from the

idea that money must necessarily be a thing, and that thing, possessed of the intrinsic value of its face or stamp.

As the body of man possesses no more of intrinsic value than a lump of earth of its weight, so should the body of money possess no more intrinsic value than its weight of the cheapest product of earth.

It is not the body of man, or the material of which it is made, that constitutes the wealth of the soul, but that invisible element, or spirit, breathed into it, and stamped upon its face, by the sovereign power of the universe.

A lump of gold weighing 25.8 grains, troy, is not a dollar. It will not pay a dollar of debt in any country on the globe. It is not money. But without taking from, or adding to, it a particle of matter, we pass it under the mint dies, and behold it comes out a living, legal tender, debt-paying dollar.

We lay it on the railroad track, allow a train of cars to run over it, and although it has lost none of its weight, fineness or intrinsic value, the dollar has fled, it is no longer money, and will not legally pay a debt of ten cents.

Where has the dollar gone?

Where, and what, was that element, or principle called money, or a dollar?

In its crude natural state it did not possess it. It went under the mint dies and came out with a soul of money—a living legal tender. It possessed a new, and a debt-paying function, which it did not before possess.

Under the car wheel it lost that function, or quality. Its legal tender spirit was driven out of it. It became a dead commodity. Its money soul had departed.

Now, what is money?

Not the material body of 25.8 grains of metal, for although that still existed before it went to the mint, and after the car wheels passed over it, the money principle was not in it. Money, then, is not material, nor does it possess intrinsic value; for the intrinsic value of 25.8 grains of gold was not changed from the time it came from the ore bed till its flattened form was taken from under the car wheel.

If money, then, is the spirit of legal tender breathed into an organic or material form by the sovereign power of the government, as the spirit of man is breathed by God into the soul's clayey tenement, why clamor for a body, or hope to obtain an equal in intrinsic value to the spirit that inhabits it?

As Pagans worship a material deity of wood or stone, so let financial idolators, who cannot comprehend or grasp the idea of the spirit of money, worship the image of gold and silver, while a higher wisdom, a more refined civilization, and a more exalted manhood abandon this Pagan materialism, and substitute the true and the living.

VALUE.

E. P. Elder, in his treaties on political enconomy, says:

"Money is no more a standard of the value of the things exchanged than is any other commodity."

Speaking of the precious metals, Adam Smith says:

"Constantly varying in their own value, they can never be made an accurate measure of the value of other commodities."

Colwell, in his Ways and Means of Payment, says:

"Another attribute generally given to the precious metals is that they are a *standard of value.*

"This is inaccurate.

"Gold cannot, in the mint, be made the standard for silver, nor can silver be made the standard for gold. Much less, taking the whole range of articles for human consumption, can they be a standard of value to which all can be referred. The term standard is, then, inaccurately applied, when it is used with any signification. If gold is a standard at all, it is a standard of payment, but not of value."

We can measure a quart of milk with a quart measure, and that measure will measure that amount a thousand different times, and during as many different years. But who ever heard of a dollar, no matter how "honest" it was, or how universally the world recognized it as such, that would measure, or represent, the value of a given amount of wheat any two years, or even two days, in succession?

If money measures values, there would be no necessity for "price currents," "market reports," goods marking, or bantering in trade. When we wish to measure the value of anything, we do not approach it with coin or legal tender. An experienced lapidary is better than all the gold in Christendom to determine the value of a jewel. If we want a piece of property appraised, we do not employ gold, but intelligent experience, and sound judgment. After intelligence has ascertained the value, we express it in money terms. The unit of value, the dollar for instance, is used to express the value which intelligence has determined. We measure value, then, with brains, and express it in terms of money, as we measure yards by the stick, and express them in numbers. So money is no more the measure of values than figures are the measure of yards.

Price is the relation of commodities to the money of account. *Value* is the relation of commodities to the labor, or force, usually required to produce them.

Adam Smith says:

"Labor, never varying in its own value, is alone the ultimate and real standard by which the value of all commodities can, at all times and places, be estimated and compared. It is their real value; money is their nominal price only."

Carey defines value as "*simply the measure of resistance that labor and skill meet in subduing natural objects to human use.*"

The value of commodities is not changed by high or low price. For instance, wheat may be a dollar a bushel in gold in Canada, and two dollars a bushel in greenbacks in the United States. Supposing a Canadian farmer and an Illinois farmer meet in New York with a cargo of fifty bushels of wheat each, the Canadian receiving one dollar per bushel in gold, and the Illinois farmer two dollars per bushel in greenbacks. Have they received equal value, or the representative of equal value? Certainly, for the $50 of gold will purchase the same quantity of *labor*, dry goods, groceries or other commodities that the $100 of greenbacks will. The only difference is, the greenbacks will pay twice the amount of debts in the United States that the gold will in Canada, but their purchasing power is no greater. The larger the volume of money, the more active its circulation, the more lively and the better times are, and the higher prices are. It matters not how high prices are in the currency of the country, it does not change the value relation between labor and commodities. The proceeds of the sale of high priced commodities in this country, will purchase no more or less of English manufactures, than the proceeds of the sale of the same commodities in England, or Germany, where prices may be 50 per cent. less. Wheat may be five dollars per bushel in American money, and but one dollar in English money, while its value may be the same in each country, measured by the purchasing power of its proceeds.

The money of the country should be sufficiently abundant to render its circulation free and easy, and readily obtainable at all times. The question of great importance is, after the volume of money and general prices are once established, to keep them uniform and unvarying. If prices drop, debtors are wronged. If they advance above what they were when the debt was contracted, the creditor is wronged. All debts should be paid in a money having the same purchasing power, no more nor less, than money possessed at the time the obligation was incurred. It is the great decline in prices, and the appreciation of money, giving creditors double the value of their dues, robbing debtors of half the value of their labor and products, that has given rise to the greenback movement.

To pay to-day, when prices are down to a gold valuation, debts contracted when prices corresponded to thirty or forty dollars per capita of circulation, is an outrageous swindle, nothing short of robbery upon every debtor and tax-payer in the nation. Why should nine-tenths of the people be robbed for all time to come, for the sake of feathering the nests and double paying the other tenth, who neither produce wealth, nor contribute to the support of the government by whose laws they receive their unjust gains?

If there were no debts drawing fixed amounts of interest, the gold basis for money would have no advocates. The mountains of the world's debt, whose fixed interest yields colossal annual fortunes to their owners, were created almost wholly when prices were very high, and money very cheap, and to double the value of these debts, and the purchasing power of their annual income, the dollars in which it has to be paid have been doubled in value by limiting currency to a gold basis and depressing prices to a gold standard. This injustice is what the greenback party aims to overcome by cutting loose from gold and greenback equivalency, and lessening the purchasing power of money, by increasing its volume.

PRICES.

Prices are the estimate of mankind of the relative value of one thing to another, *as compared with money.* The term "price" is ordinarily employed to denote the amount of value possessed by a given thing expressed in terms of money. Thus, when we say "wheat is worth a dollar a bushel," a dollar is the price of a bushel of wheat. But while we constantly use language in such a way as to imply that the value of the thing to which we affix the "price" is the sole fact we wish to determine, in reality, we put a price on the money as much as we do on whatever we "price." When we say "corn is worth a half a dollar a bushel," we virtually say that the price of a dollar is two bushels of corn. The average scale of prices measures the value of money as effectually as money measures the prices of commodities. The scale of prices is governed chiefly by two influences.

First, the volume of legal tender money in circulation; for, increase the volume, and the price of labor rises, and that raises the price of commodities. Diminish the amount of money, and wages and commodities fall in price. Money is like everything else. The scarcer it is, the dearer it is, and the more labor or commodities it takes to purchase a given sum.

Second, the extent to which public and private credit is employed in the form of notes, checks, bills of exchange, etc. It is not the amount of money in *existence* which determines prices, so much as the *amount in active circulation*. From 1866 to 1873 the circulating medium was diminished by the funding of over a thousand million greenbacks and treasury notes, still prices were kept up by the substitutions of inflated credits in place of money until the crash of the latter year produced a sudden and actual contraction of money, and credit, of over a thousand million dollars in a day, which caused prices to fall like the forest before a cyclone.

Prior to this time, prices had become established, and all debts and contracts were made with reference to these prices. But the contraction of the currency enhanced the value of money, depreciated prices, and robbed every man who sustained the relation of debtor, or contractor, whose obligations were incurred on the scale of prices previously existing.

CHAPTER V.

COLONIAL MONEY.

From "Sumner's Reminiscences of Colonial Times," we learn that for many generations after the first settlement of the Colonies, the work of production was slow and laborious, and the surplus products, at least such as could find their way to foreign markets, were hardly sufficient to procure in return the common necessaries of life. The small sums of money brought to the country by the settlers were soon exhausted, sent abroad for merchandise; and trade, for the most part, had to be carried on by the inconvenient method of barter. The Indians found along the shores of Long Island Sound, were more advanced in civilization than those further north, and used a circulating medium of exchange, consisting of beads of two kinds, one white, made out of the end of a periwinkle shell, and the other black, made out of the dark part of a clam shell. They were rubbed down and polished, and, when artistically arranged in strings or belts, formed objects of real beauty. These beads circulated among the Indians as money, one black bead being reckoned as worth two white ones, and were known as *Wampum*. The Colonists came to use them, first in their trade with the Indians, and then among themselves. In Massachusetts they became by custom, the common currency of the colony, and were made a legal tender in small sums. The first issue of paper money made in the Colonies, was made by Massachusetts in 1690, six years before the establishment of the Bank of England. An expedition had been sent out against Canada, and, returning without spoils, and in a state of misery, the soldiers were clamorous for their pay. So £7,000 were issued in notes from 5s. to £5. The form of these notes or bills was as follows:

"This indented bill of ten shillings, due from the Massachusetts colony to the possessor, *shall be in value equal to money*, and shall be accordingly accepted by the treasurer, and receivers subordinate to him in all public payments, and for any stock at any time in the treasury." They circulated at par with coin for twenty years, until redeemed. In 1703, another issue of £15,000 was authorized, which were made a legal tender for private debts. In 1716, another issue to the amount of £150,000 was authorized, to be distributed among the different counties of the province, and to be put into the hands of five trustees in each county, to be appointed by the legislature, to be let out on real estate security in the county in specific sums for the space of ten years, at 5 per cent. per annum. Another act for £50,000, in bills, was passed in 1720, which resulted in clearing Massachusetts of debt in 1773. In 1720, bills were issued by the colony of Rhode Island, and were made legal tender for all debts. The colony of Connecticut issued similar bills at various times between 1709 and 1731. New York began to issue bills in 1709; Pennsylvania, in 1723; Maryland, in 1733; Delaware, in 1739; Virginia, in 1755; and South Carolina, in 1703. The first emission of bills by Virginia bore 5 per cent. interest, and, according to Jefferson, in a very short time not one of them was to be found in circulation. They were locked up for the interest. "We then," says Jefferson, "issued bills *bottomed on a redeeming tax,* but bearing no interest—these were readily received, *and never depreciated a farthing.* Several hundred thousand dollars of this colonial paper money remained in circulation more than twenty years *at par with gold,* with no other basis, or advantage, than being receivable for debts and taxes."

But in 1751, Parliament, controlled by the money power of Great Britain, and becoming alarmed at the prosperity and growing independence of the colonies, passed an act forbidding the issue of any more paper money, and in 1763 all colonial acts for issuing paper money were declared by act of Parliament void. Dr. Franklin visited England and protested against the act, but without avail. He stated to the British authorities that before the issue of colonial money, the colonies were stripped of gold and silver. That there were great difficulties for the want of money, as trade had to be carried on by the extremely inconvenient method of barter. But that the introduction of colonial paper money had given new life to business, promoted greatly the settlement and development of the country, whereby the provinces had greatly increased in inhabitants, and their exports had been increased tenfold.

This Parliamentary prohibition, more than anything else, led to the discontent which resulted in the Revolution. The colonial legal tender greenback system caused rich and powerful states to spring up in the wilderness as if by magic, but then, as now, it was liable to educate society into a better system than that of specie, and make production independent of the usurer. It had to be strangled. The shylocks of Change Alley feared its influence upon the institutions of the old world, and as the ruling powers of all monarchies are but the tools of the Money Power, Parliament had to obey.

During the Revolutionary struggle. the colonies or states issued what has since been known as continental money, a description of which, from the pen of Warwick Martin, is given in the following chapter.

CHAPTER VI.

CONTINENTAL MONEY

ACT OF JUNE 25, 1775.

This act was passed more than one year before independence was declared. It authorized the issue of $2,000,000 of notes, which read as follows: "This note entitles the bearer to receive —— Spanish mill dollars, or the value thereof in gold or silver, according to the resolution of Congress of the 10th of May, 1775."

We need not say that that was neither money nor a promise to pay money emanating from any individual State or nation. The note authorized the party holding it to receive therefor Spanish mill dollars, or their equivalent in gold or silver; but it did not obligate any person, State or nation to pay said dollars, or other coin.

THE ACT OF JULY 25, 1775.

This act provides for the issue of another $1,000,000 of these notes. The act of December 26, 1775, also provides for the issue of $3,000,000 more of said notes, making $6,000,000 issued before Independence day.

This act also provided for the sinking, as it was termed, of all notes issued under acts of Congress. Each colony was to appoint a treasurer, who should give security. Each colony was to provide ways and means to sink its portion of the bills of credit authorized by Congress.

The amount to be redeemed by each colony was to be in proportion to population.

A census was to be taken to ascertain the number of people in each colony. Until this was completed, the whole number of people in the colonies was assumed at 3,000,000 souls. The estimated number in each colony is given, and the amount of liability of each for the bills is stated. The bills were not to be redeemed by the States united as a nation, but by the States in their individual capacity—each State acting for itself.

Each colony was to commence redeeming the notes in 1779, and close in 1783—being eight years from the time they were issued. The treasurers of the colonies were required to receive the bills for taxes imposed to take them up, but not for any other taxes. This was a strange provision, tending to depreciate.

On the 28th of December, 1779, Congress took notice of a report then in circulation, to the effect that Congress never intended to redeem the notes. Congress pronounced this an unfounded charge, which did them great injustice, and greatly injured the bills in the estimation of the people. They passed an act pledging the faith of the United Colonies for the payment of these bills.

On December 31, 1779, Congress ordained that the $15,000,000 due from the colonies be paid, and that eighteen years be granted them instead of four, as previously provided, in which to make the balance of the payments, and that the amount of each annual payment be limited to $6,000,000, commencing in 1780.

About $200,000,000 of this money were issued. We can not, in this article, refer to all the acts in proof. We point out the defects in this money, and show the causes of its depreciation in the following manner:

The States were contending with the greatest nation on earth. Her armies had generally been victorious on land. She was conceded to be the mistress of the seas. The States were poorly prepared for war with such a power. They had no army, no navy, no fortifications, no arms, no ammunition, no credit, no money. The odds were immensely against them, viewed from a military standpoint. The contest was not only doubtful, but from any standpoint except justice and right, was overwhelmingly in favor of Great Britain. Under these circumstances it would have been difficult to maintain a State paper circulation at par had Congress adopted the best method of doing it. But with the means adopted, it is astonishing that any success attended their efforts to keep the Government circulation at par.

At the time $6,000,000 of this money were issued, independence had not been declared. The States were still colonies, and the people and Congress subjects of Great Britain, styling themselves in their communication to the throne, "Your Majesty's most faithful subjects." They were engaged in petitioning for and demanding their rights as "British subjects." They were also preparing to defend their rights and maintain them, if denied to them by the mother country. To raise and equip an army for that purpose, was at first their only object in issuing these bills of credit. At this time the United States was not a nation. The power delegated to Congress by the States extended only to soliciting and demanding a restoration of rights, and to prepare for war, if need be. Congress was little else than an advisory counsel to the States. They possessed no power to impose and collect taxes or duties, and did not attempt it. They exacted that the States should impose taxes and collect them; but the States could comply with the wishes of Congress in this behalf, or neglect to do so, and some of them did the latter.

The bills of credit emitted by Congress were not made legal tender in payment of private debts, and were not made receivable for debts due Congress or the colonies. Congress had no debts due them. They collected no duties on imports, or internal revenue. These impositions and collections were confined to the States. To Congress it was all outgo and no income. They made their own money, and paid it out to equip and sustain the army, and to support a limited civil service. There was but one means through which the money issued and paid out by the Continental Treasurer could get back into his hands. Of this we shall speak hereafter.

Previous to 1779 the faith of the States, as expressed by Congress, was pledged for the redemption of the bills emitted; but the faith of Congress, or of a National Government of any kind, was not pledged. The law did not, at any time, read that Congress would pay, or that the Treasurer would pay, but that the States as individuals, not collectively, would pay. Everybody knew that the duty of paying or redeeming the bills devolved upon the States in their individual capacity, not upon Congress or a nation.

Each State was bound only for its portion. The debt was divided among the States according to population. This fact, at the beginning of 1799, or thereabout, was extensively circulated among the people, to the prejudice of Congress, and to the depreciation of the bills. Congress noticed the change, and pledged the faith of the United States for the redemption of the bills, and soon after commenced giving certificates of indebtedness bearing interest for them.

But another most fatal mistake in the issue of this money was in making it payable not only in coin, but in that which was at a premium over other coin. It should not have been redeemable in coin of any kind; it should have been made legal tender—lawful money. The States had only about $5,000,000 of coin, all told. It was impossible to make the redemption in coin, and no such promise should have been given. If no coin had been promised in the law, or in the notes, no one would have expected coin, and it would not have been demanded. But the law expressly promised coin. When the people presented the notes at the treasury of a State, or that of Congress, and demanded the fulfillment of the promise, and learned that the coin could not be paid, the credit of the notes was injured—though the people stood the disappointment, and continued to receive and pay the money until another injurious circumstance occurred.

Very unwisely, the Continental money was not made as though intended to circulate as money. For the purpose of giving it credit above other notes, it was made payable in coin, which was at a premium. The failure to pay coin for it, as promised, reduced it somewhat in value; and the failure of the States to redeem it, as provided by law, reduced it still lower. The extension of time in which the States were to redeem the notes, from four years after 1779 to nineteen years after that time, had a still greater depressing effect.

The fact that the printing of the notes was, of necessity, poorly done, caused them to be counterfeited in large quantities, so that few persons could know the good notes from the counterfeits. The people feared to receive them. This counterfeiting was a trick of the enemy to destroy the money.

At the time these notes began to depreciate, it was the darkest in the Revolution. Our armies had not been successful in battle. The British had been reinforced. The contest, with men of weak faith, was doubtful. The people did not need to be told that if the cause failed the money would be worthless. The cause of the colonies depended upon sustaining the money of the colonies. Great Britain well knew this; and for the purpose of destroying the Revolution, the armies of the Crown, with the aid of British gold and silver, and their allies, the Tories, used all their powers to cut off from the colonies the sinews of war, and thus to destroy the American cause. Much of the depreciation of the bills of credit was owing to these efforts.

Had this money been both issued and redeemable by the nation or Government; had the Government possessed the power to impose duties on imports and internal taxes, and to collect them; had the bills been made, by the act creating them, legal tender in payment of all private debts and receivable for debts due the nation and individuals, with power in the General Government to make its authority respected; had nothing been said in the law or in the notes about paying in specie, as was done on the issue of our treasury notes, and no provision been made for the States to receive them in coin, not more than $50,000,000 need to have been issued. The money paid out would have returned to the treasury for taxes and duties, and could have been re-paid out. This would have obviated the necessity of issuing three-fourths of the bills issued, and kept those out at par, or nearly so, with coin. But whether par with coin or not, they would have been a sure, sound circulation, with which the loyal people would have been satisfied.

But our fathers, though great and wise in counsel, and brave and patriotic in battle and trial, do not appear to have understood the proper method of conducting the finances of a great people in time of war. They were misled by the idea that a people in a protracted war could sustain a specie currency, or one based upon currency, and that when the able-bodied men of the nation were in camp or on the battle-field, instead of at the plow or anvil, and the productive industries of the country were prostrate, millions upon millions could be collected from the people to supply armies, or to redeem a currency by which they were supplied. Their fatal error was in making their bills payable in premium coin, on demand, and providing that the money should be redeemed in eight years, by taxes collected from an impoverished people, instead of issuing the bills as a permanent circulation, making them legal tender and par with coin by receiving and paying them for everything for which coin was paid and received. What would have been the result if, in 1862 and 1863, the United States, with all their resources and power, had pursued the policy of our father in 1775 and 1776. It is impossible to compute the millions lost by the American people in the last 100 years by the specie delusion. But this money was wanting in all these monitary characteristics. At all times, when debts were to be paid by the Continental Congress, it was necessary to issue new money, instead of paying therefor that which had been received into the Treasury for taxes or duties, or in exchange for interest certificates and bonds. The circulation therefore increased to four times the wants of trade and commerce, and became, for this and the other reasons assigned, depreciated.

But depreciated and imperfect as this money was, it enabled our fathers to achieve their and our independence. But for the Continental money the Revolution would have been a failure. It enabled Congress to equip and sustain armies until 1780, when other nations espoused our cause and loaned us money, and aided in fighting our battles. For four long years of war this was our only money. In 1780 and 1781 France became our ally and loaned us $5,000,000 in coin.

We confess to a want of admiration of those statesmen who compare the United States of America in 1879 to the Continental government of 1775 and 1776, and the paper issues of the Continental Congress, with those of the United States at this time; and insist that because the former money was a partial failure the latter must of necessity be. We have little or no confidence in the honesty or patriotism of those hired authors who now, at the bidding of Wall Street, point to the example of the Continental government as a warning to the greatest nation on earth not to issue paper money. Let them be reminded of the following facts:

Our fathers were not at the time a nation. They had pledged their lives, their fortunes and their sacred honor in support of their right to be independent. We, through their sacrifices, have been a nation nearly 100 years. They numbered only 3,000,000 of souls; we number 50,000,000. Thirteen States composed the confederation; we number thirty-eight States and ten Territories. Their western boundary was the Mississippi River; ours is the Pacific Ocean. They had no fortifications, no army, no navy, no canals, no railroads, no steamboats, no steamships, no constitution nor laws made thereunder; no legislative, judicial, and executive departments of the

Government; no national duties on imports, no national internal revenue, no manufactories, no experienced artisans, no money, no credit, no army, no navy, and their foreign commerce was at the time cut off. We have fortifications at every assailable point; can in a short time put a million of brave men under arms, well equipped, and can cover the ocean with our ships. Our canals connect our inland seas with the ocean. The whole Union is chequered with railroads, connecting all parts of the country, even the Atlantic and Pacific. Our manufacturing establishments are found in every State of the Union. Our machine shops have been supplied with the most experienced artisans. Our agricultural products enable us to export $500,000,000 per annum. Our duties on imports amount to $200,000,000 annually; our internal revenue to more than $100,000,000. Our production of the precious metals amounts to $70,000,000 per year. In view of these facts, how preposterous to compare the United States in 1879 with the Continental Government in 1776, and their issues of paper money with those of the United States now. The Continental Government failed to meet its obligations. The Government of the United States under the Constitution never has. In 1776 the Continental Government had established no credit at home or abroad. The Government of the United States has established a first-class credit both at home and abroad. A currency issued by the Government of the United States, made legal tender in all parts of the nation, paid out for all debts due by the Government, and received into the treasury for all debts due the nation, can never be at discount.

Mr. Calhoun, in a few words, expresses the difference between Continental money and United States Treasury notes. He says the former was a promise to pay without revenue, but the latter is a promise to receive for revenue, with an abundance of revenue to receive. We add that the former promise was not made by a nation to be fulfilled by a nation. The latter is made by a nation having the ability to perform.

THE FIRST BANK OF THE UNITED STATES UNDER THE CONSTITUTION.*

This bank was chartered by Congress in 1791. The capital was $10,000,000. One-fifth of the stock was owned by the United States and $8,000,000 by the people. Six of the eight millions were Government indebtedness; and $2,000,000—money. The tenth section of the charter made the notes of the bank those of the nation, by providing that for twenty years they should be received for all dues to the Government.

This institution was the depository of all Government money, the fiscal agent of the United States, the commissioner of all Government loans, received all the revenues of the nation, paid all the debts of the Government, and its notes were made by the 14th section of the act, receivable for all obligations due the Government for twenty years, or during the life of the charter. The bank always paid coin when demanded, but the notes were legal tender to the Government; and, therefore, satisfactory to the people, whether the bank paid coin or not. This was made plain by the law, and was demonstrated in the last four years of the life of the charter, when the most bitter controversy was carried on between the bank and the President and Cabinet.

The bank, it was charged, had attempted to control,

---
*Warwick Martin.

and had controlled elections in the State, and was then laboring to control those of the nation. Reports charging the bank with corruption, and even insolvency, were circulated; but the notes of the institution were legal tender for all debts due the United States, and on that account were preferred to coin by the people. The charter of this bank expired, by limitation, in 1836.

We solicit especial attention to the fact that the two banks of the United States, which existed for forty years, were and are the only banks of issue in the United States, or in any part of the commercial world, which never suspended specie payments. We ask every thinking man, why was this so? We ask each one to give to himself a candid answer to the question. It is impossible for him to say that it was simply because said banks were better fortified by coin in our new country, than institutions of the old world were. On the contrary no bank of issue, not even the Bank of England or these banks, kept more coin than one dollar to twenty of liabilities, including circulation and deposits. Coin lying idle in banks pays no interest, and banks wish something which will pay interest. The reason can not be found in anything but in this, that the strong arm of the United States was under and around these institutions; the Government owned a large portion of the stock, having five directors in the institution, and had contracted with these banks and with the people that the United States would always receive their notes for all obligations to the nation. In the United States, and throughout the world, the notes, drafts and obligations of these institutions carried with them the name and credit of the new, but great Republic. Had these institutions possessed nothing to depend upon but specie payment, they would have shared the fate of all banks of issue. These banks were the United States Treasury and the Treasury was the banks.

Do not suppose that we approve the chartering of these institutions by Congress. We are opposed to all such charters and connections. There was no necessity for creating these banks. Congress should have followed the advice of Jefferson instead of Hamilton. The Treasury should have issued all the paper money of the country, and made it a full legal tender, as it did the copper, silver and gold, money. Its name, power, revenue and credit should have been used to sustain its own money, instead of being thus loaned to sustain a private corporation and individual interests. Its paper issue, made full legal tender, would have commanded more respect and confidence everywhere than the notes of these banks thus guaranteed by the nation. They never would have been at a discount for coin; they would generally have been at a premium therefor. Gold, silver and Treasury notes should have been made by law full legal tender, and the one could never have been at any considerable premium over the other. Being all equal in law, the one most convenient would have the best.

The law placed the Government money in this bank, and there it remained subject to the warrants of the treasurer. The bank received the Government revenues, and paid the Government debts. In reality, the bank was the Treasury; and so far as finance was concerned, the Government was the bank. The name and credit of the United States accompanied every note throughout the world. All the copper, silver, gold and paper money of the nation was in this bank. The Government kept no money at the Treasury. The people who held and used the notes did not inquire whether the bank paid or did not pay coin. It was a matter of indifference to them. They did not wish coin. The notes which the Government had bound itself to receive for all dues for twenty years, whether the bank paid coin or not, were satisfactory to them. They did not look to or regard the bank. They confided in the Government, which did not deceive them. In those days the Government kept contracts made with people, as well as with nations and institutions. There was little or no demand for coin in business. It, therefore, went into the bank, and into the Treasury, which was the bank. The notes went out —the coin went in. When drafts of the treasurer upon the bank were presented, for which coin could be demanded, the notes were generally paid instead of coin, being preferred because of safety, uniformality and convenience. The coin remained in the bank—the notes went out among the people.

Men of business will not use coin in large quantities if they can obtain instead thereof reliable paper money. This money always has, and always will meet this demand. The charter of this bank expired in 1811.

THE SECOND BANK OF THE UNITED STATES, CHARTERED BY CONGRESS IN 1816.

This bank had $35,000,000 capital, so-called. The Government owned $7,000,000 of the stock, the people $28,000,000. Twenty-one millions of this $28,000,000 consisted of Government indebtedness; $7,000,000 were coin and the notes of the State banks, supposed to be good, though suspended. The bank was also given 25 branches in the States. The charter which passed Congress in 1815, provided that $15,000,000 of the capital of the bank should be United States Treasury notes, issued during the war, and then used as money by the Government and the people. Mr. Madison vetoed this bill because of this provision. He insisted that to give the bank said Treasury notes would be to furnish it with $15,000,000 of money instead of bonds, and to deprive the United States of that amount of money. The charter was changed the next winter, and bonds were taken by the bank instead of Treasury notes. The bank wished the Treasury notes instead of bonds, because they were legal tender for all debts due the United States. The bonds were not legal tender for anything. This bank paid $1,500,000 for its charter.

Being based on specie, and authorized to issue thereon four dollars of paper to one of coin in reserve, the volume of its outstanding issue was constantly fluctuating between thirty and a hundred million of dollars, keeping values irregular, and trade and business in a constant tremor of uncertainty. The result was prostration one day, and stimulation the next. The price of wheat was one year as low as 20 cents per bushel in Kentucky, and pork $1 per barrel in Pittsburgh.

Ruinous sacrifices of property at sheriff sales followed a year of apparent prosperity. To stop this condition of things, and to strike down a dangerous political power, Jackson, in 1832, organized himself into a greenback party, and declared a war of extermination against this enemy of the people.

Contemporaneous history informs us that at this time "the press of the country was completely subsidized; congress, as well as state legislatures, bowed in abject submission to the mandates of this Money Power; and even the supreme court of the United States did not escape its contaminating influence. The people were perfectly helpless, and the outlook of American freedom was dark, indeed."

Millions of dollars belonging to depositors were squandered to corrupt the people and defeat Jackson's second election.

Statesmen, congressmen, politicians, and editors, all succumbed to its influence. Hon. W. D. Kelley, in a speech in 1875, said:

"In Philadelphia, the bank would order the business men to hold public meetings in its behalf, in order that it might ascertain who were its friends, and who were courageous enough to stand by the President in his efforts to redeem the people, and then in turn would appoint places for the assembling of different trades, in order that the employers might see who of their workmen had opinions which they dared maintain."

The two political parties were divided. Like the Republican and Democratic parties of to-day, the Republican and Federal parties of that day had their bank and anti-bank advocates. Jackson's war was not, as many suppose, against paper money, but against the right and policy of banks to issue it. He contended that the Government alone had the right to issue money. Before, during and after his administration, United States treasury notes were issued and in circulation, and although their issue was bitterly opposed, and their constitutionality denied by the bank party, they were strongly advocated by the anti-bank party, and not only the constitutionality of their issue, but their legal tender qualities were affirmed by the supreme court in the case of Thorndike against the United States.

Jackson's new anti-bank party took the name of Democrat.

Berkey says:

"The bank itself was a colossal Money Power—its arms in every state—by means of branches—its power over country banks—its power over the business community—over public men who were its debtors and retainers—its organization under a single head, issuing its orders in secret to be obeyed in all places, and by all subordinates at the same moment. Such was the formidable array on the side of the bank."

The Republican party that had elected Jackson was demoralized and disheartened by the division this issue had created.

Still old Hickory was firm, unyielding and uncompromising.

He gathered his little Democratic band around him, and when the second campaign opened, he sent them out to educate and save the people, with nothing to rely upon but the goodness of his cause, and the intelligence and patriotism of the people. He made no concessions, and formed no coalitions with either of the old parties, but marched straight on to victory or to death. Benton, in his "Thirty Years in Congress," says that the bank spent $3,000,000 in bribing and subsidizing members of congress, newspaper editors, politicians, brokers, jobbers and men of influence, to defeat Jackson and purchase a re-charter.

But justice and Jackson prevailed, the bank power was destroyed, and Democracy was triumphant.

When we now consider, that through the stupidity of the people, and the bribery of those in authority, another bank power, sixty-six times the strength of the old one, has grown up in our midst, it will be seen that the struggle for its destruction will be formidable, but if successful, the victory will be great.

STATE BANKS.

"The old United States Bank was succeeded by hundreds of State banks all over the country. They were not chartered by the United States, but by the States of the Union. The nation did not agree to receive their notes for anything. The people soon learned this fact. They professed to pay coin for all liabilities. For some time they met all coin demands upon them, but the people had no assurance that their notes would be received by the Government for all dues, if they failed to pay coin, as they had, with the United States bank notes. It was not long until bank notes in circulation were presented at the counters of the banks for coin. Coin was again seen among the people and in the business of the country. The notes went into the banks; the coin went among the people. The condition of things was reversed. Confidence in the State banks weakened; their coin became less and less, until they failed to pay coin."

The extent to which these banks were enabled to loan their credit by means of the specie basis will appear from an examination of the following table, copied from the *Merchants' Magazine* and the report of the commissioners of the banks of Connecticut for a period of twelve years, from 1837 to 1849. The condition of the Connecticut banks may be taken as an average of the banks of the country:

Year.	Capital.	Circulation.	Total Liabilities.	Specie.	Loans and discounts.
1837	$8,744,697 50	$3,996,325 30	$15,715,964 50	$415,386 10	$13,246,495 08
1838	8,754,467 50	1,930,552 45	12,302,613 11	535,447 86	9,760,246 80
1839	8,832,223 00	3,987,815 45	14,942,779 31	502,180 15	12,286,946 97
1840	8,878,245 00	2,330,589 95	12,930,572 40	959,032 52	10,418,630 87
1841	8,873,927 50	2,784,721 45	13,866,373 45	454,298 61	10,914,673 36
1842	8,876,317 57	2,555,638 33	13,465,052 32	471,238 08	10,683,412 37
1843	8,580,393 50	5,379,947 02	12,914,124 66	438,752 92	9,798,392 27
1844	8,292,238 00	3,490,903 06	14,572,681 32	454,430 30	10,842,955 35
1845	8,359,748 00	4,102,444 00	15,243,235 79	453,658 79	12,477,196 06
1846	8,475,630 00	3,565,347 06	15,882,685 25	481,367 09	13,032,600 78
1847	8,675,742 00	4,437,631 06	15,784,782 04	462,165 52	12,781,857 43
	95,273,623 57	38,549,475 13	157,550,872 44	5,168,657 95	126,292,888 33
1849	8,985,917 00	4,511,571 00		575,676 00	13,740,591 00
	$104,259,546 57			$5,744,633 95	$140,033,189 33

```
Average Capital..............................$8,688,295 55
Average Liabilities..........................13,129,230 37
Average Specie...............................   478,719 70
Average Loans and Discounts..................11,669,457 44
```

By the foregoing table it will be seen that the average amount of specie held by the banks in the State of Connecticut, for the twelve years, was $478,719, while the average amount of their loans to the public, during that period, was $11,669,457—more than twenty-four and one-third times as much money as the banks had specie. The annual interest on $11,669,457 was $700,167. If they could have loaned only their specie, the interest would have amounted to but $28,723. The banks gained from the public annually $671,444 above the interest on their specie; and, in the twelve years, $8,057,328. They collected this interest in advance, and made their dividends half yearly to their stockholders; therefore, it is proper to compound this interest half yearly, which would swell their gains to nearly $12,000,000, that is to say $1,000,000 interest annually. These were actual gains, as much realized by these banks as if they had produced and sold annually $700,167 worth of agricultural products. (The statements of the banks of any of the large cities, published from time to time in the newspapers, will disclose a similar inflation of credit at the present time. The fact that the National Banks do not redeem their notes in specie makes no difference. They are banks of issue and belong to the specie basis system all the same.)

The banks of the United States have been compelled to suspend specie payments at various times, as follows, to wit: In 1809, 1814, 1819, 1825, 1834, 1837, 1839, 1841, 1857, 1861, and in 1873 currency payment. These suspensions have invariably occasioned great public distress, and in several instances have involved the entire country in bankruptcy and ruin, from which it took years to recover. In March, 1809, a legislative committee of the State of Rhode Island made an examination into the affairs of the Farmers' Exchange Bank of Gloucester, and it was found that the bank had $580,000 of its notes in circulation, and only $86.16 in its vaults for their redemption. Before the end of the year a general suspension of the banks of New England took place, and it was discovered that they were nearly all in the same condition—no specie and nothing to show but the worthless notes of speculators.

The National Banking Act of 1863 placed a tax of ten per cent. upon all State bank notes, which had the effect of driving these issues out of circulation and winding up the banks.

CHAPTER VII.

THE BANK OF VENICE.

Notwithstanding the bank advocates raise their voices in holy horror against the idea of the Government engaging in anything like a banking business, it is nevertheless a fact that the Venetian Government was the first banker, and established the first bank on record. It was a bank, too, that not only did all the banking business of that republic, but of a large proportion of the civilized world. It existed for over six hundred years, during which time it never failed or suspended, and was, according to historians, "the admiration of all people, the chief instrument of finance, and the chief facility for the commerce of a large portion of the continent." The duration of its prosperous existence, the unparalleled facilities it afforded to enterprise, the strength and power it gave to the Government, the great favor with which its medium met, and the premium it commanded over the precious metals, prove it to have been based upon a system of more than ordinary merit, and one that students of financial science would do well to study with particular care.

In the year 1171 a war between the Venetian republic and the Grecian empire gave rise to the Bank of Venice as our late civil war gave rise to our greenback system, the currency or exchange medium in both cases being precisely of the same nature, and possessing the same basis and qualities. After having exhausted every other financial resource, the Venetian Government was obliged to have recourse to what is falsely called a forced loan. Like our Government during the late war, it needed soldiers, guns, ammunition, ships, mules, horses and other things necessary to carry on a successful campaign, and as all of these things must be paid for, money must be had, and as the Government had none, it proposed to borrow it of its own citizens in such sums as each felt able and disposed to contribute. For these sums loaned to the Government, the individuals loaning them were simply credited on the books of the Government treasury, and these credits were made transferable in part, or in whole, and thus became a medium of exchange, and a substitute for money in the payment of debts. The difference between the Venetian system, and the greenback system was, the Venetians gave their credits for money, and with the money purchased supplies and paid for services, while our Government gave its greenback credit tokens direct for what it needed, without the use of money. The policies and systems were identical, except the greenback system is more simple, as it avoids the unnecessary handling of coin.

The Venetian greenbacks were simply inscriptions of credit. A man who had credit at the Venetian treasury used it in the purchase of goods or the payment of debts, just as we use greenbacks. If he owed a man a thousand ducats, more or less, he transferred to his creditor that amount of his claims against the Government. These credits, too, were irredeemable by the Government. Colwell says: "Reimbursement of the loan ceased to be regarded as either necessary or desirable. Every creditor was reimbursed when he transferred his claim on the books of the bank."

Thus the cost of their war, like that of our own, was not felt, as the money expended was immediately replaced by a currency of Government credit. The entire public debt was in the shape of a medium of exchange.

The Bank of Venice was simply a Government bureau, having charge of this fund, similar to our bureau of the comptroller of the currency. It kept the records of the owners and transfers of this fund for the benefit of the commercial business of the country. The credit of this bank, which was the most popular medium of exchange the world ever had, commanded a premium over coin for two reasons: first, security from loss or robbery, and its superior convenience of handling, and second, from its perfect security against the prevailing fraud of counterfeiting and debasement of coin. The volume of these credits was not restricted to the original loan, but was enlarged as the demand for the fund increased. We may judge of the high estimation in which this ideal money of Venice was held when history informs us that from the commencement, coin was continually being deposited for bank credit, knowing that it would never be returned to the depositor. Colwell says " If individuals could make purchases and pay debts by transfers in bank, the public treasury could well afford to receive it in payment of its dues, as it would only be equivalent to taking up its own obligations. Thus, the more these credits were employed, the more the demand for them increased, the more rapidly money flowed into the Treasury, and the more readily the Government could afford to receive payment of its revenues in the funds of the bank."

Thus, for near seven hundred years, existed a system

of finance, based upon public credit, with entire confidence on the part of the people, and admirable prudence and good faith on the part of the Government, converting the entire public debt into a currency or medium of exchange, which really made a public debt a public blessing, and produced a degree of prosperity never before or since reached by any people. The only difference between the Venetian system and our greenback system is, that the Venetian money was ideal, represented by transferable credits on the bank books, and ours is ideal, represented by greenback credit tokens transferable by passing from hand to hand. The principle was the same, the basis the same, and were it not for the bank sharks that infest the times, endeavoring to cry down, browbeat and discredit a system so safe, just and beneficial to the public welfare, in order that they themselves may have the advantage of controlling the currency of the country, resumption and specie payments would never be dreamed of.

Stephen Colwell's digest of fourteen authorities leads to the following deductions, as will be seen by perusal of his able work:

First—It proves that there was a national bank of Venice founded on a loan of two millions of ducats spent by the State in 1171, and the bank existed within the memory of living men, a period of 626 years, during which time it was gradually enlarged over seven hundred per cent.

Second—That A. D. 1423 it was modified by law to prevent fluctuation.

Third—That the four per cent. interest previously paid was abolished.

Fourth—That all promise of reimbursement, other than transfer of credit receipts, was abolished.

Fifth—That the nation "took the coin of its loans one time for all" in the nation's bank, giving a credit receipt only.

Sixth—That no coin was kept as a specie basis of credit, or for strengthening the nation. They were immediately paid out.

Seventh—That no promise to pay any coin was made after 1423, for nearly 400 years of its continuance.

Eighth—That this "fiat" or legal credit was that in which all coins were expressed—the fixed standard of payment—and thus the principal money of account; specie being for retail coin or export commodity and legal tender at 20 per cent. discount.

Ninth—That the premium fixed by law of 20 per cent. premium over the Venetian gold ducat, so celebrated for its fineness in export, was a real superiority of legal money of account over the commodity gold, and over gold currency.

Tenth—That it was not dependent on any promise of convertibility or redemption in gold, as no claim for any gold was acknowledged in the National Bank.

Eleventh—That it continued for nearly four hundred years with all these extraordinary attributes, producing no financial derangements and no opposition; but on the contrary grew until it exceeded the money per capita of any nation in Europe, ancient and modern, and was the pride of Venice, the envy of Europe.

Twelfth—That it only fell when Napoleon conquered Venice, when it had reached an issue exceeding $16,000,000 of Government credit or money for 200,000 people, excluding the dependencies of Venice.

Thirteenth—That Napoleon could not, and did not find a ducat in its vaults, as there had never been a pretence of any. That he would have taken gold if it was there, is clear, and thus have been strengthened to further enslave Venice.

Fourteenth—That the interest alone saved on each million ducats was $6,250,000,000,000 at four per cent. for 400 years, savings bank interest.

These facts, if true, mean something, and fair argument is better than calling hard names, because the American people love light and truth and fair play.

CHAPTER VIII.

METALLIC MONEY.*

"For ages gold and silver have been esteemed precious metals, containing a large amount of intrinsic value, although their inadequacy to supply natural wants is manifest, when we imagine a man, with a bag of coins, on a desert island, and without the power to exchange them for other articles. These metals have intrinsic, or actual value, and this value consists in their utility for utensils and ornaments; their malleability, ductility and beauty rendering them, for some purposes, superior to all other metals. But it will be confessed, that we could far better dispense with them than with any of the abundant metals, which are in more general and constant use, and the loss of which would seriously impair our comfort.

"In early ages, gold and silver were, doubtless, selected for the material of money on account of their scarcity, and the amount of labor necessary to procure them; the same reason that led the American Indians to select the beaver skin for a standard of value, by which the value of all other skins and commodities was estimated. It has been already explained, that gold and silver, when used as money, cease to have any other use. These metals have, however, received the sanction of Governments as the material of money. The laws require

---

*Kellog.

coins used as a public tender shall contain a certain weight of the authorized metal—without which they are illegal, and cannot be enforced as a tender. But the only reason they are not received is, that they are unsanctioned by law. If coins of base metal were endowed by law with the properties of money—that is, were made representatives of actual value, capable of accumulating by interest and a public tender for debts, they would answer every purpose of money, equally well with coins of pure metal. They could represent, measure, accumulate and exchange property, and these are the sole properties and uses of money.

"If money be a commodity, why do Governments pretend to fix a value upon coins, and not upon any other commodity, although it be made of gold or silver? If a definite value be assigned to one commodity by legal enactment, a definite value should also be legally assigned to every other commodity, that each may sustain a just relation according to the amount of labor necessary to manufacture or produce it. If money be a commodity, goods sold might as well be made payable in other commodities, sugar, beef, etc., as in money. Why not as well sell money on time, payable in goods, as goods on time, payable in money? If money be a commodity, why should the Government force the public to convert every other commodity into this one to pay debts? If the sale and purchase of all other commodities will cause debts to exist, why should one commodity only be competent to pay them? And why should the value of every other commodity be determined by this one commodity? If money be a commodity, why does the Government reserve the right to coin it, making its private coinage a criminal offense?

Why not let any one make it, and dispose of it in market as of any other commodity? If money be merchandise, why is it, that it can be at all times exchanged for property and products, in any part of the country, and that all other more necessary commodities are at certain times esteemed almost worthless, compared with it? It is answered, that it is because it is made by law a legal tender in payment for debts—that it has this superiority over every other commodity. But the very answer proves that it is not a commodity; for a legal tender is a creation by law of certain properties which do not naturally belong to any substance, but which are made to represent all substances, and to control their exchange."

NOT A STANDARD OF VALUE.

It is utterly impossible to make gold uniform as a standard or measure of value: It being a commodity and bearing a commercial value, it rises and falls in market like any other production.

The act known as the Peel Act, of 1845, made gold receivable at the Bank of England at the rate of three pounds, nineteen shilling, and nine pence per ounce of pure metal. Doubleday's Financial History of England, page 277, has the following statement of the fluctuations of gold in that country for the ten years from 1810 to 1820, compared with the present standard price by the Peel Act. £3, 19s, 9d:

1810	£4, 5s, 0d	1816	£3, 18s, 6d
1811	£4, 17s, 1d	1817	£4, 0s, 0d
1812	£5, 8s, 0d	1818	£4, 1s, 5d
1813	£5, 10s, 0d	1819	£4, 3s, 0d
1814	£5, 1s, 0d	1820	£3, 17s, 10½d
1815	£4, 12s, 9d		

*I insert the following comparative table of English money from Sir Frederick Eden. The unit, or present value, refers of course to that of the shilling before the last coinage, which reduced it:

		Value of pound sterling present money.			Proportion.
Conquest,	1066	2	18	1½	2.906
28 E. I.,	1300	2	17	5	2.871
18 E. III.,	1344	2	12	5¼	2.622
20 E. III.,	1346	2	11	8	2.583
27 E. III.,	1353	2	6	6	2.325
13 H. IV.,	1412	1	18	9	1.937
4 E. IV.,	1464	1	11	0	1.55
18 H. VIII.,	1527	1	7	6¾	1.378
34 H. VIII.,	1543	1	3	3¼	1.163
36 H. VIII.,	1545	0	13	11½	0.698
37 H. VIII.,	1546	0	9	3¾	0.466
5 E. VI.,	1551	0	4	7¾	0.232
6 E. VI.,	1552	1	0	6¾	1.028
1 Mary,	1553	1	0	5¾	1.024
2 Eliz.,	1560	1	0	8	1.033
43 Eliz.,	1601	1	0	0	1.000

English law had decided and assumed to compel an ounce of gold to be worth £3, 19s, 9d, according to the stamp they had put on an ounce of their *pure* gold metal.

The stamp put on a piece of metal by a Government mint, is supposed to indicate its value, or to express its measuring quality or purchasing power under the law. But by the above table it will be seen that in 1810 an ounce of pure gold by the same stamp-counting measure of value was worth, bought, and was received at £4, 5s. in 1812, £5, 8s, and on up, in 1813, to £5, 10s, and then down, in 1820, to £3, 17s, 10½d; and this was not as compared with any paper money, but with itself, in value at different periods of only a few months apart.

The wealth concentrating and labor impoverishing machine of the British Government being drawn on, in 1810, for an ounce of pure gold, would count out £4, 5s

*Note by Hallam.

worth, as footed up by the stamp on the coins; drawn on for an ounce of pure gold in 1812, it would count out £5, 8s worth, drawn on in 1844 for the same, it would count out £3, 17s, 10½d worth—unless it had suspended, as it has made a rule of doing periodically, as the *gold basis* has always done.

How did it happen that the absolute measures fluctuated so that it could not swallow as much of itself at one time as another? And this is the absolute money standard that our popular preachers, bondholders and shylocks worship. Did the ounce weigh less, and then more, changing the fixed law of gravitation, during 1810 and 1812, or did the value of the metal, gold, itself by law the arbitrary measure of value, change?

The following statistics, compiled by W. Kimball, of New Haven, Conn., show the price of gold, flour and beef from 1860 to 1874, during which period the volume of currency swell from about $400,000,000 to near $2,000,000,000, and was contracted again to $779,000,000, and gold fluctuated all the way from 1.00 to 2.85.

YEAR.	GOLD.	FLOUR.	BEEF.
1860	$1.00	$5.25	$10.75
1861	1.00	5.50	9.00
1862	1.00 to 1.37	5.47	12.00
1863	1.37 to 1.72½	5.87	12.50
1864	1.72 to 2.85½	6.30	13.25
1865	1.46¼	9.72	20.00
1866	1.41	7.60	19.00
1867	1.37	9.42	13.50
1868	1.36	8.70	15.00
1869	1.24	5.70	14.00
1870	1.10	4.92	14.00
1871	1.08	5.50	12.50
1872	1.11	6.00	10.00
1873	1.12	5.55	11.00
1874	1.13	5.95	10.37

Accompanying this table are the following comments and conclusions:

"These figures demonstrate that the value of gold, as money, has not been governed by the volume of currency, and that it is not the price of gold that governs the value of products or confidence among business men, or the stability of their commercial relations.

"Money represents ideal values; its standard is regulated by ideal conceptions of the people using it, or the power using it must have the force to cause its acceptance. Uncivilized tribes use shells, beads, etc. *Heathen nations use metallic coins.* As civilization advanced, coin was found inadequate to meet the wants of commercial exchange, and to meet the ideal conception of that age, a currency was founded on a coin basis, issuing three or more dollars for one of coin."

Professor Jevons, in "Money, Mechanism and Exchange," shows from statistics read before the London Statistical Society in 1865, that the value of gold between 1789 and 1809, fell in the ratio of 100 to 54, or by 46 per cent. From 1806 to 1859 it rose again in the extraordinary ratio of 100 to 245, or by 145 per cent., "rendering Government annuities and all fixed payments almost two and a half times as valuable as they were in 1809, prostrating and paralysing industries in the same ratio that debts and fixed incomes became more valuable, and gold increased in value and purchasing power." After 1846 the gold discoveries in California and Australia increased the world's annual supply from $61,000,000 that year to $181,000,000 in 1851, diminishing its value and producing power 36 per cent. Since 1846 the annual product of gold has steadily diminished in quantity from $124,000,000 that year to about $80,000,000 in 1877.

The New York *Public*, a prominent financial newspaper of the bullion school, furnishes statistics to demonstrate that the purchasing power of gold has increased 34 per cent. since 1873, and that there has been a corresponding shrinkage in wages of labor and the general prices of products.

The London *Economist* of a late date is also of the opinion that gold has been advancing in value since 1873. To establish this conclusion, it takes the average prices of 22 articles in 1845 to 1850 at 100, and makes a comparison, of which the following are the principal points: From 1850 to 1857 there was a rise from 100 to 136; to 1859, a fall to 115; to 1864 a rise to 172; to 1869, a fall to 121; a temporary advance in 1870 to 122; and in the succeeding years fluctuations as below: 1871, 118; 1872, 129; 1873, 134; 1874, 131; 1875, 136; 1876, 123; 1877, 123; 1878, (December) 104.

It will be observed that the figures of the *Economist* show an increase in the value of gold from 1873 to 1878 of 30 per cent. while the calculation of the *Public* puts the rise in gold at 34 per cent. One figures upon commodities in London, and the other in New York.

The effects of shrinking and swelling values of money upon the industrial and commercial prosperity of a country are most disastrous.

The greatest prosperity, and the highest moral, intellectual and material development of a nation are promoted by the use of money unchanging in value. The falling value of money, induced by an increase of its quantity, has invariably been followed by an increased business activity and general prosperity, and *vice versa*.

It was scarce and dear money that cast over the world the pall of the Dark Ages, and not till the discovery of America unlocked the vaults of Potosi, in 1570, increased the volume of money, diminishing its purchasing power, and advancing the prices of labor and products, did the torch of civilization light up the world, or the shackles of feudalism fall from the limbs of society.

What is meant by dear and cheap money? What is the standard, above which we are to know it is dear, and below which it is cheap?

We have our zero, above or below which the mercury is a sure indicator of temperature. The ocean level is the standard of altitude, and the equator of latitude. These standards are unvarying and reliable.

We are told that gold is a standard of value. It can not be a standard of its own value, and as it is subject to all the changes and fluctuations of other products it is unreliable as a standard of other values

Uniformity of general prices, is the only reliable standard of money value.

All things being equal, the average value of commodities will remain steady and uniform, with a steady and uniform volume of money. This is self-evident, and the only question is, how can the purchasing power of money be fixed and permanently maintained?

Only by substituting for the precious metals a domestic medium of exchange, whose volume, and purchasing as well as debt-paying power, are within the control of the Government for the benefit of labor and enterprise.

What matters it if gold is one, or one thousand per cent. premium? As a domestic money we have no use for it, and our business prosperity should not be jeopardized by being linked to its ever-varying and uncertain fortunes.

Gold has nearly doubled in value and purchasing power since 1864. We need a cheaper money, within the reach of every hand of toil.

COINAGE ACTS.

(Compiled and digested by W. L. Fawcett.)

The following includes all the clauses of all the laws of the United States (and the previous Confederation of States) from 1781 to 1876, as they relate to the *Weight, Fineness* and *Legal-Tender Value* of United States and foreign coins. This summary is intended as historic of the policy of the Government in regard to gold and silver coins and the relative values of the two metals:

Articles of Confederation between the States, adopted March 1, 1781.

§ 1. The United States in Congress assembled shall also have the sole and exclusive right and power of regulating the alloy and value of coin struck by their own authority or by that of the respective States, fixing the standard of weights and measures throughout the United States.

[By act of the Congress of the Confederation passed August 8, 1786, and by the ordinance of October 16, 1786, a silver dollar, containing 375.64 grains of pure silver, was established as the "unit of account," though the Confederation had not established any mint, and no such coins as were specified by the act were coined anywhere. The dollar thus established was intended to be the equivalent of 4s. 6d. sterling, but fell short of it by about two per cent.]

The Constitution, adopted September 17, 1787.

The Congress shall have power—

§ 2. To borrow money on the credit of the United States.

§ 3. To coin money, regulate the value thereof, and of foreign coin, and fix the standard of weights and measures.

No State shall coin money; emit bills of credit; make anything but gold and silver coin a tender in payment of debts; pass any *ex post facto* law, or law impairing the obligation of contracts.

Act April 2, 1792.

That the money of account of the United States shall be expressed in dollars or units, dimes or tenths, cents or hundredths, and mills or thousandths, a dime being the tenth part of a dollar, a cent the hundreth part of a dollar, a mill the thousandth part of a dollar, and that all accounts in the public offices and all proceedings in the courts of the United States shall be kept and had in conformity to this regulation.

§ 4. That a mint for the purpose of a national coinage be and the same is established; to be situate and carried on at the seat of government of the United States for the time being.

§ 5. There shall be, from time to time, struck and coined at said mint, coins of gold, silver and copper, of the following denominations, values and descriptions, viz.: *Eagles*—each to be of the value of ten dollars or units, and to contain 247½ grains of pure, or 270 grains of standard gold. *Half eagles*—each to be of the value of five dollars or units, and to contain 123¾ grains of pure, or 135 grains of standard gold. *Quarter eagles*—each to be of the value of two dollars and a half dollar, and to contain 61⅞ grains of pure, or 67½ grains of standard gold. *Dollars or units*—each to be of the value of a Spanish milled dollar, as the same is now current, and to contain 371¼ grains of pure, or 416 grains of standard silver. *Half dollars*—each to be of half the value of the dollar or unit, and to contain 185⅝ grains of pure, or 208 grains of standard silver. *Quarter dollars*—each to be of one-fourth the value of the dollar or unit, and to contain 92 13/16 grains of pure, or 104 grains of standard silver. *Dismes*—each to be one-tenth of the value of a dollar or unit, and to contain 37½ grains of pure, or 41¾ grains of standard silver. *Half dismes*—each to be of the value of one-twentieth of a dollar, and to contain 18 9/16 grains of pure, or 20¾ grains of standard silver. *Cents*—each to be of the value of one hundredth part of a dollar, and to contain 11 pennyweights of copper. *Half cents*—each to be of the value of half a cent, and to contain 5½ pennyweights of copper.

§ 6. The proportional value of gold to silver in all coins which shall, by law, be current as money within the United States shall be as fifteen to one, according to quantity in weight of pure gold and pure silver; that is to say, every fifteen pounds weight of pure silver shall be of equal value in all payments with one pound weight of pure gold, and so in proportion as to greater or less quantities of the respective metals.

Act February 9, 1793.

§ 7. At the expiration of three years next ensuing from the time when the coinage of gold and silver, agreeably to the act entitled "An act establishing a mint and regulating the coins of the United States," shall commence at the mint of the United States (which shall be announced by proclamation of the President of the United States), all foreign gold coins and all foreign silver coins, except Spanish milled dollars and parts of such dollars, shall cease to be legal tender as aforesaid. (See § 13.)

§ 8. All foreign gold and silver coins, except Spanish milled dollars and parts of such dollars, which shall be received in payment for moneys due to the United States after the said time when the coining of gold and silver coins shall begin at the mint of the United States, shall, previously to their being issued in circulation be coined anew, in conformity to the act entitled "An act establishing a mint and regulating the coins of the United States." (See § 19.)

Act March 2, 1799.

§ 9. All foreign coins and currencies shall be estimated at the following rates, viz.: Each *pound sterling* of Great Britain at four dollars and forty-four cents ($4.44); each *livre tournois* of France at eighteen and a half cents (18½); each *florin* or *guilder* of the Union Netherlands at forty cents (40); each *mark-banco* of Hamburg at thirty-three and one-third cents (33⅓); each *rix dollar* of Denmark at one hundred (100) cents; each *real* of plate and each *rial of vellon* of Spain, the former at ten cents and the latter at five cents each; each *milree* of Portugal at one dollar and twenty-four cents; each *pound sterling* of Ireland at four dollars and ten cents; each *tale* of China at one dollar and forty-eight cents; each *pagoda* of India at one dollar and ninety-four cents; each *rupee* of Bengal at fifty-five and one-half cents; and all other denominations of money, as nearly as may be to the said rates or the intrinsic value thereof, compared with money of the United States.

§ 10. All duties and fees to be collected shall be payable in money of the United States, or in foreign gold and silver coins at the following rates, that is to say: the gold coins of Great Britain and Portugal of the standard prior to the year 1792 at the rate of one hundred cents for every twenty-seven grains of the actual weight thereof; the gold coins of France, Spain and the dominions of Spain, of the standard prior to the year 1792, at the rate of one hundred cents for every twenty-seven grains and two-fifths of a grain of the actual weight thereof; Spanish milled dollars at the rate of one hundred cents for each dollar, the actual weight whereof shall not be less than seventeen (17) pennyweights and seven (7) grains—and in proportion for the parts of a dollar; crowns of France at the rate of one hundred and ten cents for each crown; the actual weight whereof shall not be less than eighteen (18) pennyweights and seventeen (17) grains—and in proportion for the parts of a crown, *Provided*, that no foreign crowns shall be receivable which are not by law a legal tender for the payment of all debts—except in consequence of a proclamation by the President of the United States authorizing such foreign coins to be received in payment of duties and fees as aforesaid.

Act March 3, 1801.

§ 11. The foreign coins and currencies hereinafter mentioned shall be estimated in the computation of duties at the following rates: each sicca rupee of Bengal and each rupee of Bombay at fifty cents, and each star pagoda of Madras at one hundred and eighty-four cents.

Act April 10, 1806.

§ 12. Foreign gold and silver coins shall pass current as money within the United States, and be a legal tender for the payment of all debts and demands at the several and respective rates following, and not otherwise, viz.: The gold coins of Great Britain and Portugal of their present standard at the rate of one hundred cents for every twenty-seven grains of the standard weight thereof; the gold coins of France, Spain and the dominions of Spain, of their present standard, at the rate of one hundred cents for every twenty-seven grains and two-fifths of a grain of the actual weight thereof. Spanish milled dollars at the rate of one hundred cents for each, the actual weight whereof shall not be less than seventeen (17) pennyweights and seven (7) grains, and in proportion for the parts of a dollar. Crowns of France at the rate of one hundred and ten cents for each crown, the actual weight whereof shall not be less than eighteen (18) pennyweights and seventeen (17) grains, and in proportion for the parts of a crown. And it shall be the duty of the Secretary of the Treasury to cause assays of the foreign gold and silver coins of the description made current by this act, and which shall issue subsequently to the passage of this act, and shall circulate in the United States—at the mint aforesaid, at least once in every year, and to make report of the result thereof to Congress, for the purpose of enabling Congress to make such coins current—if they shall deem the same to be proper—at their real standard value.

§ 13. That the first section of the act entitled "An act regulating foreign coins and for other purposes," passed the 9th day of February, 1793, be and the same is hereby repealed, and the operation of the second section of the same act is hereby suspended for and during the space of three years from the passage of this act. (See §§7-8.)

Act March 3, 1823.

§ 14. The following gold coins shall be received in all payments on account of public lands at the several and respective rates following and not otherwise, viz.: the gold coins of Great Britain and Portugal of their present standard, at the rate of one hundred cents for every twenty-seven grains, or eighty-eight cents and eight-ninths (88 8-9) per pennyweight; the gold coins of France, of their present standard, at the rate of one hundred cents for every twenty-seven and one-half grains or eighty-seven and a quarter (87 ¼) cents per pennyweight, and the gold coins of Spain, of their present standard, at the rate of one hundred cents for every twenty-eight and a half grains, or eighty-four cents per pennyweight.

§ 15. It shall be the duty of the Secretary of the Treasury to cause assays of the foregoing coins to be made at the mint of the United States at least once in every year, and make report of the result thereof to Congress.

Act June 25, 1834.

§ 16. The following silver coins shall be of the legal value, and shall pass current as money within the United States, by tale for the payment of all debts and demands at the rate of one hundred cents to the dollar, that is to say, the *dollars* of Mexico, Peru, Chili and Central America, of not less weight than four hundred and fifteen grains each, and those re-stamped in Brazil of the like weight, of not less fineness than ten ounces fifteen pennyweights of pure silver in the troy pound of twelve ounces of standard silver; and the five-franc pieces of France, when of not less fineness than ten (10) ounces and sixteen (16) pennyweights in twelve ounces troy weight of standard silver, and weighing not less than three hundred and eighty-four grains each—at the rate of ninety-three (93) cents each.

§ 17. The following gold coins shall pass current as money in the United States, and be receivable in all payments by weight, for the payment of all debts and demands at the rates following, that is to say; the gold coins of Great Britain, Portugal and Brazil, of not less than twenty-two (22) carats fine, at the rate of ninety-four cents and eight-tenths of a cent ($94\frac{8}{10}$) per pennyweight; the gold coins of France, nine-tenths fine, at the rate of ninety-three cents and one-tenth of a cent ($93\frac{1}{10}$) per pennyweight, and the gold coins of Spain, Mexico and Columbia, of the fineness of twenty (20) carats, three grains and seven-sixteenths ($3\frac{7}{16}$) of a grain, at the rate of eighty-nine cents and nine-tenths of a cent ($89\frac{9}{10}$) per pennyweight.

Act January 18, 1837.

§ 18. The standard for both gold and silver coins of the United States shall hereafter be such that of one thousand parts by weight nine hundred shall be of pure metal and one hundred of alloy, and the alloy of silver coins shall be of copper, and the alloy of the gold coins shall be of copper and silver, provided that the silver do not exceed one-half the alloy.

§ 19. Of the silver coins, the *dollar* shall be of the weight of $412\frac{1}{2}$ grains; the *half dollar* of the weight of $206\frac{1}{4}$ grains; the *quarter dollar* of the weight of $103\frac{1}{8}$ grains; the *dime*, or tenth part of a dollar, of the weight of $41\frac{1}{4}$ grains, and the *half dime*, or twentieth part of a dollar, of the weight of $26\frac{5}{8}$ grains.

§ 20. And that dollars, half dollars, quarter dollars, dimes and half dimes shall be legal tenders of payment according to their nominal value for any sums whatever.

§ 21. Of the gold coins, the weight of the *eagle* shall be 258 grains; that of the *half eagle* 129 grains, and of the *quarter eagle* $64\frac{1}{2}$ grains.

§ 22. And that for all sums whatever the eagle shall be a legal tender of payment for ten dollars, the half eagle for five dollars, and the quarter eagle for two and a half dollars.

Act July 27, 1842.

§ 23. In all payments by or to the treasury, whether made here or in foreign countries where it becomes necessary to compute the value of the pound sterling, it shall be deemed equal to four dollars and eighty-four cents ($4.84).

Act March 3, 1843.

§ 24. The following gold coins shall pass current as money in the United States and be receivable by weight for the payment of all debts and demands at the rates following, that is to say; the gold coins of Great Britain, of not less than nine hundred and fifteen and a half thousandths ($915\frac{1}{2}$-1,000) in fineness, at ninety-four cents and six-tenths ($94\frac{6}{10}$) of a cent per pennyweight, and the gold coins of France, of not less than eight hundred and ninety-nine thousandths ($\frac{899}{1000}$) in fineness, at ninety-two cents and nine-tenths of a cent ($92\frac{9}{10}$) per pennyweight.

The following foreign silver coins shall pass current as money within the United States and be receivable by tale for the payment of all debts and demands at the following rates, that is to say; the Spanish pillar dollars, and the dollars of Mexico, Peru and Bolivia, of not less than eight hundred and ninety-seven thousandths ($\frac{897}{1000}$) in fineness and four hundred and fifteen (415) grains in weight, at one hundred cents each, and the five-franc pieces of France, of not less than nine hundred thousandths ($\frac{900}{1000}$) in fineness and three hundred and eighty-four (384) grains in weight, at ninety-three (93) cents each.

Act March 3, 1849.

§ 25. There shall be from time to time struck and coined at the mint of the United States and the branches thereof—conformably in all respects to law, and conformably in all respects to the standard for gold coins now established by law—coins of gold of the following denominations and value, viz.: *Double eagles*, each to be of the value of twenty dollars or units, and *gold dollars*, each to be of the value of one dollar, or unit.

§ 26. For all sums whatever the double eagle shall be a legal tender for twenty dollars, and the gold dollar shall be a legal tender for one dollar.

§ 27. In adjusting the weights of gold coins henceforward the following deviations from the standard weight shall not be exceeded in any of the single pieces, namely: in the double eagles, the eagle and the half eagle, one-half of a grain; and in the quarter eagle and gold dollar, one quarter of a grain; and that in weighing a large number of pieces together, when delivered from the chief coiner to the treasurer, and from the treasurer to the depositors, the diviation from the standard weight shall not exceed three pennyweights in one thousand double eagles; two pennyweights in one thousand eagles; one and one-half pennyweights in one thousand half eagles; one pennyweight in one thousand quarter eagles, and one-half of a pennyweight in one thousand gold dollars.

Act March 3, 1851.

§ 28. It shall be lawful to coin at the mint of the United States and its branches a piece of the denomination and legal value of three cents, or three-hundredths of a dollar, to be composed of three-fourths silver and one-fourth copper, and to weigh twelve (12) grains and three-eighths ($\frac{3}{8}$) of a grain; that it shall be a legal tender in payment of debts for all sums of thirty cents and under.

Act February 21, 1853.

§ 29. That the weight of the *half dollar*, or piece of fifty cents, shall be one hundred and ninety-two (192) grains; and the *quarter dollar*, *dime* and *half dime* shall be respectively one-half, one-fifth and one-tenth of the weight of the half dollar.

§ 30. The silver coins issued in conformity with the above section shall be legal tenders in payment of debts for all sums not exceeding five dollars.

§ 31. From time to time there shall be struck and coined at the mint of the United States and the branches thereof, conformably in all respects to the standard of gold coins now established by law, a coin of gold of the value of *three dollars or units*.

§ 32. And that hereafter the three cent piece now authorized by law shall be made of the weight of three-fifteenths of the weight of the half dollar, as provided in said act, and of the same standard of fineness. And said act, entitled "An act amendatory of existing laws relative to the *half dollar, quarter dollar, dime and half dime*," shall take effect and be in full force from and after the first day of April, 1853, anything to the contrary notwithstanding.

Act February 21, 1857.

§ 33. The standard weight of the *cent* coined at the mint shall be seventy-two (72) grains, or three-twentieths of an ounce troy, with no greater deviation than four grains in each piece; and said *cent* shall be composed of eighty-eight (88) per centum of copper and twelve (12) per centum of nickel. And the coinage of the *half cent* shall cease.

Act February 21, 1857.

§ 34. The pieces commonly known as the quarter, eighth and sixteenth of the Spanish *pillar dollar* and of the Mexican dollar shall be receivable at the Treasury of the United States and its several offices, and the several postoffices and land offices, at the rates of valuation following, viz.: the fourth of a dollar, or piece of two reals at twenty cents; the eighth of a dollar, or piece of one real, at ten cents; and the sixteenth of a dollar, or half real, at five cents.

§ 35. *All former acts* authorizing the currency of foreign gold or silver coins, and declaring the same a legal tender in payment of debts, *are hereby repealed;* but it shall be the duty of the director of the mint to cause assays to be made from time to time of such foreign coins as may be known to commerce, to determine their average weight, fineness and value, and to embrace in his annual report a statement of the results thereof.

Act April 22, 1864.

§ 36. The standard weight of the cent coined at the mint of the United States shall be forty-eight grains, or one-tenth of one ounce troy, and said cent shall be composed of ninety-five per centum of copper and five per centum of tin and zinc in such proportions as shall be determined by the director of the mint; and there shall be from time to time struck and coined at the mint a two-cent piece of the same composition, the standard weight of which shall be ninety-six grains, or one-fifth of an ounce troy, with no greater diviation than four grains to each piece.

§ 37. The said coins shall be a legal tender in any payment, the one cent coin to the amount of ten cents, and the two cent coin to the amount of twenty cents; and it shall be lawful to pay out said coins in exchange for the lawful currency of the United States (except cents or half cents issued under former acts of Congress) in suitable sums, by the treasurer of the mint, and by such other depositaries as the secretary of the treasury may designate.

Act March 3, 1865.

§ 38. There shall be coined at the mint of the United States a *three cent piece* composed of copper and nickel in such proportion— not exceeding twenty-five (25) per centum of nickel—as shall be determined by the director of the mint, the standard weight of which shall be thirty grains, with no greater deviation than four grains to each piece.

§ 39. The said coin shall be a legal tender in any payment to the amount of sixty cents; and it shall be lawful to pay out said coins in exchange for the lawful currency of the United States (except cents or half cents or two cent pieces issued under former acts of Congress) in suitable sums, by the treasurer of the mint, and by such other depositaries as the secretary of the treasury may designate. *Provided*, that from and after the passage of this act no issues of fractional notes of the United States shall be of less denomination than five cents.

§ 40. The one and two cent coins of the United States shall not be a legal tender for any payment exceeding four cents in amount (previous laws to the contrary repealed).

Act May 16, 1866.

§ 41. There shall be coined at the mint of the United States a five cent piece, composed of copper and nickel in such proportion—not exceeding twenty-five centum of nickel—as shall be determined by the director of the mint, the standard weight of which shall be seventy-seven and sixteen hundredths grains, with no greater deviation than two grains to each piece.

§ 42. Said coins shall be a legal tender in any payment to the amount of one dollar; and it shall be lawful to pay out said coins for lawful currency of the United States, in suitable sums, by the treasurer of the mint, and by such other depositaries as the secretary of the treasury may designate.

§ 43. That from and after the passage of this act no issue of fractional notes of the United States shall be of less denomination than ten cents.

§ 44. It shall be lawful for the treasurer and the several assistant treasurers of the United States to *redeem in national currency*, under such rules and regulations as may be prescribed by the secretary of the treasury, the coins herein authorized to be issued when presented in sums of not less than one hundred dollars.

Act March 3, 1871.

§ 45. That the secretary of the treasury is required to redeem in lawful money all copper, bronze, copper-nickel and base-metal coinage of every kind hitherto authorized by law, when presented in sums of not less than twenty dollars.

Act February 12, 1873.

§ 46. That the gold coins of the United States shall be a One Dollar Piece, which, at the standard weight of twenty-five and eight-tenths ($25\frac{8}{10}$) grains shall be the *Unit of Value;* a Quarter Eagle, or two and a half dollar piece; a Three Dollar Piece; a Half Eagle, or five dollar piece; an Eagle, or ten dollar piece; and a Double Eagle, or twenty dollar piece. And the standard weight of the Gold Dollar shall be twenty-five and eight-tenths grains; of the Quarter Eagle sixty-four and one-half grains; of the Three Dollar Piece seventy-seven and four-tenths grains; of the Half Eagle one hundred and twenty-nine grains; of the Eagle two hundred and fifty-eight grains; of the Double Eagle five hundred and sixteen grains, which coins shall be a legal tender in all payments at their nominal value when not below the standard weight and limit of tolerance provided in this act, and that when reduced in weight below said standard and tolerance shall be a legal tender in proportion to their actual weight.

Any gold coins of the United States, if reduced by natural abrasion not more than a half of one per cent. below the standard weight after twenty years' circulation, and at a ratable proportion for any less period, shall be received at their nominal value at the United States treasury.

§ 47. The silver coins of the United States shall be a Trade Dollar, a Half Dollar, a Quarter Dollar, a Dime. And the weight of the Trade Dollar shall be four hundred and twenty (420) grains troy; the weight of the Half Dollar shall be twelve *grams* and one-half of a *gram;* the Quarter Dollar and the Dime shall be respectively one-half and one fifth the weight of said half dollar; and *said coins* shall be a legal tender at their nominal value for any amount not exceeding five dollars in one payment.

§ 48. The standard for both gold and silver coins of the United States shall be such that of one thousand parts by weight nine hundred shall be of pure metal and one hundred of alloy. The alloy of the silver coins shall be of copper. The alloy of the gold coins shall be of copper, or of copper and silver, but the silver shall in no case exceed one-tenth of the whole alloy.

§ 49. The minor coins of the United States shall be a Five Cent Piece, a Three Cent Piece and a One Cent Piece. The alloy for the five and three cent pieces shall be of copper and nickel, to be composed of three-fourths copper and one-fourth nickel. The alloy of the one cent piece shall be ninety-five per centum of copper and five per centum of tin and zinc, in such proportions as shall be determined by the director of the mint. The weight of the five cent piece shall be seventy-seven and sixteen hundredths grains troy; of the three cent pieces thirty grains, and of the one cent piece forty-eight grains.

§ 50. No coins, either of gold, silver or minor coinage, shall hereafter be issued from the mint other than those of the denominations, standards and weights set forth in this title.

§ 51. Silver coins, other than the trade dollars, shall be paid out at the several mints and at the assay office in New York City in exchange for gold coins at par, in sums not less than one hundred dollars.

§ 52. Nothing herein contained shall, however, prevent the payment of silver coins at their nominal value for silver parted from gold, as provided in this title, or for change less than one dollar in settlement of gold deposits.

§ 53. In adjusting the weights of the gold coins the following deviations shall not be exceeded in any single piece: In the double eagle and the eagle, one-half of a grain; in the half eagle, the three dollar piece, the quarter eagle and the one dollar piece, one-fourth of a grain, and in weighing a number of pieces together, when delivered by the coiner to the superintendent and by the superintendent to the depositor, the deviation from the standard weight shall not exceed one-hundredth of an ounce in five thousand dollars in double eagles, eagles, half eagles or quarter eagles, or in one thousand dollars in three dollar pieces or one dollar pieces.

§ 54. In adjusting the weight of the silver coins the following deviations shall not be exceeded in any single piece: In *the dollar*, the half dollar, the quarter dollar and in the dime, one and one-half grains, and in weighing a large number of pieces the deviations shall not exceed two-hundredths of an ounce in one thousand *dollars*, half dollars, or quarter dollars, and one-hundredth of an ounce in one thousand dimes.

§ 55. In adjusting the weight of the minor coins provided by this title, there shall be no greater deviation allowed than three grains for the five cent piece, and two grains for the three and one cent pieces.

§ 56. That all other acts and parts of acts pertaining to the mints, assay offices and coinage of the United States, inconsistent with the provisions of this act are hereby repealed: *Provided*, That this act shall not be construed to affect any act done, right accrued, or penalty incurred under former acts, but every such right is hereby saved.

Act March 3, 1873.

§ 57. The value of the sovereign, or pound sterling, shall be deemed equal to four dollars eighty-six cents and six and one-half mills; and all contracts made after the first day of January, 1874, based on an assumed par of exchange with Great Britain, of fifty-four pence to the dollar, of four dollars forty-four cents and four-ninths cents to the sovereign, or pound sterling, shall be null and void.

Act March 3, 1875.

§ 58. That there shall be from time to time coined at the mints of the United States, conformably in all respects to the coinage act of 1873, a coin of silver of the denomination of twenty cents, and of the weight of five grams. That the twenty cent piece shall be a legal tender at its nominal value for any amount not exceeding five dollars in any one payment. That in adjusting the weight of the twenty cent piece, the deviation from the standard weight shall not exceed one and one-half grains.

Act July 13, 1876.

§ 59. That the trade dollar shall not hereafter be a legal tender.

COIN IN THE UNITED STATES.

Estimate of the amount of coin in the country from 1854 to 1876. (Official report of Treasury Department.)

	Coin in Banks.	Total in the Country.
1854	$59,410,000	$240,000,000
1855	55,945,000	....
1856	59,714,000	....
1857	59,272,000	....
1858	60,705,000	....
1859	....	240,000,000
1860	....	....
1861	....	....
1862	....	....
1863	....	....
1864	....	....
1865	....	....
1866	....	....
1869	....	....
1870 (October)	6,000,000	121,000,000
1871 (October)	6,000,000	116,000,000
1872 (October)	5,000,000	102,000,000
1873 (October)	5,000,000	109,000,000
1874 (October)	5,500,000	110,000,000
1875 (October)	5,000,000	100,000,000
1976 (June)	6,000,000	102,000,000

The amount of gold and silver in the United States treasury, on Nov 1, 1879, was as follows:

Gold Coin	$171,517,713
Silver Coin	50,078,620
Total	$221,596,333

The Director of the mint in his report for this year, estimates that the amount of coin in the country on June 30, 1879, was as follows:

Estimated amount June 30, 1878	$327,781,898
Net gold coinage for the year	39,290,009
Net silver coinage for the year	26,518,642
Importation of silver	5,180,015
Total	$398,770,564
Deduct net exportation of gold	228,881
Total estimated amount	$398,541,683

Of which,

Estimated amount of gold $286,490,698
Silver coin $112,050,985

Added since June 30 to November 1, of silver $9,405,370; of gold $19,259,799, making the stock of coin in the country at the latter date, $427,206,852.

THE WORLD'S ANNUAL PRODUCTION.

GOLD AND SILVER.

The following is the *Journal des Economists* table of the production of gold and silver each year since 1852:

	Gold, Millions.	Silver, Millions.	Total Gold and Silver, Millions.
1852	$182½	$40½	$223
1853	155	40½	195½
1854	127	40½	167½
1855	135	40½	175½
1856	147½	40½	188
1857	133	40½	173½
1858	124½	40½	165
1859	124½	40½	165
1860	119	40½	159½
1861	114	42½	156½
1862	107½	45	152½
1863	107	49	156
1864	113	51½	164½
1865	120	52	172
1866	121	50½	171½
1867	116	54	170
1868	120	50	170
1869	121	47½	168½
1870	116	51½	167½
1871	116½	61	177½
1872	101½	65	166½
1873	103½	70	173½
1874	90½	71½	162
1875	97½	62	159½

Assumed progress of the annual consumption of gold in the arts, by the loss and abrasion of coins, and by the loss, wear and accumulation of jewelry:

(W. L. Fawcett.)

Year.	Millions	Year.	Millions
1839	25	1857	55
1840	25.5	1858	59
1841	26	1859	63
1842	26.5	1860	67
1843	27	1861	71
1844	27.5	1862	74
1845	28	1863	77
1846	28.5	1864	81
1847	29	1865	85
1848	29.5	1866	89
1849	30	1867	92
1850	32	1868	93
1851	34	1869	97
1852	37	1870	101
1853	40	1871	105
1854	43	1872	109
1855	47	1873	110
1856	51	1874	108

Gold, silver and base metal coin and gold and silver bullion in circulation and in banks in all Europe.

	Gold.	Silver and Base Metal.
Great Britain	$442,500,000	$ 80,000,000
France	650,000,000	350,000,000
Germany	380,000,000	370,000,000
Austria		200,000,000
Russia		250,000,000
Italy		145,000,000
Spain	300,000,000	200,000,000
Sweden		70,000,000
Belgium		38,000,000
Switzerland		5,000,000
All other States of Europe		360,000,000
	$1,872,500,000	$2,060,000,000

(*From Dr. Linderman's Official Report.*)

Annual Product of gold and silver from the American mines.

Year.	Gold.	Silver.	Total.
1870	$50,000,000	$16,000,000	$ 66,000,000
1871	43,500,000	23,000,000	66,500,000
1872	36,000,000	28,750,000	64,750,000
1873	36,000,000	35,750,000	71,750,000
1874	40,000,000	32,000,000	72,000,000
1875	40,000,000	32,000,000	72,000,000
1876	44,300,000	41,500,000	85,700,000
1877 (Wells, Fargo & Co.'s est.)			100,000,000

COINAGE FOR THE YEAR 1879.

(*From the Report of the Secretary of the Treasury.*)

The value of the gold coinage executed during the year was	$40,986,912 00
Of standard silver dollars	27,227,500 00
Of subsidiary silver coin	342 50
Of minor coin	97,798 00
Total	68,312,592 50

The bullion production from the mines of the United States for the last year is estimated by the Director to be nearly eighty million dollars, the proportions of gold and silver being about equal. The year's total production is less than that of the preceding year, caused by a diminution in the yield in the mines of Nevada, which was not compensated by increased production in other places.

The Director estimates the coin in the country on October 31, 1879, at $305,750,497 of gold, and $121,456,355 of silver. The bullion in the mints and New York assay office at that date awaiting coinage, amounted to $49,931,035 of gold, and $4,553,182 of silver, making the total amount of coin and bullion $481,691,069.

The total amount of silver dollars coined to November 1, 1879, under the act of February 28, 1878, was

$45,206,200, of which $13,002,842 was in circulation, and the remainder, $32,203,358, in the Treasury at that time.

The total amount of specie imported from January 1, 1879, to November 15, is $75,512,392, of which $65,124,200 has arrived since August 1. The production of precious metals for the fiscal year 1879 are estimated by the Director of the Mint at $79,711,990, of which $38,899,858 is gold, and $40,812,132 is silver.

The following table shows the amount of bullion held by the Bank of England in each year from 1870 to 1879:*

(£=5 dollars.)		(£=5 dollars.)	
1870	$103,900,000	1875	$119,600,000
1871	117,950,000	1876	143,500,000
1872	112,900,000	1877	126,850,000
1873	113,500,000	1878	119,200,000
1874	111,450,000	1879	150,942,980

The amount of coin held by the Bank of France on December 31 of each year from 1870 to 1878, and also on October 30, 1879, is shown by the following table:†

Date.	Gold Coin and bullion. (5 fr.=$1.)	Silver coin and bullion. (5 fr.=$1.)	Total.
Dec. 31, 1870	$ 85,740,000	$ 13,700,000	$ 99,440,000
Dec. 31, 1871	110,680,000	16,240,000	126,920,000
Dec. 31, 1872	131,740,000	25,520,000	158,260,000
Dec. 31, 1873	122,260,000	31,260,000	153,520,000
Dec. 31, 1874	204,220,000	62,640,000	266,860,000
Dec. 31, 1875	234,860,000	101,000,000	355,860,000
Dec. 31, 1876	306,080,000	127,720,000	433,800,000
Dec. 31, 1877	235,420,000	173,080,000	408,500,000
Dec. 31, 1878	196,720,000	211,620,000	408,340,000
Oct. 30, 1879	169,000,000	241,800,000	410,800,000

*Page 412 of the Statistical Society, June, 1879.

†From the *Bulletin de Statistique*, as quoted in the *Bankers' Magazine*, New York, vol. xiii, page 740, except the item for the present year, which was obtained from the *Financial Chronicle* of New York, of November 15, 1879.

The following is a statement of different nations, not including the United States, with their estimated populations, classified according to their metallic standards:

SILVER-STANDARD COUNTRIES.

	Population.
Russia	76,000,000
Austria	36,000,000
Egypt	4,500,000
Mexico	8,000,000
Central America	2,600,000
Ecuador	1,300,000
Peru	3,400,000
China	400,000,000
British India	237,144,456
	768,944,456

As Russia and Austria both have legal tender paper money, their population will be *non-effective* in relation to the matter in hand, until they resume specie payments, or commence to hoard specie with a view to such payments. With that deduction, the population actually using the silver standard is 656,944,456.

DOUBLE-STANDARD COUNTRIES.

	Population.
Greece	1,400,000
Roumania	4,000,000
Colombia	2,900,000
Venezuela	1,600,000
Chili	1,900,000
Uruguay	400,000
Paraguay	1,200,000
Japan	33,000,000
Holland	3,700,000
France	36,200,000
Belgium	5,100,000
Switzerland	2,700,000
Italy	26,800,000
Spain	16,400,000
	137,300,000

As Italy has not only a legal tender paper money, but substantially no metallic money in circulation, its population may be set down as *non-effective*, thus reducing the population of this group to 110,500,000. In Holland, France, Belgium, Switzerland, and Spain, containing a population of 64,100,000, the coinage of silver is either limited or entirely suspended.

GOLD-STANDARD COUNTRIES.

	Population.
Great Britain	32,000,000
Canada, Cape of Good Hope, and Australian Colonies	7,000,000
Germany	42,000,000
Norway	1,700,000
Sweden	4,300,000
Denmark	1,800,000
Portugal	4,000,000
	92,800,000

The average value of the standard gold dollar, in legal tender paper dollars, during the month of July in each year, from 1864 to 1878, and also on January 1, 1879:

1864.	1865.	1866.	1867.	1868.	1869.	1870.	1871.
Cts. 258.1	Cts. 142.1	Cts. 151.6	Cts. 139.4	Cts. 142.7	Cts. 136.1	Cts. 116.8	Cts. 112.4

1872.	1873.	1874.	1875.	1876.	1877.	1878.	1879.
Cts. 114.3	Cts. 115.7	Cts. 110.0	Cts. 114.8	Cts. 112.1	Cts. 105.8	Cts. 100.6	Cts. 100.0

WHY AND HOW SILVER WAS DEMONETIZED.

The scheme for the demonetizing of one of the so-called precious metals originated with the money or creditor class, not for the public good or general welfare, but was prompted solely by selfishness on the part of that class.

It originated soon after the rich gold discoveries of California and Australia, at a time when it was thought that the increased production of the precious metals would seriously affect the value of money by the anticipated rise in general prices.

In 1857, in his work ("Fall of Gold") Chevalier said:

> "The quantity of gold annually thrown on the general market approaches, in round numbers, a milliard of francs ($200,000,000). For a long series of years California and Australia must produce such quantities as to render a *marked decline in its value inevitable*.
>
> "It is absolutely certain that a production so vast should be accompanied with a *great reduction in its value.*
>
> "In no direction can a new outlet be seen sufficiently large to absorb the extraordinary production of gold, so as to prevent *a fall in its value.*
>
> "Unless, then, we possess a very robust faith in the immobility of human affairs, *we must regard the fall in the value of gold as an event for* which we should prepare *without loss of time."*

Under this and similar appeals from different parts of Europe, by the money and creditor class, who saw, in the near future, their coin and their securities depreciating in value relatively as the poor man's labor, and the producer's wealth increased through the increased volume of money, Germany, Austria and several other countries demonetized gold.

On this subject the Congressional monetary commission says:

> "The movement in Europe for the general demonetization of gold would have become general, but for the resistance of France. It was changed in 1865 into a movement for the demonetization of silver.
>
> "But this change from demonetizing gold to demonetizing silver was more of form than of substance. The object aimed at by both was a disuse of one of the money metals, *to protect the creditor classes* and those having *fixed incomes* against a fall in the value of money, and a *rise in general prices, of labor and property.*"

The commission adds:

> "This is the pith and marrow of the monetary discussions of the past twenty years. In all the European discussions after 1848, and prior to the German demonetization of silver and its consequences, the point made was not that either metal had depreciated *relatively to the other*, but that by reason of extraordinary supplies of gold from California and Australia about 1865, and by new supplies of silver

from Nevada, both metals had depreciated *relatively to labor and commodities*, and that kings, princes and office holders, having *fixed incomes*, and the creditor class, having *fixed annuities*, were being injured by a *rise in the price of labor and commodities*."

The laboring and producing classes were getting the better of the idle, non-taxed and non-producing classes. So long as the double standard existed, a new supply of either metal was an addition to and only affected the general mass of money, and not the relative value of the metals. The "fall in gold" which Chevalier lamented in 1857, *was its fall in relation to property*. In order, therefore, to protect the "income classes" it was claimed to be necessary to demonetize one of the metals, and *gold*, being the metal which then promised the most abundant yield, was selected for the purpose.

It was not a fall in gold *relatively to silver*, which caused Germany to demonetize gold in 1857, neither was it a fall in the value of silver in 1871–73 which induced several countries in Europe and the United States to demonetize silver.

The principal causes which led these countries to adopt finally the gold standard and reject the silver, was, first, the persistence with which England clung to the gold, made a European union upon a single metal other than gold impossible; and second, the discoveries of the Nevada silver mines.

We can readily see how the creditor class of kingdoms and empires, and that class of born and law perpetuated rulers who depend upon "fixed incomes," could thus outrage and impose upon the laboring and producing classes, who have no voice in the legislation of their respective countries; but it is astonishing that a free people, exercising absolute sovereignty, should be so blind to their own interest as to allow the "creditor" and "fixed income" class thus to rob and destroy them.

The sole object of the resumption of gold payments and the demonetization of silver in the United States as in Europe, was to *enhance the value of the creditors' principal and interest*, and the "fixed incomes" of the salaried officials, by low and degrading prices of labor and production. The demonetization of silver in the United States was a fraud upon the people, if not upon Congress and the administration.

From the report of the Silver Commission we obtain the following facts, also. The Act of February 12, 1873, is a long act of sixty-seven sections, regulating all the details of the mint: It does not demonetize the old silver dollar, or any of the silver coins of standard weight issued prior to 1874. *The silver dollar is not named in it*, and it would escape the casual observation that the dollar was in any way affected by it.

Precisely what the act did, was to authorize the coinage of silver half dollars, quarters, and dimes below standard weight, and of a new silver coin for Asiatic commerce, above standard weight, called the "trade dollar," and prohibited these coins from being legal tender for more than five dollars in any one payment.

None of these coins were legal tender for more than that amount under the act of February 25, 1853. It contained no prohibition of the coinage of the old silver dollar, except the following, which would not likely attract the attention of anyone:

"No coins shall hereafter be issued from the mint other than the denominations, standards and weights herein set forth."

The act of February 12, 1873, did not demonetize, nor affect in any manner, the legal tender functions of the full-weighted silver coins that had been minted prior to its passage, but the 17th section deprived silver bullion of its right of being coined into full legal tender money on either Government or private account.

In no section of the act was it specifically pointed out or referred to, that the effect of the act was to change the standard of values of gold and silver, to gold alone.

The act when passed was not read, except by title, and that title, instead of expressing its real character, read: "*An act revising and amending the laws relating to the mint, assay offices and coinage of the United States.*"

It is notorious that this transcendent change in the money systems of the country, affecting the most vital interests, was carried through without the knowledge or observation of the people. It was neither demanded by the resolutions of public meetings or political conventions, nor asked for in petitions from the people. In its relations to a double or single standard it was hardly mentioned in the House, and not at all in the Senate.

The press of the country was silent, and for three years it rested unobserved by the public.

The actual demonetization of silver, coined and uncoined, was not completed until 1874, in June, by the following section (3586) of the Revised Statutes:

"*The silver coins of the United States* shall be a legal tender at their nominal value for any amount not exceeding five dollars in any one payment."

Whereas the act of February 12, 1873, did not demonetize or in any way affect the silver dollar of 1853, or authorize its discontinuance, or prevent its coinage, the above clause was *interpolated into the Statutes by the revisers*, and as the statutes thus revised were enacted in bulk, the demonetization of the silver dollar was effected.

CHAPTER IX.

NATIONAL BANKS.

DIGEST OF THE ORIGINAL ACT.

The National Banking law provides: First: That any number of persons not less than five may form an association for carrying on the business of banking.

Second: That any such association shall have corporate power, to have succession for the period of twenty years, to make contracts, to sue and be sued, etc.

Third: The capital of such associations shall not be less than $50,000 in places whose population does not exceed six thousand; not less than $100,000 in places whose population exceeds six thousand; and not less than $200,000 in places whose population exceeds fifty thousand.

Fourth: The aggregate amount of circulation is fixed at $354,000,000, to be apportioned as follows: $150,000,000 among the several states and territories according to representative population; $150,000,000 to be distributed by the secretary of the treasury according to his discretion; and the remaining $54,000,000 to such states and territories, having less than their share, as may make application prior to July 12, 1871.

Fifth: No association is authorized to commence business until it shall have deposited United States bonds to the amount of $30,000 with the treasurer of the United States.

Sixth: Every such association is entitled to receive from the comptroller of the currency circulating notes to the amount of ninety per cent. of the capital stock, if it does not exceed $500,000; eighty per cent. if it exceeds $500,000, but does not exceed $1,000,000; seventy-five per cent. if it exceeds $1,000,000, but does not exceed $3,000,000; and sixty per cent. if it exceeds $3,000,000.

THE LEGAL TENDER OF BANK NOTES.

Section 23 of the Act provides that such notes (bank notes) shall circulate the same as money; and the same shall be received at par in all parts of the United States in payment of taxes, excises, public lands, and all other dues to the United States, except for duties on imports; and also for all salaries and other debts and demands owing by the United States to individuals, corporations, and associations within the United States, except interest on the public debt, and in redemption of the national currency.

Section 32 provides that every association formed or existing under the provisions of this act shall take and receive at par, for any debt or liability to said association, any and all notes or bills issued by any association existing under and by virtue of this act.

NATIONAL BANK CIRCULATION.

(From Report of Comptroller of the Currency, 1879.)

The act of February 25, 1863, and the subsequent act of June 3, 1864, authorized the issue of $300,000,000 of national bank circulation, which was increased by the act of July 12, 1870, to $354,000,000. The act of June 20, 1874, authorized any national bank desiring to withdraw its circulating notes, in whole or in part, to deposit lawful money with the treasurer of the United States in sums of not less than $9,000, and to withdraw a proportionate amount of bonds held as security for such notes; and the act of June 14, 1875, repealed all previous provisions restricting the aggregate amount of national bank circulation, and required the secretary of the treasury to retire legal tender notes to an amount equal to eighty per cent. of the national bank notes thereafter issued, until the amount of such legal tender notes outstanding should be $300,000,000 and no more. That provision of the act which required a reduction of United States legal tender notes was, however, repealed by the the act of May 31, 1878. Subsequent to the passage of the act of June 20, 1874, and that of January 14, 1875, which latter act authorized the retirement and re-issue of national bank notes at the pleasure of the banks, the circulation steadily decreased in volume until the year 1877, the total decrease in this interval being $30,869,655. During the year ending November 1, 1878, there was an increase of $4,216,684, and during the year ending November 1, 1879, a further increase of $14,742,503, as will be seen from the following table, which exhibits the total outstanding circulation, not including mutilated notes in transit, on the 1st day of November of each year for the last thirteen years, and also upon the dates of the acts above named:

November 1, 1867	$299,153,296	November 1, 1874	$351,927,246
November 1, 1868	300,002,234	January 14, 1875	351,861,450
November 1, 1869	299,910,419	November 1, 1875	345,586,902
November 1, 1870	302,607,942	November 1, 1876	321,150,718
November 1, 1871	324,810,656	November 1, 1877	316,775,111
November 1, 1872	341,512,772	May 31, 1878	321,232,099
November 1, 1873	348,382,046	November 1, 1878	320,991,795
June 20, 1874	349,894,182	November 1, 1879	335,134,504

Since the passage of the act of June 20, 1874, $90,229,886 of legal tender notes have been deposited in the treasury by the national banks, for the purpose of reducing their circulation, and $81,136,362 of bank notes have been redeemed, destroyed, and retired.

From the date of the passage of the act of January 14, 1875, to that of the act of May 31, 1878, which prohibited the further cancellation of legal tender notes, $44,148,730 of additional circulation was issued, and legal tender notes equal to eighty per cent. thereof, or $35,318,984, was retired, leaving the amount authorized $346,681,016, which is the amount of legal tender notes now outstanding.

The amount of additional circulation issued for the year ending November 1, 1879, was $22,933,490, of which $7,494,170 was issued during the months of September and October. The amount issued to banks organized during the year was $2,615,440; the amount retired was $8,190,987; the actual increase for the year being $14,742,503. During the year ending November 1, 1879, lawful money to the amount of $10,319,398 was deposited with the treasurer to retire circulation, of which amount $2,936,063 was deposited by banks in liquidation. The amount previously deposited under the act of June 20, 1874, was $65,164,523, and by banks in liquidation $14,745,965, to which is to be added a balance of $3,813,675 remaining from deposits made by liquidating banks prior to the passage of that act. Deducting from the total, $94,043,561, the amount of circulating notes redeemed and destroyed without reissue ($81,136,362), there remained in the hands of the treasurer on November 1, 1879, $12,907,199 of lawful money for the redemption and retirement of bank circulation.

SECURITY OF CIRCULATING NOTES.

The following table exhibits the classes and amounts of United States bonds held by the Treasurer on the 1st day of November, 1879, to secure the redemption of the circulating notes of the national banks:

Class of Bonds.	Authorizing act.	Rate of Interest.	Amount.
Loan of February, 1861, (81s)	February 8, 1861	6 per cent	$2,221,000
Loan of July and Aug., 1861 (81s)	July 17 and Aug. 5, 1861	....do....	33,971,750
Loan of 1863 (81s)	March 3, 1863	....do.....	18,549,500
Consols of 1867	March 3, 1865	....do.....	33,240
Consols of 1868	....do	....do.....	75,000
Ten-forties of 1864	March 3, 1864	5 per cent	7,119,500
Funded Loan of 1881	July 14, 1870, and Jan. 20, 1871.	....do.....	124,182,100
Funded Loan of 1891	....do	4½ pr cent	34,866,950
Funded Loan of 1907	....do	4 per cent	138,318,400
Pacific Railway bonds	July 1, 1862, and July 2, 1864.	6 per cent	4,465,000
Total			364,802,400

CURRENCY OUTSTANDING.

Treasury notes outstanding	$346,681,016
National bank notes outstanding	337,181,418
Gold in the Treasury, less certificates held by the banks	157,960,193
Silver in the Treasury	50,078,620
Coin in the banks (October 2)	42,173,731
Total	$934,074,978

The following table gives the circulation of the Bank of France and its branches, with the number of pieces, and the denomination in francs and dollars, on January 30, 1879:

Number of pieces.	Denominations	Value of each piece in dollars.	Amount in francs.	Amount in dollars. (Fr.—20 cents.)
5	5,000 francs.	1,000	25,000	5,000
1,382,379	1,000 francs.	200	1,382,379,000	276,475,800
753,599	500 francs.	100	376,799,500	75,359,900
3,087	200 francs.	40	617,400	123,480
5,046,031	100 francs.	20	504,603,100	100,920,620
316,166	50 francs.	10	15,808,300	3,161,660
29,525	25 francs.	5	738,125	147,625
426,537	20 francs.	4	8,530,740	1,706,148
206,653	5 francs	1	1,033,265	206,653
1,245	Forms out of date.	....	436,400	87,280
8,165,227		....	2,290,970,830	458,194,166

The following table shows the capital, surplus, dividends, and total earnings of all the national banks, for each half-year from March 1, 1869, to Sept. 1, 1879:

Period of six months, ending	No. of banks.	Capital.	Surplus.	Total Dividends.	Total Net Earnings.
Sept. 1, 1869	1,481	$401,650,802	$82,105,848	$21,767,831	$29,221,184
Mar. 1, 1870	1,571	416,366,991	86,118,210	21,479,095	28,996,834
Sept. 1, 1870	1,601	425,317,104	91,630,620	21,080,343	26,808,885
Mar. 1, 1871	1,605	428,699,165	94,672,401	22,295,150	27,343,162
Sept. 1, 1871	1,693	445,999,264	98,286,591	22,125,279	27,315,311
Mar. 1, 1872	1,750	450,693,706	99,431,243	22,859,826	27,502,549
Sept. 1, 1872	1,852	465,676,023	105,181,942	23,827,289	30,572,891
Mar. 1, 1873	1,912	475,918,688	114,257,288	24,826,061	31,926,478
Sept. 1, 1873	1,955	488,100,951	118,113,848	24,823,029	33,122,000
Mar. 1, 1874	1,967	489,510,343	123,469,859	23,529,998	29,541,120
Sept. 1, 1874	1,971	489,938,284	128,364,039	24,929,307	30,036,811
Mar. 1, 1875	2,007	493,568,831	131,560,637	24,750,816	29,136,007
Sept. 1, 1875	2,047	497,834,833	134,123,649	24,317,785	28,800,217
Mar. 1, 1876	2,076	504,209,491	134,467,595	24,811,581	23,997,921
Sept. 1, 1876	2,081	500,482,271	132,251,078	22,563,829	20,540,231
Mar. 1, 1877	2,080	496,651,580	130,872,165	21,803,969	19,592,962
Sept. 1, 1877	2,072	486,324,860	124,349,254	22,117,116	15,274,028
Mar. 1, 1878	2,074	475,609,751	122,373,561	18,982,390	16,946,696
Sept. 1, 1878	2,047	470,231,806	118,687,134	17,959,223	13,658,893
Mar. 1, 1879	2,043	464,413,996	116,744,135	17,541,054	14,678,660
Sept. 1, 1879	2,045	455,132,056	115,149,351	17,401,867	16,873,200

The following table exhibits by denominations the circulation of the Imperial Bank of Germany on January 1, 1879, in thalers and marks, which have been converted into our currency:

Thalers.				Marks.			
Number of pieces.	Denominations	Value of each piece in dollars.	Amount in dollars. (Thaler 75 cents.)	Number of pieces.	Denominations	Value of each piece in dollars.	Amount in dollars. (Mark 25 cents.)
194	500 thalers.	375 00	72,750	218,444	1,000 marks.	250	54,611,000
2,517	100 thalers.	75 00	188,775	207,018	500 marks.	125	25,877,250
1,745	50 thalers.	37.50	65,456	3,395,059	100 marks.	25	84,876,487
9,194	25 thalers.	18.75	172,388				
9,311	10 thalers.	7.50	69,836				
22,962			569,205	3,820,521			165,364,737

BANK TAXATION.

Banks of all kinds, National and otherwise, are subject to the following tax:

On capital beyond the average amount invested in bonds, one-half of one per cent.

On average deposits, one-half of one per cent.

On circulation, one per cent. per annum.

Total annual tax paid by the banks on circulation since 1864:

1864	$53,096 97
1865	733,247 59
1866	2,106,785 30
1867	2,868,636 78
1868	2,946,343 07
1869	2,957,416 73
1870	2,949,744 13
1871	2,987,021 69
1872	3,193,570 03
1873	3,353,186 13
1874	3,404,483 11
1875	3,283,105 89
1876	3,091,795 76
1877	2,899,037 09
1878	2,948,047 08
1879	3,009,647 16
Aggregating	42,785,464 51

According to the last report of the Comptroller of the currency, page 47, the amount of taxes paid by the national banks on their circulation, for 1879, was $3,009,-647.16. The Government paid the banks for the same period $17,152,396.75 interest on the bonds deposited as security for circulation (page 23), or $14,142,749.59 more than the Government received in taxes on circulation. The national banks also pay taxes on their capital and deposits the same as state, savings and private banks. The only tax paid by them, and not paid by other banks, is the tax on circulation, on which they receive from the Government more than four times as much as they return.

On deposits the national banks paid, in 1879, $3,309,-668.90. Other banks paid during the same period on deposits $2,354,911.74. On capital the national banks paid $491,920, while other banks paid $830,068—nearly twice as much as the national banks.

The following table exhibits, by denominations, the amount of national bank and legal tender notes outstanding on November 1, 1879:

Denominations.	1879.			1878.	1877.
	Amount of national bank notes	Amount of legal tender notes.	Aggregate.	Aggregate.	Aggregate.
Ones	$3,567,200	$19,320,302	$22,887,502	$24,652,750	$28,606,915
Twos	2,092,498	18,938,365	21,030,863	22,915,066	26,883,428
Fives	97,911,820	61,611,033	159,522,853	148,116,015	146,437,048
Tens	109,736,240	71,711,318	181,447,558	168,968,071	161,459,711
Twenties	72,652,160	68,793,773	141,445,933	131,785,709	126,290,995
Fifties	21,324,900	24,853,045	46,177,945	47,658,995	52,363,815
One Hundreds	26,911,600	31,428,180	58,339,780	58,331,470	58,976,670
Five Hundreds	641,500	22,446,500	23,088,000	31,159,000	35,956,000
One Thousands	283,000	22,828,500	23,111,500	33,794,500	34,380,500
Five Thousands		3,250,000	3,250,000		
Ten Thousands		2,500,000	2,500,000		
Add for fractions of notes not presented or destroyed	13,586		13,586	11,561	*1,010,800
Totals	335,134,504	347,681,016	682,815,520	667,333,137	672,365,882
Deduct for legal tender notes destroyed in Chicago fire		1,000,000	1,000,000	1,000,000	
Totals	335,134,504	346,681,016	681,815,520	666,333,137	672,365,882

*Includes $1,000,000 destroyed in Chicago fire; denominations unknown.

ORIGIN OF BANK NOTES.

A device for regulating the value of coin. For centuries they were not redeemable, but bore a premium.

Jevons informs us that the bank note system had its origin in Italy, from five to seven centuries ago. In those days the circulating medium consisted of a mixture of coins of various and unknown quality and value, and much of it clipped and debased.

In receiving money the merchant had to weigh and estimate the fineness of each coin, or be to the trouble and expense of having it assayed, and much trouble, loss of time and risk of fraud thus arose.

It became, therefore, the custom in the mercantile republics of Italy to deposit such money in bank, where its value was accurately estimated, *once for all*, no more to go into circulation, and the amount placed to the credit of the depositor.

The banks of Hamburg and Amsterdam were established on a similar system. The coins placed to the credit of individuals in those banks were called *bank money*. It was "*banked*," set, or placed there to remain, and instead of being used in ordinary transactions of commerce, *paper representatives*, or transferable certificates of the value and amount of the deposit were used instead.

In some instances, as the Bank of Venice, payments were made by the parties attending the bank at a particular hour, and ordering transfers of credit to be made in the bank books.

These transfers of credit constituted the currency, or circulating medium of the republic.

It was always of full value, often commanding a premium, while all trouble and errors of counting and valuing it were avoided.

This system avoided all losses of money by robbery or shipwreck and piracy. It avoided the nefarious practice of abstracting from the value of the coins by plugging, sweating and counterfeiting, and above all it saved the loss of deterioration by wear of circulation, which is estimated at three per cent. each year.

Paper transfers were attended by no such risk.

Being legal tender, and known to represent the actual value of their face, they possessed all the commercial value of the thing represented, besides the additional value of their convenience and safety.

For five hundred years this was the currency of Italy, under which her wealth and commerce surpassed that of any other nation on the globe.

If one of earth's productions was ample security on which to base the currency of Italy, which carried her through centuries of uninterrupted prosperity, how much more ample is the deposit of the domain itself, with all its productions, for the basis of our medium of exchange!

No banker or bullionist complains of bank currency, which is nothing more or less than transferable tokens of credit.

The banker deposits with the comptroller of the currency his bonds, and he becomes a creditor of the Government, nothing more or less, to the amount so deposited.

For convenience sake, and as evidence that the Government is indebted to him, he asks that the aggregate of his credit may be cut up into small denominations, to be transferred to third parties, and pass from hand to hand in the ordinary transactions of business.

Every person to whom one of these bits of paper is paid becomes a creditor to the Government to the amount represented by it.

The injustice of this system is, that the banker, after he has transferred nine-tenths of his claim against the

Government to third parties, he not only continues to draw interest on the whole amount, while those to whom he has transferred his claim, get no interest, but are compelled to pay the banker interest on that portion of the public debt he has parted with.

THE CONSTITUTIONALITY OF BANK MONEY.

No one will deny that bank notes are intended, and in fact are, a substitute for money. Their necessity grows out of a deficiency of money. Congress has authority, which it derives from the constitution, to coin money and regulate the value thereof.

If authority exists anywhere to coin a substitute, it must rest with that branch of the Government authorized to coin the real. The very fact that congress delegates the power to banks, and the fact that banks claim to derive their power from congress, to issue paper substitutes for coin, are admissions that congress possessed the power, else how could it confer what it did not possess?

All the powers of congress are derived from the constitution, and if that instrument confers the power to coin money substitutes, it is implied in that clause conferring power to coin money. Has congress a right to delegate its control over the coinage of gold and silver to private corporations? If not, whence does it derive its authority to delegate to banking associations its control over coin substitutes? Congress could not grant the substitute prerogative to the banks unless it first possessed it. If it ever possessed it, it held it as a trust, to exercise for the benefit of the people as their agent. If it never possessed the substitute prerogative, it could not confer it upon banks, hence, they exercise a usurped power. If congress does possess the prerogative, it has no more right to delegate it than it has to delegate the power to coin money.

Is the right to issue, regulate and control the currency of the country a natural individual right, or a function of sovereignty?

If a natural individual right, is not the monopoly of it by the national banks in violation of the spirit of our republican form of Government which was instituted to protect all men in the full enjoyment of their natural rights, instead of depriving them of one of them?

If it is a function of sovereignty, how can it be exercised by any except such as are chosen by the sovereign people from time to time to exercise it?

If congress has a right to confer the monetary function of sovereignty upon a hereditary succession, has it not the same right to dispose of any and all sovereign powers in the same manner?

The two great arms of national sovereignty are the purse and the sword; if it is wise to confer one upon a hereditary succession, why not dispose of the other in the same manner?

If it is safe to trust the monetary prerogative of the nation to the present generation of bankers and their heirs and assigns forever, without regard to fitness and qualification, why not trust the war power of the Government to the present generation of brigadiers, their heirs and assigns forever?

Viewed in its true light, is not the national banking system a long step towards the establishment of sovereignty based upon hereditary succession, is it not a big block wrenched from the temple of liberty and planted as the corner stone of imperialism, a powerful element of sovereignty crowned with the divine right of kings?

As the Federal Government possesses no powers except such as were delegated to it by the people and enumerated in the constitution, was not the bank act, conferring and perpetuating delegated powers upon foreigners and aliens, a gross betrayal of trust, if not treason against the people?

Has the Government a constitutional right to delegate powers entrusted to it, especially to be exercised by it for the people?

If not, is not the national bank act a palpable violation of the constitution, and its enforcement a usurpation of power not warranted by that instrument?

The answer to these inquiries are left to the intelligent reader.

If bank notes are money, from whence do they derive their money qualities?

If the Government can create money for the banks, why not for itself and the people?

If greenbacks are money, how can the power of the Government to create money be denied?

If greenbacks are not money, did the bondholders ever loan any money to the Government, having loaned nothing but greenbacks?

If the *debts* of a nation are good security on which to base its money, why is not its *wealth* better?

If the Government chooses to farm out its control over the currency to private parties, why not grant the privilege to those who need it in the production of wealth, instead of giving it to an idle monopoly to rob, blackmail and oppress the producers of wealth?

Why should the money power that has accumulated

colossal fortunes solely through Government protection and favoritism, be exempt from all Government support, when those out of whom it has made these fortunes are compelled to bear all the public burdens in addition to being robbed?

When orders went forth from the treasury department at Washington, through the New York clearing house, to the Wall Street gold exchange, to turn the gold dial to 100, and let it remain there till further orders—what was resumption but the fiat of John Sherman?

If it is as inconsistent to re-issue a United States note after it has once been redeemed as it would be to re-issue a note of hand after it had been paid, as the goldites claim, why will not the same principle apply to bank notes?

If the right to pay the bonds in greenbacks is denied on the ground that one debt cannot be paid with another, then have any of the soldiers been really paid, or any of the millions of debts and mortgages, that have been cancelled with greenbacks and bank notes?

CHAPTER X.

LEGAL TENDER PAPER MONEY.

Nearly all civilized nations recognize the sovereign right of Government to make its treasury notes legal tender. In the following table we follow the figures of the Director of the mint, adding thereto the statement of the amounts of paper money which is legal tender in the countries named:

Countries.	Gold.	Silver full tender.	Total paper.	Paper legal tender.
United States	$305,750,497	$15,206,200	$683,943,799	$346,601,000
Great Britain	618,619,013		209,148,875	200,000,000
Sweden	15,000,000		11,680,000	11,680,000
Norway	10,000,000		10,300,000	10,300,000
Denmark	20,000,000		18,900,000	18,900,000
France	733,400,000	366,700,000	466,755,000	
Austria	43,200,000	27,360,000	322,938,854	128,993,411
Italy	17,000,000		315,000,000	305,000,000
Russia	108,000,000		587,907,562	360,000,000
Spain	130,000,000	40,000,000	33,795,000	40,000,000
Peru	62,000	1,819,900	13,900,000	13,900,000
Brazil			91,000,000	91,000,000
Canada	6,291,385		29,047,742	10,674,850
Japan	30,000,000	10,000,000	114,000	100,000,000
Turkey			100,000,000	100,000,000

The authorities for these statements of the amount of legal tender paper money in these countries, are as follows: United States, debt statement; Great Britain, weekly report Bank of England; Sweden, American Almanac, 1879, page 242; Norway, Report of Silver Commission, page 518; Denmark, Report of Silver Commission, page 169; Austria, Silver Commission, page 114; Italy, Silver Commission, page 243; Russia, United States Mint Report, page 101; Peru, Silver

Commission, page 114; Brazil, same, 158; Canada, Report of United States Mint, 1879, page 30; Japan, Report on Foreign Relations, 1879, page 386; Turkey estimated.

The universal experience of all Governments is that gold, as the exclusive legal tender money, is not sufficient to enable any people to carry on their domestic and foreign trade, and that where the quantity of full legal tender silver coin is not, in addition to the gold, in large quantities, or is excluded altogether, then there must be an issue of legal tender paper, either by the Government direct, or by the banks under the authority of the Government, as is the case in England and the Scandinavian States. So thoroughly is this supported by the experience of other nations that if by judicial or other proceedings the present legal tender greenbacks of this country shall be forced into retirement, an amendment to the Constitution, authorizing the issue of paper money having a legal tender quality will become a national necessity.

THE GREENBACK.

At the breaking out of the rebellion, the Government found itself destitute of the means necessary to carry on a gigantic war, and unable to procure such means from ordinary sources. It applied to the great banks of the country, and found that aid from that source was too limited, and to uncertain, to be depended upon. The banks finally agreed that, if specie payments could be indefinitely suspended, they would supply the Government with an unlimited amount of their promises to pay—their non-interest bearing bank notes—in exchange for the Government's interest-bearing promises to pay—coin bonds.

When the Government saw that the war had to be carried on without the use of coin—with paper money based upon credit—it conceived the idea that its own credit, coupled with its sovereign power of conferring the legal tender quality upon its evidences of indebtedness, was far better, cheaper, and more reliable than that of the banks.

This idea was embodied in the first legal tender act, and reported to the House by the Ways and Means Committee, January 7, 1862.

Its constitutionality received the approval of the Attorney General, and its announcement met with popular and unparalleled favor, as it was destined to meet the nation's needs.

The greenback has the safest, most reliable, and permanent basis of any money in the world.

No man ever accepts money in payment, with a view, or for the purpose of obtaining its basis. It must be borne in mind that gold and silver coin require the same kind of basis to give them their money value, that greenbacks do. Without the basis that underlies coin, the precious metals would be comparatively worthless. Let the civilized world demonetize these metals, and for all the uses society has for them, they would not command their weight in blank greenback paper.

The moment their fiat money value is taken from them they will cease to be even ornamental, for the beauty-loving eye of unbiased nature sees greater splendor in colored glass than in gold or silver.

What is the basis of gold and silver? During the financial crisis of England in 1847, when legal tender debt-paying money was in urgent demand, no man could borrow a £5 note on a thousand dollars' worth of silver. Why? Because the basis of silver coin had been removed by demonetization, and although it was intrinsically as valuable as ever, it did not possess money functions. It was a dead body without the legal tender soul. The basis of man is his immortal spirit; when that takes its flight, the body becomes valueless, like demonetized metal. In Calcutta, where silver only is legal tender, during a money stringency in 1864, it was impossible to borrow a dollar on gold; and merchants who had hundreds of thousands of gold coin, were obliged to allow their notes to go to protest, because they could not borrow $10 of silver on a bushel of gold. The question is not, "What kind is the dollar," but "What will it do?" Has it the legal tender basis under it, and does it possess debt-paying functions? Henri Cernuschi, an eminent French writer on finance, author of "Bi-metallic Money," said before the congressional monetary commission in 1877:

"*Money is a value created by law.* Its basis is legal and not material. It is, perhaps, not easy to convince one that the value of metallic money is created by law. *It is, however, the fact.* If you suppose that gold and silver are not money—are not legal tender—their value is lost."

In reference to legal tender greenbacks, Mr. Cernuschi says:

"Many people suppose their value depends upon the promise of the Government to repay them in metal one day or other. This promise does not add to the purchasing power of paper money. It makes no difference of what material money is composed, whether it is costly or otherwise; THE LAW OF LEGAL TENDER GIVES VALUE TO MONEY, *and that value is increased or diminished in proportion as its volume is greater or less.*"

Men accept money in payment, not to use, but to exchange for something they can use. They require a basis as surety, that the money will perform this office.

Bank notes, not a legal tender, having no legal value, simply a representative of legal value, must have that legal value as a basis, or they fail even to be representatives. Not so with greenbacks or coin. Their basis is the law, making them a tender for taxes and debts, public and private; and as long as the law continues their basis is secure. The basis of bank notes, if coin, is treacherous. It may take wings and fly to foreign countries, leaving its representative worthless. But the basis of the greenback is anchored in the laws of the land, and in every debt of the nation, public and private. Bank currency is always considered safe when based on thirty-three per cent. of its face in redemption material, and when based on a reserve of resumption material in excess of its face, it commands a premium over the par of the basis. Greenbacks being legal tender are based on the public and private credit of the country. Every dollar of it is redeemable in debts and taxes as good as gold, and if $150,000,000 of coin in the country is ample to carry $600,000,000 of paper at par, it is strange if fifteen thousand millions of private and corporate debts, and $1,000,000,000 of annual taxes cannot carry $2,000,000,000 of greenbacks at par with those debts and taxes.

The basis of coin is the credit of the nations, or the faith and confidence which the public have that the different nations will retain the enforced coin standard. Metal coins are simply representatives of the monetized credit of all nations, while greenbacks are representatives of the coined credit of the United States, each being current money within the jurisdiction of the nation or nations which thus represent their monetized credit, and no further. Coin money does not strengthen a Government as greenbacks do. The whole fabric of our Government might tumble to the ground without loss to the holders of gold, whose metal is as valuable in Europe as here. In fact, wars, panics, financial crashes, revolutions and periods of bankruptcy are harvest seasons for gold owners, who rather encourage such disasters than otherwise. But with greenbacks it is different. They are based upon the laws of the United States alone, hence, with the destruction of our Government they would become worthless.

Were the legal tender money of the United States limited to greenbacks alone, they would afford the most perfect safeguard to the perpetuity of the Government that could be conceived of, for every man, even if he lacked patriotism, would be impelled by self-interest to support and defend the Government that gave *value* to his money, as much as he would to defend the *box* that contained it. So by all the arguments of reason and philosophy the greenback is the best and most securely based money in the world.

LEGAL TENDERS CONSTITUTIONAL IN TIME OF PEACE AS WELL AS IN TIME OF WAR—EVERY OBJECTION ANSWERED BY THE SUPREME COURT.

The newspapers and orators in the interest, if not in the employ, of the bankers and bondholders, argue that the Supreme Court of the United States decided the legal tender act unconstitutional in time of peace It will, however, be found that the court rendered no such decision. The substance of the decision bearing on this point was that the mode or manner of providing the means for the maintenance of the Government was a legislative and not a judicial question, and as it is as much the duty of Congress to provide the means for maintaining the Government in time of peace as in time of war, its power must be the same in both cases. This is common sense as well as common honesty.

The cases of Knox vs. Lee, and Parker vs. Davis were consolidated and brought before the Supreme Court, and, at the request of the court, the question of the constitutionality of the legal tender acts was to be fully argued, and finally settled by the court, so that the question should be forever put at rest. In this case the court held that the legal tender acts were constitutional as applied both to past and future contracts. The court says:

"Before we can hold the legal tender acts unconstitutional we must be convinced they were not appropriate means, or means conducive to the execution of any or all of the powers of Congress or the Government, not appropriate in any degree (for we are not judges of that degree of appropriation) or we must hold they were prohibited."—12 Wallace, U. S. Supreme Court Reports, page 509.

"The degree of the necessity for any congressional enactment, or the relative degree of its appropriateness, is for consideration in Congress, not here. *When the law is not prohibited*, and is really calculated to effect any of the objects intrusted to the Government, to undertake here to inquire into the degree of its necessity, would be to pass the line which circumscribes the judicial department, and to tread on legislative ground.—*Ibid*, 542.

It will be seen that the question is not decided upon the contingency of war, but the whole matter of the necessity of any constitutional enactment is left to congress. The court says:

"The constitution was intended to frame a Government as distinguished from a league or compact, a Government supreme in some particulars over States and people. *It was designed to provide the same currency having a uniform legal value in all the States.* It was for this reason the power to coin money and regulate its value *was conferred upon the Federal Government*, while the same power to emit bills of credit was *withheld from the States*. The States no longer can declare what shall be money or regulate its value. *Whatever power there is over the currency is vested in congress. If the power to declare what is money is not in congress it is annihilated.*"—Ibid, 545.

"And generally when one of such powers was expressly denied

to the States only, it was for the purpose of rendering the federal power *more complete and exclusive;* how sensible, then, its framers must have been that emergencies might arise when the precious metals *might prove inadequate to the necessities of the Government and the demands of the people*—when it is remembered that paper money was almost exclusively in use in the States as a medium of exchange, and when the great evil sought to be remedied was the want of uniformity in the current value of money, it might be argued, we say, that the gift of power to coin money and regulate the value thereof, was understood as conveying general power over the currency and which had belonged to the States and which they had surrendered."—Ibid, 546.   *   *   *   *

"*By the obligation of a contract to pay money is to pay that which law shall recognize as money when the payment is to be made.*

"If there is anything settled by decision it is this, and we do not understand it to be controverted. No one ever doubted that a debt of one thousand dollars, contracted before 1834 could be paid by *one hundred eagles* coined after that year, though they contained *no more gold than ninety-four eagles when the contract was made, and this is not because of the intrinsic value of the coin, but because of its legal value.* The eagles coined after 1834 were not money until they were authorized by law, and had they been coined before, without a law fixing their legal value, they could no more have paid a debt than uncoined bullion, or cotton or wheat. Every contract for the payment of money is necessarily subject to the constitutional power of the Government over the currency, whatever that power may be, and the obligation of the parties is, therefore, assumed with reference to that power."—Ibid, 548–9.

"If therefore, they (the legal tenders) were what we have endeavored to show, appropriate ends, they were not transgressive of the authority vested in congress."—Ibid, 552.

"It is hardly correct to speak of a standard value. The constitution does not speak of it. It contemplates a standard for that which has gravity or extension; but value is an ideal thing. The Coinage Acts fix its unit as a dollar, but the gold or silver thing we call a dollar is, in no sense a standard of a dollar, it is a representative of it. There might never have been a piece of money of the denomination of a dollar.   *   *   *   *

"It will be seen that we hold the acts of congress constitutional as applied to contracts made before or after their passage."—Ibid, 553.

For the information of those who profess to believe that the court was packed to procure a decision confirming the constitutionality of the legal tender act, I will give the opinion of Chief Justice Marshall, who in the case of McCullough vs. Maryland, says:

"When the act *is not prohibited*, and is calculated to effect any of the objects intrusted to the Government, to undertake here to inquire into the degree of its necessity *would be to pass the line which circumscribes the judicial department, and to tread on legislative ground.*"

THE BONE OF CONTENTION.

Seventeen years, side by side, the greenback has proved itself under all circumstances fully equal to the bank note. There is no instance on record where the bank note has been preferred, and no instance where the greenback has been refused in the ordinary commercial transactions of the country. It is an established fact, which no one will dispute, that as a medium of exchange, a tool of trade, the greenback, has established its equality at least, with the best bank note ever issued. The bank note has no qualities which render it superior to the greenback. On the other hand, does the greenback possess any virtues or qualities not possessed by the bank note, which recommend it as superior to the bank note?

It does. There are three important considerations why the greenback should displace the bank note entirely.

1. It is legal tender between man and man, which the bank note is not.

2. When the greenback is issued, it serves the Government as money for the amount its face represents, saving the people that amount of taxation. When the Government prepares a million dollars of greenbacks, it has come in possession of that amount of money without drawing it from society, by direct or indirect taxation. It is so much clear gain for the people. The substitution of greenbacks for the amount of bank notes now outstanding would be a net gain of $337,181,418 to the Government, and save in taxation that amount to the taxpayers.

3. It costs nothing to keep the greenback in circula-

tion. The expense of printing, is all that attaches to it, and that is not greater than the cost of printing the bank note, which the Government also has to pay; but the bank note costs an average of 5 per cent. per annum, the amount of interest the people are compelled to pay on the bonds upon which it is based. Already the *industries of the country have redeemed every bank note in circulation, in gold;*—by paying since 1863, $350,000,000 of gold interest on the bonds held by the Government, as security for the bank circulation. The Government furnishes the security for the bank note, and the people pay the bank for the use of it. No one denies but at least $1,000,000,000 of currency is necessary for this country when enterprise is in its full tide of activity. If the competing greenback was out of the way, there is not the least doubt but the bank currency would be immediately inflated to that sum, or more. The great issue now is, which kind of paper money shall prevail.

The banks are determined to drive out all competition, that they may have the benefit of the entire circulation. The Greenback party is equally determined that the people shall have the benefit of it, by allowing the Government to issue the whole amount, and save, not only that amount from taxes, but forty or fifty millions every year of interest which they will be compelled to pay on the bonds upon which the bank note must be based.

The pecuniary stake at issue between the Greenback party and the Bank party is $1,000,000,000 cash down, and at least $40,000,000 a year for all time to come.

If the opposition prevail, the Government will lose the $350,000,000 of greenbacks now in circulation, by being obliged to redeem and retire them; a perpetual bank tax of forty or fifty millions a year will be saddled upon the country, and to get the $1,000,000,000 of bank currency into circulation, $3,000,000,000 of property will have to be mortgaged to the banks, and an annual interest of not less than $100,000,000 paid them, time without end.

There is another consideration of no less importance than those already alluded to, in connection with this matter, and that is the political danger of depriving the people of the right to control so important and dangerous a power as the monetary prerogative; and conferring it upon a hereditary and alien dynasty. There is more truth than poetry in the declaration that "money is power." He who holds the purse, commands the sword of any nation, and nine-tenths of the public debt, which constitutes the foundation of our banking system, is in the control of foreign capitalists, who hate democracy, and flourish best in the soil of imperialism. Are the people of America prepared to surrender their sovereignty into the hands of aliens and tyrants?

Some one objects to the greenback full legal tender, because it is irredeemable—and claims the superiority of the bank note because it is redeemable. Money is fit for nothing else, it can be used for no other purpose while it remains money. No matter of what it is composed. Money is created to pay for labor, and debts, and to exchange commodities, and needs redemption no more than a horse or a steamboat. We might object to buying farms, and stock, and tools, because they are irredeemable. The righteous need no redemption—only the damned—hence it is well for the bank note that salvation has been provided for it, and its savior and redeemer, so far, has been the greenback, which never fell, but is the redeemer of all things temporal, even the nation itself.

CHAPTER XI.

THE PUBLIC DEBT.

The following table exhibits the classification of the interest-bearing indebtedness of the United States, on August 31, 1865, and on the 1st of July annually, including interest-bearing treasury notes used as currency, as reported by Secretary Sherman, January 1, 1880:

[From Report of Secretary of Treasury.]

Date.	6 per cent. bonds.	5 per cent. bonds.	4½ per cent. bonds.	4 per cent. bonds.	Total.
Aug. 31, 1865	$908,518,091	$199,792,100			$1,108,310,191
July 1, 1866	1,008,388,469	198,528,435			1,206,916,904
July 1, 1867	1,421,110,719	198,533,435			1,619,644,154
July 1, 1868	1,841,521,800	221,588,400			2,063,110,200
July 1, 1869	1,886,311,300	221,589,300			2,107,930,600
July 1, 1870	1,764,932,300	221,589,300			1,986,521,600
July 1, 1871	1,613,897,300	274,236,450			1,888,133,750
July 1, 1872	1,374,883,800	414,567,300			1,789,451,100
July 1, 1873	1,281,238,650	414,567,300			1,695,805,9 0
July 1, 1874	1,213,624,700	510,628,050			1,724,252,750
July 1, 1875	1,100,865,550	607,132,750			1,707,998,300
July 1, 1876	984,999,650	711,685,800			1,696,685,450
July 1, 1877	854, 21,850	703,266,650	$140,000,000		1,697,888,500
July 1, 1878	738,619,000	703,266,650	240,000,000	$98,850,000	1,780,735,650
July 1, 1879	310,932,500	646,905,500	250,000,000	679,878,110	1,887,716,110

The interest-bearing public debt is a burden which never ought to have been imposed upon the nation. It is the most stupendous fraud and swindle ever perpetrated upon a free people. It was conceived in fraud, and brought forth in iniquity. It was a scheme to rob and enslave 40,000,000 of people after they had emancipated 4,000,000 at the sacrifice of rivers of blood and millions of treasure.

Before the legal tender act had passed the threshold of legislation, it was met by the money sharks of Wall

Street. There was no stealings in it for the money power. There was no seam left open for the grappling irons of the financial pirate. There was no tap, from which the usurer could suck the blood of toil. It met violent organized opposition. From whom? From the soldier, who was risking his life in defence of his country? No. From the farmer, who supplied food and mules? From the manufacturer, who furnished guns, wagons, army blankets, or ships of war? No. Not one of all the employes, or creditors of the Government, from the President down to the army teamsters, but what rejoiced at the prospect of receiving the Government's own legal tender money, in exchange for anything he had to sell, or any service he could render during the war, be it six months or seven years.

Who, then, opposed the coinage of free legal tender money? Why, the banks and the money power. What interest was it to them? What had they to do with this new money? Had they anything to sell to the Government? Not a thing. Were they going to enlist, and wanted pay other than greenbacks? No; not a recruit from that quarter.

We will show you how and why they opposed it. We are told that on the 11th of January, only four days after the introduction of the bill, the wolf-howl that had, during the time, echoed from bank to bank, called to Washington a convention of the Money Power, consisting of four delegates from the New York banks, three from Philadelphia, and three from Boston.

They saw in the legal tender bill a scheme that would cut off all future chance for them to rob the people. They saw it would transfer the monopoly of the money from their hands, to the control of the people.

They saw in it a precedent which, if permitted to be tested, would ever afterward enable the Government to relieve itself and the people, without being obliged to submit to the extortions of the usurer.

In short, they saw the handwriting of their downfall, and the emancipation of labor and production, written on the legal tender greenback.

If the nation's necessities compelled it to resort to its own bills of credit, they must go forth under sentence of death to fight the battles of the country.

What arguments were used, or what undue influences were brought to bear upon the law-makers of the Government, will probably never be known. The result is a matter of record. Every greenback that went out to fight the nation's battles, was accompanied by a bond-shark, to gobble it up, as soon as it had performed its service. The act of 1862, authorizing the issue of the first $150,000,000 of greenbacks, authorized $500,000,000 of bonds to absorb them.

There never was a day, after the passage of the first legal tender act, but what the Government was in possession of all the money it needed, of its own creation, without borrowing a dollar, or selling a bond.

The only object of the bond was to enable the money sharks again to get control of the money of the country, which they never could do without the bond. The Government established the fact that it could meet all its obligations, purchase all its supplies, and defray every expense, by its own legal tenders; and if so, what was the necessity of borrowing?

You answer, that the bonds were necessary to absorb the excess, occasioned by the extraordinary demands of the war.

I deny that there ever was an excess. Let only him dare assert it, who had more than he could find use for.

Even if there was an excess, the bonds did not diminish it. The excess has only been transferred from the pockets of laborers and wealth producers, to those of usurers, importers and international dealers.

Every bond is used as money. They are used by English capitalists, to buy American cotton and bread stuffs, and by American dealers to purchase, import, and glut our market with what our own labor should produce, but cannot; for the want of the very money which was destroyed, that these bonds might live.

Just in proportion as the people's money has been contracted, that of the money king has been inflated.

Just as contraction and specie limitation weakens and impoverishes the masses, bond inflation strengthens and enriches the few.

That their inflated paper bond money may be current all over the world, they require it to draw interest, and that they may be relieved of the burden of such interest, they compel labor and its products to pay all the taxes.

The difference to the people of America, between the greenbacks, before they were converted into bonds, and the bonds, is as follows:

The fifteen hundred million dollars of greenbacks, earned their owners nothing while lying idle. To be profitable every $500 had to give a laborer a year's employment, and the total amount kept three million laborers constantly at work.

In bonds, they earn their owners full as much, while resting in their safes; but throw three millions of men out of employment, and compel property owners, who receive no benefit from them, not only to support the three millions of idle laborers, and their families, but to pay the bondholders $100,000,000 annually, for the fun of the thing. The people and tax payers have got tired of this. If they are to be taxed to support the Government, they claim the benefits of the Government and taxation. When bonds are given for the loan of money, and that money circulated among the people, they can afford to bear the burdens of the debt; but when such bonds are given, to absorb and destroy the people's money, thus creating new burdens, by destroying the very means necessary to bear those already existing, the sufferers will refuse to submit to the outrage, and will certainly take the first opportunity to relieve themselves. It matters not what the result may be, the American people have drank too deep at the fount of liberty, to submit to be enslaved by the bond fraud schemes of Europe, and now give fair notice that if the same money that purchased the bond, will not pay it, the entire fraud will be repudiated.

THE PUBLIC DEBT OF FRANCE AND AMERICA.

The public debt of France is represented by interest-bearing obligations, called *Rentes*, which are issued in small denominations, as low as 100 francs ($20), and held mostly by the peasantry and laboring population, as savings investments. In 1867 the debt of France was held by 1,095,683 persons, averaging about $2,000 each. It is now still more widely distributed, Spofford, librarian of congress, claiming that "half the families in France have money in public funds." The debt is, therefore, no burden to the people. Its interest goes to the masses of the taxpayers.

In England, on the other hand, her great debt of

$3,850,000,000 is in the hands of only 126,331 persons, thus averaging more than $30,000 each. In America the public debt is also in the hands of a few, with this difference: In both England and France the Government obligations are taxed *pro rata* with all other investments, and have to bear their proportion of the public burdens, while in America they are exempt from all taxation, thus throwing their entire burden upon those who reap no profit from them.

The real object of our bonded debt was to provide a foundation for a huge national banking system, as the basis of a colossal money power, who, by controlling and monopolizing the monetary prerogative of the nation, could control values, and through usury, absorb the wealth and surplus earnings of labor and enterprise.

The fact that the vast sum required to carry on the late war, which aggregated nearly $7,000,000,000, all but about $500,000,000 was provided by the issue of United States legal tenders and treasury notes, and from the legitimate revenues of the Government, such as duties on imports, internal revenue, sales of public lands and income taxes, and all this, without being perceptibly felt by the taxpaying industries of the country, is evidence that the entire amount might have been paid in the same manner, without a bond to disgrace the credit of the nation, or to check the march of prosperity which an ample volume of Government currency had set in motion.

And when we consider that the country has had to pay already over $1,600,000,000 of interest on the public debt, it is proof positive that the bonds were wholly unnecessary, and have been a curse to the extent of the interest already paid upon them, besides fostering, and building up a giant monied oligarchy, the most dangerous for civil liberty, and our republican institutions that can be conceived.

The money kings siezed the opportunity, when our Government was in distress, when it was struggling with a giant foe in front, to stab it in the rear. They took this opportunity to compel the nation to disgorge its interest-bearing obligations, and to saddle a monstrous perpetual debt upon the people as a future means of robbing the wealth producers after they should have returned from the field of victory and blood, to their avocations of peace. Now for the proof.

Nominally, the bonds were due and payable in twenty years from date of issue. On the 2d of February, 1863, John Sherman reported the National bank bill in the Senate. This bill, which is the act now in existence, provided for a national currency, BASED ON UNITED STATES BONDS. It was recommended by Secretary Chase, December, 1862, but was not acted upon, *for the want of bonds as a basis.*

Bonds must be provided.

But the legal tender act as introduced by Thad Stevens, and passed the House of Representatives February 6, 1862, would do away with the necessity of both bonds and national bank currency, so it was defeated in the Senate through the influence of the eastern bankers.

The greenback would be too good. With a paper circulation confined to greenbacks, what could the bankers do, and what would banking be worth? Hence the greenbacks were purposely depreciated. Bonds were provided to absorb them.

Fifteen different varieties of treasury notes were issued, all convertible into bonds, at par, but the bonds were withheld until the nation's paper had been so depreciated by the people's agents in high places, that one dollar of gold would purchase two or three dollars of treasury notes, every one of which was par for bonds.

Speaking of the national banking proposition, Mr. Chase said in his report, in 1862:

> "The central idea of the measure is the establishment of a sound uniform currency throughout the country *upon the foundation of national credit* (in other words, upon a national debt), *making this the settled policy of the country.*"

As the bonds were due and payable in twenty years, at furthest, it could hardly be called *a settled policy*, whose foundation was intended to be removed at the expiration of that time. Four years later, in December, 1866, Hugh McCulloch, then secretary of the treasury, in his annual report, said:

> "The national banking system *was intended*, while not invading the rights of the States, nor damaging private interests, *to furnish the people with* A PERMANENT PAPER CIRCULATION. The United States notes were intended to meet a temporary emergency *and to be retired when the emergency had passed.*"

Now, the foundation of the national currency being the public debt, and the expressed declaration that this system of currency was to be the fixed and permanent policy of the country, is positive proof that the original intention was to make the bonds permanent, perpetual and never payable.

In 1869, when the credit-strengthening act was passed, changing the payment of the bonds from greenbacks to coin, there was outstanding, $1,500,000,000 of 5.20 bonds, all to become due and payable within the next twelve years.

At that time the coin resources of the Government were no more than sufficient to enable it to meet its current interest obligations, nevertheless congress obligated it to pay *fifteen hundred millions of gold and silver.*

This was an apparent impossibility. It was intended to be such.

The act was for the express purpose of immortalizing the public debt, that it might never be paid.

But when Nevada opened her rich vaults of silver and made it possible to pay the debt in accordance with the new terms imposed, that metal was demonetized, and payment limited to gold.

It may seem strange to some that the bond-holders should desire such legislation as would absolutely defeat payment to them.

But they regard the bonds as the best paying investment they could put their money into.

First. They are untaxed, and their annual interest is twice the average profits of money invested in productive industry.

Second. While lying idle, drawing this interest, they furnish collaterals for the loan of 90 per cent. of their value from the Government at 1 per cent., which the holders can re-loan to enterprise at from 10 to 15 per cent. per annum.

The bondholders have the strongest possible inducement to perpetuate the public debt.

The public debt of France is as near a "public blessing" as any debt can be. It is distributed among all the people, who use it both as a safe and profitable investment for their small savings, and as a medium of exchange.

It imposes no unjust or unequal burdens. It pays its own way. It is not used as the basis for banking or to foster any monopoly or money oligarchy.

To say that our bonds were issued and sold to raise money to carry on the war, is absurd and false.

It was a year and a half after they were authorized before they were put upon the market, and when they were offered, it was not because the Government needed the money.

This is the proof:

On the 3d of March, 1863, before a bond had been issued, the Secretary of the Treasury was authorized to issue $900,000,000 of legal tenders and other treasury notes—$300,000,000 for the current year, and $600,000,000 for the year following; and not until the May following were the bonds authorized by act of Feb. 25, 1862, offered for sale.

This $900,000,000 of new issue were thrown into circulation in order to depreciate the currency, so that bonds could be had cheap, and it had the effect. The Government did not place its bonds on the market because it needed money, but it did authorize an inordinate volume of money in order to depreciate it, as well as that already out, so as to enable the money sharks to buy up their future banking basis for a song; and then, in order to get the Government issues out of the way, so the bank sharks could have full swing, the people's money was destroyed as fast as it was paid into the treasury for bonds, which resulted in the losses, bankruptcies, ruin, desolation and death, of the panic of 1873, and subsequently.

CHAPTER XII.

FINANCE LEGISLATION FROM 1860 TO 1876.

SUMMARY OF LAWS.
[From Gold and Debt.]

Act June 22, 1860.

[This act authorized the issue of $21,000,000 of 6 per cent. bonds to be used in the redemption of outstanding treasury notes.]

Act December 17, 1860.

That the President of the United States be authorized to cause treasury notes to be issued for such sums as the exigencies of the public service may require, but not to exceed at any time the amount of ten millions ($10,000,000). That such notes shall be redeemed after the expiration of one year. They shall bear interest, six per cent. per annum.

Act February 8, 1861.

That the President of the United States be authorized to borrow, on the credit of the United States, a sum not exceeding twenty-five millions ($25,000,000). That stock shall be issued for the amount so borrowed, bearing interest not exceeding six per centum per annum, and to be reimbursed within a period not beyond twenty years and not less than ten years.

Act March 2, 1861.

That the President of the United States be, and hereby is, authorized, at any time within twelve months from the passage of this act, to borrow, on the credit of the United States, a sum not exceeding ten millions of dollars: *Provided*, That no stipulation or contract shall be made to prevent the United States from reimbursing any sum borrowed under the authority of this act at any time after the expiration of ten years from the 1st day of July next, by the United States giving three months' notice, to be published in some newspaper published at the seat of Government, of their readiness to do so; and no contract shall be made to prevent the redemption of the same at any time after the expiration of twenty years from the said 1st day of July next, without notice. That stock shall be issued for the amount so borrowed, bearing interest not exceeding six per cent. per annum.

Act July 17, 1861.

That the secretary of the treasury be authorized to borrow, on the credit of the United States, within twelve months, a sum not exceeding $250,000,000, for which he is authorized to issue *coupon bonds* or registered bonds or treasury notes in such proportion as he may deem advisable. The bonds to bear interest not exceeding seven per cent. per annum, payable semi-annually, irredeemable for twenty years, and after that at the pleasure of the United States, and the treasury notes to be of denominations not less than $50, payable three years after date, with interest at the rate of seven and three-tenths per cent. per annum. And the secretary may also issue, in exchange for coin, treasury notes of a less denomination than $50, not bearing interest but payable on demand at the assistant treasuries of the United States—or treasury notes bearing interest at the rate of 3.65 per cent. per annum, payable in one year from date and exchangeable at any time for treasury notes (7.30s) for $50 and upward.

That the secretary is authorized, whenever he shall deem it expedient, to issue, in exchange for coin or in payment of public dues, treasury notes of any of the denominations hereinbefore specified, bearing interest not exceeding six per cent. per annum, and payable at any time not exceeding twelve months from date; that the amount of notes so issued shall at no time exceed $20,000,000.

Act August 5, 1861.

That the secretary of the treasury is authorized to issue bonds of the United States, bearing interest at six per cent. per annum, and payable at the pleasure of the United States after twenty years from date. If any holder of treasury notes bearing interest at the rate of seven and three-tenths per cent. per annum desire to exchange the same for said bonds, the secretary may, at any time before the maturity of said treasury notes, issue to said holder, in payment thereof, an amount of said bonds equal to the amount due on said treasury notes; nor shall the whole amount of such bonds exceed the whole amount of treasury notes bearing seven and three-tenths per cent. interest issued under said act (of July 17, 1861).

Act February 12, 1862.

That the secretary of the treasury, in addition to the $50,000,000 of notes payable on demand of denominations not less than five dollars, authorized by the acts of July 17 and August 5, 1861, is authorized to issue like notes to the amount of $10,000,000—said notes shall be deemed part of the loan of $250,000,000 authorized by said acts.

Act February 25, 1862.

That the secretary of the treasury is hereby authorized to issue, on the credit of the United States, one hundred and fifty millions of dollars of United States notes, not bearing interest, payable to bearer, at the Treasury of the United States, and of such denominations as he may deem expedient, not less than five dollars each: *Provided, however,* That fifty millions of said notes shall be in lieu of the demand treasury notes authorized to be issued by the act of July seventeen, eighteen hundred and sixty-one; which said demand notes shall be taken up as rapidly as practicable, and the notes herein provided for substituted for them: *And provided further,* That the amount of the two kinds of notes together shall at no time exceed the sum of one hundred and fifty millions of dollars, and such notes herein authorized shall be receivable in payment of all taxes, internal duties, excises, debts and demands of every kind due to the United States, except duties on imports, and of all claims and demands against the United States of every kind whatsoever, except for interest upon bonds and notes, which shall be paid in coin, and shall also be lawful money and a legal tender in payment of all debts, public and private, within the United States, except duties on imports and interest as aforesaid. And any holders of said United States notes depositing any sum not less than fifty dollars, or some multiple of fifty dollars, with the treasurer of the United States, or either of the assistant treasurers, shall receive in exchange therefor duplicate certificates of deposit, one of which may be transmitted to the secretary of the treasury, who shall thereupon issue to the holder an equal amount of bonds of the United States, coupon or registered, as may by said holder be desired, bearing interest at the rate of six per centum per annum, payable semi-annually, and redeemable at the pleasure of the United States after five years, and payable twenty years from the date thereof. And such United States notes shall be received the same as coin, at their par value, in payment for any loans that may be hereafter sold or negotiated by the secretary of the treasury, and may be re-issued from time to time as the exigencies of the public interest shall require.

That to enable the secretary to fund the floating debt of the United States he be authorized to issue, on the credit of the United States, bonds to an amount not exceeding $500,000,000, redeemable at the pleasure of the United States after five years, and payable twenty years after date, bearing interest at the rate of six per cent. per annum.

Sinking Fund Act, February 25, 1862.

That all duties on imported goods shall be paid in coin, or in notes payable on demand, heretofore authorized to be issued and by law receivable in payment of public dues, and the *coin* so paid shall be set apart as a special fund and shall be applied as follows:

First, To the payment in coin of the interest on the bonds and notes of the United States.

Second, To the purchase or payment of one per centum of the entire debt of the United States to be made within each fiscal year after the first day of July, 1862, which is to be set apart as a sinking fund, and the interest of which shall in like manner be applied to the purchase or payment of the public debt as the secretary of the treasury shall from time to time direct.

Third, The residue thereof to be paid into the treasury.

Act March 17, 1862.

That the secretary may purchase coin with any of the bonds or notes of the United States authorized by law, at such rates and upon such terms as he may deem most advantageous to the public interest.

(By Sec. 2 of this act, the demand notes authorized by the acts of

July 17, 1861, and February 12, 1862, are declared lawful money and a legal tender, same as the treasury notes issued under act of February 25, 1862.)

Pacific Railroad Bonds, Act July 1, 1862.

Sec. 5. That for the purposes herein mentioned the secretary of the treasury shall, upon the certificate in writing of said commissioners of the completion and equipment of forty consecutive miles of said railroad and telegraph, in accordance with the provisions of this act, issue to said company bonds of the United States of one thousand dollars each, payable in thirty years after date, bearing six per centum per annum interest (said interest payable semi-annually), which interest may be paid in United States treasury notes or any other money or currency which the United States have or shall declare lawful money and a legal tender, to the amount of sixteen of said bonds per mile for such section of forty miles; and to secure the repayment to the United States, as hereinafter provided, of the amount of said bonds so issued and delivered to said company, together with all interest therein which shall have been paid by the United States, the issue of said bonds and delivery to the company shall ipso facto constitute a first mortgage on the whole line of the railroad and telegraph, together with the rolling stock, fixtures and property of every kind and description, and in consideration of which said bonds may be issued; and on the refusal or failure of said company to redeem said bonds, or any part of them, when required so to do by the secretary of the treasury, in accordance with the provisions of this act, the said road, with all the rights, functions, immunities and appurtenances thereunto belonging, and also all lands granted to the said company by the United States, which, at the time of said default, shall remain in the ownership of said company, may be taken possession of by the secretary of the treasury, for the use and benefit of the United States: *Provided,* this section shall not apply to that part of any road now constructed.

Sec. 6. That the grants aforesaid are made upon condition that said company shall pay said bonds at maturity, and shall keep said railroad and telegraph line in repair and use, and shall at all times transmit dispatches over said telegraph line, and transport mails, troops and munitions of war, supplies and public stores upon said railroad for the Government, whenever required to do so by any department thereof, and that the Government shall at all times have the preference in the use of the same for all the purposes aforesaid (at fair and reasonable rates of compensation, not to exceed the amounts paid by private parties for the same kind of service); and all compensation for services rendered for the Government shall be applied to the payment of said bonds and interest until the whole amount is fully paid. Said company may also pay the United States, wholly or in part, in the same or other bonds, treasury notes, or other evidences of debt against the United States, to be allowed at par; and after said road is completed, until said bonds and interest are paid, at least five per centum of the net earnings of said road shall also be annually applied to the payment thereof.

Act July 11, 1862.

That the secretary of the treasury is hereby authorized to issue, in addition to the amounts heretofore authorized, on the credit of the United States, one hundred and fifty millions of dollars of United States notes, not bearing interest, payable to bearer at the treasury of the United States, and of such denominations as he may deem expedient: *Provided*, That no note shall be issued for the fractional part of a dollar, and not more that thirty-five millions shall be of lower denominations than five dollars; and such notes shall be receivable in payment of all loans made to the United States, and of all taxes, internal duties, excises, debts and demands of every kind due to the United States, except duties on imports and interest, and of all claims and demands against the United States, except for interest upon bonds, notes, and certificates of debt or deposit; and shall also be lawful money and a legal tender in payment of all debts, public and private, within the United States, except duties on imports and interest, as aforesaid. And any holder of said United States notes depositing any sum not less that fifty dollars, or some multiple of fifty dollars, with the treasurer of the United States, or either of the assistant treasurers, shall receive in exchange therefor duplicate certificates of deposit, one of which may be transmitted to the secretary of the treasury, who shall thereupon issue to the holder an equal amount of bonds of the United States, coupon or registered, as may by said holder be desired, bearing interest at the rate of six per centum per annum, payable semi-annually, and redeemable at the pleasure of the United States after five years, and payable twenty years from the date thereof: *Provided, however*, That any notes issued under this act may be paid in coin, instead of being received in exchange for certificates of deposit as above specified at the direction of the secretary of the treasury. And the secretary of the treasury may exchange for such notes, on such terms as he shall think most beneficial to the public interest, any bonds of the United States bearing six per centum interest, and redeemable after five and payable in twenty years, which have been or may be lawfully issued under the provisions of any existing act; may reissue the notes so received in exchange; may receive and cancel any notes heretofore lawfully issued under congress, and in lieu thereof issue an equal amount in notes such as are authorized by this act; and may purchase, at rates not exceeding one-eighth of one per centum, any bonds or certificates of debt of the United States as he may deem advisable.

Joint Resolution January 17, 1863.

That the secretary of the treasury is hereby authorized, if required by the exigencies of the public service, to issue on the credit of the United States the sum of one hundred millions of dollars of United States notes in such form as he may deem expedient, not bearing interest, payable to bearer on demand, and of such denominations, not less than one dollar, as he may prescribe, which notes so issued shall be lawful money and a legal tender, like the similar notes heretofore authorized, in payment of all debts, public and private, within the United States, except duties on imports and interest on the public debt.

Act March 3, 1863.

That the secretary of the treasury be, and is hereby, authorized to borrow, from time to time, on the credit of the United States, a sum not exceeding three hundred millions of dollars for the current fiscal year, and six hundred millions for the next fiscal year, and to issue therefor coupon or registered bonds, payable at the pleasure of the Government after such periods as may be fixed by the secretary, not less than ten nor more than forty years from date in coin, and of such denominations, not less than fifty dollars, as he may deem expedient, bearing interest at a rate not exceeding six per centum per annum, payable on bonds not exceeding one hundred dollars, annually, and on all others semi-annually, in coin; and he may in his discretion, dispose of such bonds at any time, upon such terms as he may deem most advisable, for lawful money of the United States, or for any of the certificates of indebtedness or deposit that may at any time be unpaid, or for any of the treasury notes heretofore issued or which may be issued under the provisions of this act. And all the bonds and treasury notes issued under the provisions of this act shall be exempt from taxation by or under state or municipal authority: *Provided*, That there shall be outstanding of bonds, treasury notes, and United States notes, at any time, issued under the provisions of this act, no greater amount altogether than the sum of nine hundred millions of dollars.

That the secretary of the treasury be, and he is hereby, authorized to issue, on the credit of the United States, four hundred millions of dollars in treasury notes, payable at the pleasure of the United States, or at such time or times not exceeding three years from date as may be found most beneficial to the public interests, and bearing interest at a rate not exceeding six per centum per annum, payable at periods expressed on the face of said treasury notes; and the interest on the said treasury notes and on certificates of indebtedness and deposits hereafter issued, shall be paid in lawful money. The treasury notes thus issued shall be of such denominations as the secretary may direct, not less than ten dollars, and may be disposed of on the best terms that can be obtained, or may be paid to any creditor of the United States willing to receive the same at par. And said treasury notes may be made a legal tender to the same extent as the United States notes, for their face value, excluding interest; or they may be made exchangeable under regulations prescribed by the secretary of the treasury, by the holder thereof, at the treasury in the City of Washington, or at the office of any assistant treasurer or depositary designated for that purpose, for United States notes equal in amount to the treasury notes offered for exchange, together with the interest accrued and due thereon, at the date of interest payment next preceding such exchange. And in lieu of any amount of said treasury notes thus exchanged, or redeemed or paid at maturity, the secretary may issue an equal amount of other treasury notes; and the treasury notes so exchanged, redeemed or paid, shall be cancelled and destroyed as the secretary may direct. In order to secure certain and prompt exchanges of the United States notes for treasury notes when required as above provided, the secretary shall have power to issue United States notes to the amount of one hundred and fifty millions of dollars, which may be used if necessary for such exchanges; but no part of the United States notes authorized by this section shall be issued for or applied to any other purposes than said exchanges; and whenever any amount shall have been so issued and applied, the same shall be replaced as soon as practicable from the sales of treasury notes for United States notes.

That the secretary of the treasury be, and he is hereby, authorized, if required by the exigencies of the public service, for the payment of the army and navy, and other creditors of the Government, to issue to the credit of the United States the sum of one hundred and fifty millions of dollars of United States notes, including the amount of such notes heretofore authorized by the joint resolution approved January seventeen, eighteen-hundred and sixty-three, in such form as he may deem expedient, not bearing interest, payable to bearer, and of such denominations, not less than one dollar, as he may prescribe, which notes so issued shall be lawful money and a legal tender in payment of all debts, public and private, within the United States, except for duties on imports and interest on the public debt; and any of the said notes, when returned to the treasury, may be reissued from time to time as the exigencies of the public service may require. And in lieu of any of said notes, or other United States notes, returned to the treasury, and cancelled or destroyed, there may be issued equal amounts of United States notes, such as are authorized by this act. And so much of the act to authorize the issue of United States notes, and for other purposes, approved February twenty-five, eighteen hundred and sixty-two, and of the act to authorize an additional issue of United States notes, and for other purposes, approved July eleven, eighteen hundred and sixty-two, as restricts the negotiation of bonds to market value, is hereby repealed. And the holders of United States notes, issued under and by virtue of said acts, shall present the same for the purpose of exchanging the same for bonds, as therein provided, on or before the first day of July, eighteen hundred and sixty-three, and thereafter the right so to exchange the same shall cease and determine.

That in lieu of postage and revenue stamps for fractional currency, and of fractional notes, commonly called postage currency, issued or to be issued, the secretary of the treasury may issue fractional notes of like amounts in such form as he may deem expedient, and may provide for the engraving, preparation and issue thereof in the treasury department building. And all such notes issued shall be exchangeable by the assistant treasurers and designated depositaries for United States notes, in sums not less than three dollars, and shall be receivable for postage and revenue stamps, and also in payment of any dues to the United States less than five dollars, except dues on imports, and shall be redeemed on presentation at the treasury of the United States in such sums and under such regulations as the secretary of the treasury shall prescribe· *Provided*, That the whole amount of fractional currency issued, including postage and revenue stamps issued as currency, shall not exceed fifty millions of dollars.

That the secretary of the treasury is hereby authorized to receive deposits of gold coin and bullion with the treasurer or any assistant treasurer of the United States, in sums not less than twenty dollars, and to issue certificates therefor in denominations of not less than twenty dollars each, corresponding with the denominations of the United States notes. The coin and bullion deposited for or representing the certificates of deposit shall be retained in the treasury for the payment of the same on demand. And certificates representing coin in the treasury may be issued in payment of interest on the public debt, which certificates, together with those issued for coin and bullion deposited, shall not at any time exceed twenty per centum beyond the amount of coin and bullion in the treasury; and the certificates for coin or bullion in the treasury shall be received at par in payment for duties on imports.

Act March 3, 1864.

That in lieu of so much of the loan authorized by the act of March 3, 1863, the secretary of the treasury be and is hereby authorized to borrow, on the credit of the United States, not exceeding two hundred millions of dollars during the current fiscal year, bearing date March first, eighteen hundred and sixty-four, or any subsequent period, redeemable at the pleasure of the Government after any period not less than five years, and payable at any period not more than forty years from date, in coin, bearing interest not exceeding six per centum a year—and he may dispose of such bonds at any time, on such terms as he may deem most advisable, for lawful money of the United States, or, at his discretion, for treasury notes, certificates of indebtedness or certificates of deposit issued under any act of Congress.

Joint Resolution March 17, 1864.

That the secretary of the treasury be authorized to anticipate the payment of interest on the public debt, by any period not exceeding one year, from time to time, either with or without a rebate of interest upon the coupons, as to him may seem expedient, and he is hereby authorized to dispose of any *gold** in the treasury of the United States not necessary for the payment of interest on the public debt.

Act June 30, 1864.

That the secretary of the treasury be authorized to borrow four hundred millions of dollars, and to issue bonds of the United States, redeemable at the pleasure of the Government after any period not less than five nor more than forty years from date, and bear an annual interest not exceeding six per centum, payable semi-annually in coin.

The secretary of the treasury may issue on the credit of the United States, and in lieu of an equal amount of bonds authorized by the preceding section, and as a part of said loan, not exceeding two hundred millions of dollars, in treasury notes of any denomination not less than ten dollars, payable at any time not exceeding three years from date, or, if thought more expedient, redeemable at any time after three years from date, and bearing interest not exceeding the rate of seven and three-tenths per centum, payable in lawful money

---

* This is the first instance of the use of the word "gold" instead of "coin" or "gold and silver" in any of the laws of the United States with regard to money obligations of the Government issued since 1860.

at maturity. And such of them as shall be made payable, principal and interest, at maturity, shall be a legal tender to the same extent as United States notes, for their face value, excluding interest, and may be paid to any creditor of the United States at their face value, excluding interest, or to *any creditor willing to receive them* at par, including interest.

That the total amount of bonds and treasury notes authorized by the first and second sections of this act shall not exceed four hundred millions of dollars, in addition to the amounts heretofore issued; nor shall the total amounts of United States notes, issued or to be issued, ever exceed four hundred millions of dollars, and such additional sums, not exceeding fifty millions of dollars, as may be temporarily required for the redemption of temporary loan; nor shall any treasury note bearing interest, issued under this act, be a legal tender in payment or redemption of any notes issued by any bank, banking association, or banker, calculated or intended to circulate as money.

The secretary of the treasury may issue notes of the fractions of a dollar as now used for currency, in such form, with such inscriptions, and with such safeguards against counterfeiting, as he may judge best; but the whole amount of all descriptions of notes or stamps less than one dollar issued as currency, shall not exceed fifty millions of dollars.

Amendment to Pacific Railroad Act, July 2, 1864.

That section five of said act be so modified and amended that the Union Pacific Railroad Company, the Central Pacific Railroad Company, and any other company authorized to participate in the construction of said road, may, on the completion of each section of said road, as provided in this act and the act to which this act is an amendment, issue their first mortgage bonds on their respective railroad and telegraph lines to an amount not exceeding the amount of the bonds of the United States, and of even tenor and date, time of maturity, rate and character of interest, with the bonds authorized to be issued to said railroad companies respectively. *And the lien of the United States bonds* shall be subordinate to that of the bonds of any or either of said companies hereby authorized to be issued on their respective roads, property and equipments, except as to the provisions of the sixth section of the act to which this act is an amendment, relating to the transmission of dispatches and the transportation of mails, troops, munitions of war, supplies and public stores for the Government of the United States.

Act January 28, 1865.

That in lieu of any bonds authorized to be issued by the first section of the act entitled "An act to provide ways and means for the support of the Government," approved June 30, 1864, that may remain unsold at the date of this act, the secretary of the treasury may issue, under the authority of said act, treasury notes of the description and character authorized by the second section of said act· *Provided*, That the whole amount of bonds authorized as aforesaid and treasury notes issued and to be issued in lieu thereof shall not exceed the sum of four hundred millions of dollars; and such treasury notes may be disposed of for lawful money, or for any other treasury notes or certificates of indebtedness or certificates of deposit issued under any previous act of Congress; and such notes shall be exempt from taxation by or under State or municipal authority.

Act March 3, 1865.

That the secretary of the treasury be, and he is hereby, authorized to borrow, from time to time, on the credit of the United States, in addition to the amounts heretofore authorized, any sums not exceeding, in the aggregate, six hundred millions of dollars, and to issue therefor bonds or treasury notes of the United States in such form as he may prescribe; and so much thereof as may be issued in bonds shall be of denominations not less than fifty dollars, and may be made payable at any period not more than forty years from date of issue, or may be made redeemable, at the pleasure of the Government, at or after any period not less than five years nor more than forty years from date, or may be made redeemable and payable as aforesaid, as may be expressed upon their face; and so much thereof as may be issued in treasury notes may be made controvertible into any bonds authorized by this act.

Provided, That the rate of interest on any such bonds or treasury notes, when payable in coin, shall not exceed six per centum per annum; and when not payable in coin shall not exceed seven and three-tenths per centum per annum.

Provided, That nothing herein contained shall be construed as authorizing the issue of legal-tender notes in any form.

Act April 12, 1866.

That the act approved March 3, 1865, shall be extended and construed to authorize the secretary of the treasury, at his discretion, to receive any treasury notes or other obligations issued under any act of Congress, whether bearing interest or not, in exchange for any description of bonds authorized by the act to which this is an amendment; and also to dispose of any description of bonds authorized by said act, either in the United States or elsewhere, to such an amount, in such manner and at such rates as he may think advisable, for lawful money of the United States or for any treasury notes, certificates of indebtedness or certificates of deposit, or other representatives of value which have been or which may be issued under any act of Congress, the proceeds thereof to be used only for retiring treasury notes or other obligations issued under any act of Congress; but nothing herein contained shall be construed to authorize any increase of the public debt: *Provided*, That of the United States notes not more than ten millions of dollars may be retired and cancelled within six months from the passage of this act, and thereafter not more than four millions of dollars in any one month.

Act March 2, 1867.

That for the purpose of redeeming and retiring any compound-interest notes outstanding, the secretary of the treasury is hereby authorized and directed to issue temporary loan certificates in the manner prescribed by section four of the act entitled "An act to authorize the issue of United States notes and for the redemption or funding thereof, and for funding the floating debt of the United States." approved February twenty-fifth, eighteen hundred and sixty-two; bearing interest at a rate not exceeding three per centum per annum, principal and interest payable in lawful money on demand; and said certificates of temporary loan may constitute and be held, by any national bank holding or owning the same, as a part of the reserve provided for in sections thirty-one and thirty-two of the act entitled "An act to provide a national currency, secured by a pledge of United States bonds, and to provide for the circulation and redemption thereof:" *Provided*, that the amount of such certificates outstanding at any time shall not exceed fifty millions of dollars.

Act July 25, 1868.

That for the sole purpose of redeeming and retiring the remainder of the compound-interest notes outstanding, the secretary of the treasury is authorized to issue an additional amount of temporary loan certificates not exceeding twenty-five millions of dollars, said certificates to bear three per cent. interest, payable in lawful money.

An Act to strengthen the public credit, approved March 18, 1869.

Be it enacted by the Senate and House of Representatives of the United States of America, in Congress assembled: That in order to remove any doubt as to the purpose of the Government to discharge all just obligations to the public creditors, and to settle conflicting questions and interpretations by the law by virtue of which such obligations have been contracted, it is hereby provided and declared that the faith of the United States is solemnly pledged to the payment in coin or its equivalent of all the obligations of the United States not bearing interest, known as the United States notes, and of all the interest-bearing obligations of the United States, except in cases where the law authorizing the issue of such obligations has expressly provided that the same may be paid in lawful money, or other currency than gold and silver. But none of said interest-bearing obligations not already due shall be redeemed or paid before maturity, unless at such time United States notes shall be convertible into coin at the option of the holder, or unless at such time bonds of the United States bearing a lower rate of interest than the bonds to be redeemed can be sold at par in coin. And the United States also solemnly pledges its faith to make provisions at the earliest practicable period for the redemption of the United States notes in coin.

Funding Act, July 14, 1870.

That the secretary of the treasury is hereby authorized to issue in a sum or sums not exceeding in the aggregate two hundred millions of dollars, coupon or registered bonds of the United States, in such forms as he may prescribe, and of denominations of fifty dollars, or some multiple of that sum, redeemable in coin of the present standard value, at the pleasure of the United States, after ten years from the date of their issue, and bearing interest, payable semi-annually in such coin, at the rate of five per cent. per annum; also a sum or sums not exceeding in the aggregate three hundred millions of dollars of like bonds, the same in all respects, but payable at the pleasure of the United States, after fifteen years from their issue, and bearing interest at the rate of four and a half per cent. per annum; also a sum or sums not exceeding in the aggregate one thousand millions of dollars of like bonds, the same in all respects, but payable at the pleasure of the United States after thirty years from the date of their issue, and bearing interest at the rate of four per cent. per annum; all of which said several classes of bonds and the interest thereon shall be exempt from the payment of all taxes or duties of the United States, as well as from taxation in any form by or under State, municipal or local authority; and the said bonds shall have set forth and expressed upon their face the above specified conditions, and shall, with their coupons, be made payable at the treasury of the United States. But nothing in this act, or in any other law now in force, shall be construed to authorize any increase whatever of the bonded debt of the United States.

That the secretary of the treasury is hereby authorized to sell and dispose of any of the bonds issued under this act, at not less than their par value for coin, and to apply the proceeds thereof to the redemption of any of the bonds of the United States outstanding, and known as five-twenty bonds, at their par value; or he may exchange the same for such five-twenty bonds, par for par; but the bonds hereby authorized shall be used for no other purpose whatsoever. And a sum not exceeding one-half of one per cent. of the bonds herein authorized is hereby appropriated to pay the expense of preparing, issuing, advertising and disposing of the same.

That the payment of any of the bonds hereby authorized after the expiration of the said several terms of ten, fifteen and thirty years, shall be made in amounts to be determined from time to time by the secretary of the treasury at his discretion, the bonds so to be paid to be distinguished and described by the dates and numbers, beginning for each successive payment with the bonds of each class last dated and numbered, of the time of which intended payment or redemption the secretary of the treasury shall give public notice, and the interest on the particular bonds so selected at any time to be paid shall cease at the expiration of three months from the date of such notice.

That the secretary of the treasury is hereby authorized, with any coin in the treasury of the United States which he may lawfully apply to such purpose, or which may be derived from the sale of any of the bonds, the issue of which is provided for in this act, to pay at par and cancel any six per cent. bonds of the United States of the kind known as five-twenty bonds, which have become or shall hereafter become redeemable by the terms of their issue. But the particular bonds so to be paid and cancelled shall in all cases be indicated and specified by class, date, and number, in the order of their numbers and issue, beginning with the first numbered and issued, in public notice to be given by the secretary of the treasury, and in three months after the date of such public notice the interest on the bonds so selected and advertised to be paid shall cease.

That the secretary of the treasury is hereby authorized, at any time within two years from the passage of this act, to receive gold coin of the United States on deposit for not less than thirty days, in sums of not less than one hundred dollars, with the treasurer, or any assistant treasurer of the United States authorized by the secretary of the treasury to receive the same, who shall issue therefor certificates of deposit, made in such form as the secretary of the treasury shall prescribe, and said certificates of deposit shall bear interest at a rate not exceeding two and a half per cent. per annum; and any amount of gold coin so deposited may be withdrawn from deposit at any time after thirty days from the date of deposit, and after ten days' notice and on the return of said certificates· *Provided,* That the interest on all such deposits shall cease and determine at the pleasure of the secretary of the treasury. And not less than twenty-five per cent. of the coin deposited for or represented by said certificates of deposit shall be retained in the treasury for the payment of said certificates; and the excess beyond twenty-five per cent. may be applied, at the discretion of the secretary of the treasury, to the payment or redemption of such outstanding bonds of the United States heretofore issued and known as the five-twenty bonds, as he may designate under the provisions of the fourth section of this act; and any certificate of deposit issued as aforesaid may be received at par, with the interest accrued thereon, in payment for any bonds authorized to be issued by this act.

Act January 20, 1871.

That the amount of bonds authorized by the act approved July 14, 1870, entitled "An act to authorize the refunding of the national debt," to be issued bearing five per centum interest per annum, be, and the same is, increased to five hundred millions of dollars, and the interest of any portion of the bonds issued under said act, or this act, may, at the direction of the secretary of the treasury, be made payable quarter-yearly: *Provided, however,* that this act shall not be construed to authorize any increase of the total amount of bonds provided for by the act to which this act is an amendment.

Act June 2, 1872.

That the secretary of the treasury is hereby authorized to receive United States notes on deposit without interest from bank associations, and to issue certificates therefor. The certificates issued may be held and counted by national banks as part of their reserve.

That nothing contained in this act shall be construed to authorize any expansion or contraction of the currency; and the United States notes for which such certificates are issued, or other United States notes of like amount, shall be held as special deposits in the treasury and used only for the redemption of such certificates.

Act December 17, 1873.

That for the purpose of redeeming the bonds called the loan of 1858, it is hereby declared to be the pleasure of the United States to pay all the coupon bonds of said loan on the first day of January, 1874. That the secretary of the treasury may issue an equal amount at par of principal and interest of five per cent. bonds of the funded loan under the act for refunding the national debt, approved January 20, 1871, for any of the bonds of the loan of 1858, which the holders thereof may, on or before the 1st of February, 1874, elect to exchange.

Specie Resumption Act of January 24, 1875.

§ 1. That the secretary of the treasury is hereby authorized and required, as rapidly as practicable, to cause to be coined at the mints of the United States, silver coins of the denominations of ten, twenty-five and fifty cents, of standard value, and to issue them in redemption of an equal number and amount of fractional currency of similar denominations, or, at his discretion, he may issue such silver coins through the mints, the sub-treasuries, public depositories and post-offices of the United States; and upon such issue he is hereby authorized and required to redeem an equal amount of such fractional currency until the whole amount of such fractional currency outstanding shall be redeemed.

§ 2. That so much of section 3524 of the Revised Statutes of the United States as provides for a charge of one-sixth of one per centum for converting standard gold bullion into coin is hereby repealed, and hereafter no charge shall be made for that service.

§ 3. That section 5177 of the Revised Statutes of the United States, limiting the aggregate amount of the circulating notes of the national banking associations, be and is hereby, repealed, and each existing banking association may increase its circulating notes in accordance with the existing law, without respect to said aggregate limit; and new banking associations may be organized in accordance with the existing law, without respect to the aggregate limit; and the provisions of the law for the withdrawal and redistribution of national-bank currency among the several States and Territories are hereby repealed; and whenever and so often as circulating notes shall be issued to any such banking association, so increasing its capital or circulating notes, or so newly organized as aforesaid, it shall be the duty of the secretary of the treasury to redeem the legal-tender United States notes in excess only of $300,000,000 to the amount of eighty per centum of the sum of national-bank notes so issued to any such banking association as aforesaid, and to continue such redemption as such circulating notes are issued until there shall be outstanding the sum of $300,000,000 of such legal tender United States notes, and no more. And on and after the 1st day of January, A. D. 1879, the secretary of the treasury shall redeem in coin the United States legal-tender notes then outstanding on their presentation for redemption at the office of the assistant treasurer of the United States, in the City of New York, in sums of not less than $50. And to enable the secretary of the treasury to prepare and provide for the redemption in this act authorized or required, he is authorized to use any surplus revenues from time to time in the treasury not otherwise appropriated, and to issue, sell and dispose of, at not less than par in coin, either of the description of bonds of the United States described in the act of Congress approved July 14, 1870, entitled "An act to authorize the refunding of the national debt," with like privileges and exemptions, to the extent necessary to carry this act into effect, and to use the proceeds thereof for the purposes aforesaid. And all provisions of law inconsistent with the provisions of this act are hereby repealed.

Subsidiary Silver Coin Law, Joint Resolution of Congress July 13, 1876.

§ 1. That the secretary of the treasury, under such limits and regulations as will best secure a just and fair distribution of the same through the country, may issue the silver coin at any time in the treasury, to an amount not exceeding $10,000,000, in exchange for an equal amount of legal-tender notes, and notes so received in exchange shall be kept as a special fund, separate and apart from all other money in the treasury, and be issued only upon the retirement and destruction of a like sum of fractional currency received at the treasury in payment of dues to the United States, and said fractional currency, when so substituted, shall be destroyed and held as part of the sinking fund, as provided in the act approved April 17, 1876.

§ 2. That the trade dollar shall not hereafter be a legal tender, and the secretary of the treasury is hereby authorized to limit from time to time the coinage thereof to such an amount as he may deem sufficient to meet the export demand for the same.

§ 3. That in addition to the amount of subsidiary silver coin authorized by law to be issued in redemption of the fractional currency, it shall be lawful to manufacture at the several mints, and issue through the treasury and its several offices, such coin to an amount that, including the amount of subsidiary silver coin and of fractional currency outstanding, shall in the aggregate not exceed at any time $50,000,000.

§ 4. That the silver bullion required for the purposes of this act shall be purchased from time to time at the market rate by the secretary of the treasury with any money in the treasury not otherwise appropriated, but no purchase of bullion shall be made under this resolution when the market rate for the same shall be such as will not admit of the coinage and issue as herein provided without loss to the treasury, and any gain or seigniorage arising from this coinage shall be accounted for and paid into the treasury as provided under existing laws relative to subsidiary coinage, provided that the amount of money at any time invested in such silver bullion, exclusive of such resulting coin, shall not exceed $200,000.

CHAPTER XIII.

THE BOND AGE.

The world has passed through several periods called "Ages," each characterized by some important feature of the time.

Thus, we had the Stone Age, when stone was not only used as tools for the husbandman, weapons for the warrior, but for tablets on which the events of the period and its literature were inscribed. Passing from this over to the Iron Age, the Bronze Age, the Dark Age, and the Golden Age, we find ourselves living in the Bond Age. This is characterized by its enormous inflation of credits. Civilization, the increased facilities for travel and transportation, and the enlarged diversity of the wants of the period, have greatly augmented the demands for the exchange medium, while the precious metals, "the money of the world," are being exhausted, their supply diminishing and their cost of production increasing. So urgent have been the increasing demands for an enlarged volume of exchange medium, that private, corporate, municipal and national credits have been substituted for coin, to an extent never before known in the history of the world.

Within the last twenty years the indebtedness of the world has quadrupled. It constitutes a monument terrible to contemplate.

The national, railroad and municipal debt of Europe and North America are estimated as follows:

National debts	$23,400,000,000
Railroad debts	5,000,000,000
State and municipal debts	5,600,000,000
Total	$34,000,000,000

The individual, and other corporate indebtedness will exceed the above three fold, making the interest-bearing burden of Europe and America not less than *a hundred and fifty thousand million.*

That of the United States is appalling, General A. J. Warner, of Ohio, has published a carefully prepared statement showing the increase of the municipal indebtedness from 1866 to 1876.

His figures, giving the condition of 130 cities, show that during these ten years their average debt has increased 200 per cent.; taxation, 83 per cent.; valuation, 75 per cent.; population, only 33 per cent.

That the indebtedness of eleven States, to wit.: New York, Massachusetts, Illinois, Ohio, Wisconsin, Minnesota, Kansas, Missouri, Connecticut, Georgia and Rhode Island, has increased from $286,179,060 in 1870 to $546,289,528 in 1878.

That while the debt and taxes of these states have doubled, the increase in the value of property has been slight, being from $7,172,148,175 in 1870 to $7,333,696,515 in 1878. The local or municipal indebtedness of the United States has increased from $850,000,000 in 1870 to $1,051,206,112 in 1878.

In 1866 the aggregate State debt of the United States was $390,000,000 and now eleven States owe nearly $550,000,000.

The Westminster *Review* for January, 1876, estimated that the national debts of the world then aggregated £4,598,000,000, or $22,990,000,000.

Our national debt is about $2,000,000,000.

Some other public and corporate debts have been computed by careful authorities as follows:

States	$390,000,000
Cities, towns and counties	850,000,000
Railroads	2,459,000,000
Canals	105,000,000
Total	$3,804,000,000

The figures for railroads are taken from Poor's Manual, 1876–'77. Of debts of manufacturing, mining, and other companies, no estimates have ever been attempted.

Of another form of permanent debt in this country, of mortgages upon real estate, it can only be said that it is exceedingly great.

The permanent investments of the national, State, and savings banks, insurance companies, and trust companies of New York City amounted at the commencement of the present year to about $500,000,000. These investments include $205,000,000 in real estate mortgages. According to the most recent returns from savings banks which are accessible, those in the six New England States, having $438,000,000 in deposits, had invested $228,000,000, or rather more than one-half, in real estate mortgages; those in the State of New York, having $316,677,000 in deposits, had invested $116,154,000 in the same way; and of those in New Jersey, 45 per cent. of the deposits are so invested.

It may be fairly inferred from these statements that the aggregate value of real estate mortgages held by monied institutions is very large. The value of those held by individuals must be still larger. The loans and discounts of the national banks October 2, 1876, were $927,000,000. In November, 1875, the capital of State and private banks was $209,000,000, not reckoning a large surplus, and $487,000,000 of deposits, and the savings banks had $884,000,000 of deposits. Nearly the whole of this vast aggregate must have been employed in loans of some kind. A considerable proportion of the farms in the West, especially in the newer States, are known to be mortgaged. Of the 630,099 traders and manufacturers on the book of the mercantile agency of Dunn, Barlow & Co., in 1876, 9,022 failed, with average liabilities of $21,020. If that is assumed to be the average liability of the whole 630,099, the aggregate liability would be $13,244,000,000. Those who think that the failures should be ascribed, not to a relative deficiency of assets, but to an excess of debts above the average, will reduce this estimate. But it is also to be taken into account that the books of this agency do not contain the names of all the persons described as traders and manufacturers, nor of a vast number not described as such that are large operators and debtors.

There are other forms of debt in this country, which consist of the rents reserved on long leases of either land and buildings, or land alone to be built upon by the lessees. The amount of this kind of indebtedness in the larger cities is enormous, and the effect upon it of a shrinking money is especially ruinous. The prostration of business, which destroys or greatly reduces the value of buildings hired for commercial or manufacturing purposes, does not affect the right of the landlord to exact in full the stipulated rent. The source from which it was expected to be paid may be dried up, but the liability to pay it remains undiminished. Indebtedness under long leases figures largely in the lists of debts scheduled in bankrupt courts, and largely also among the losses of those who have so far managed to keep out of such courts.

Poor's Manual states the share-capital of the railroads at $2,198,000,000, and their debts at $2,459,000,000, being a proportion of share-capital to debt of eighty-nine to one hundred. This shows a considerable excess of debt over capital stock. The financial condition of the railroads illustrates the condition of a large proportion of the corporate and individual property in the United States. The country is new and unsurpassed in natural resources, the population venturesome, ingenious and industrious, and enterprises of all kinds, from the greatest to the smallest, are undertaken by corporations and individuals on small capital. It is considered prudent for companies or individuals to undertake operations with only means enough of their own to constitute a security for loans wherewith to complete them. This view of what is prudent may or may not be well taken, but it is natural to a young and progressive people. It has made the American economical system one vast network of debts and credits, and of long debts and long credits.

CHAPTER XIV.

TABLES.

WHAT THE BONDS COST SHYLOCK, AND HIS PROFITS.

The Shylocks of the gold exchange for years kept gold up, that they might buy greenbacks cheap, to invest in bonds at par, and below is the result, showing the year, the amount of greenbacks exchanged for bonds and the amount in gold the greenbacks were purchased for:

Year.	Bonds.	Cost in gold.
In 1862	$60,982,450	$44,030,649
In 1863	160,987,550	101,890,850
In 1864	381,292,250	189,697,636
In 1865	279,646,150	208,214,090
In 1866	124,914,400	88,591,773
In 1867	421,469,550	303,215,303
In 1868	425,443,800	312,826,323
Total	$1,854,736,150	$1,248,466,624

Here is a net profit of.................. $606,269,526
Add interest since...................... 1,430,000,000

Harvest for eleven years............... $2,036,269,526

The above figures are taken from the public record and may be relied upon. The bondholders have received back more than twice the value they loaned, and still hold the bonds to draw more every year, until they mature, when they expect to receive their face in gold, or keep the blister drawing until it is paid.

Showing the values in United States money of the pure gold and silver representing respectively, the monetary units and standard coins of foreign countries, January 1, 1876.

TREASURY DEPARTMENT, WASHINGTON, D. C., *Jan. 1, 1876.*

The estimate of values contained in the following table has been made by the Director of the Mint, and is hereby proclaimed in compliance with the provisions of law:

Country	Monetary Unit.	Standard.	Value in U. S. Money.	Standard Coins.
Austria	Florin	Silver	.45.3	Florin.
Belgium	Franc	Gold and silver	.19.3	5, 10 and 20 francs.
Bolivia	Dollar	Gold and silver	.96.5	Escudo, ½ bolivar and bolivar.
Brazil	Millreis of 1,000 reis	Gold	.54.5	None.
Brit. Possessions in N. America	Dollar	Gold	$1.00	
Bogota	Peso	Gold	.96.5	
Central America	Dollar	Silver	.91.8	Dollar.
Chili	Peso	Gold	.91.2	Condor, doubloon and escudo.
Denmark	Crown	Gold	.26.8	10 and 20 crowns.
Ecuador	Dollar	Silver	.91.8	Dollar.
Egypt	Pound of 100 piasters	Gold	4.97.4	5, 10, 25 and 50 piasters.
France	Franc	Gold and silver	.19.3	5, 10 and 20 francs.
Great Britain	Pound sterling	Gold	4.86.6½	½ sovereign and sovereign.
Greece	Drachma	Gold and Silver	.19.3	5, 10, 20, 50 and 100 drachmas.
German Empire	Mark	Gold	.23.8	5, 10 and 20 marks.
Japan	Yen	Gold	.99.7	1, 2, 5, 10 and 20 yen.
India	Rupee of 16 annas	Silver	.43.6	
Italy	Lira	Gold and Silver	.19.3	5, 10, 20, 50 and 100 lire.
Liberia	Dollar	Gold	1.00	
Mexico	Dollar	Silver	.99.8	Peso or dollar, 5, 10, 25 and 50 centavo.
Netherlands	Florin	Gold and Silver	.38.5	Florin; 10 guilders, gold, $4.01.9)
Norway	Crown	Gold	.26.8	10 and 20 crowns.
Peru	Dollar	Silver	.91.8	
Portugal	Millreis of 1.000 reis	Gold	1.08	2, 5 and 10 millreis.
Russia	Ronbel of 100 copecs	Silver	.73.4	¼, ½ and 1 rouble,
Sandwich Islands	Dollar	Gold	1.00	
Spain	Peseta of 100 centimes	Gold and Silver	.19.3	5, 10, 20, 50 and 100 pesetas.
Sweden	Crown	Gold	.26.8	10 and 20 crowns.
Switzerland	Franc	Gold and Silver	.19.3	5, 10 and 20 francs.
Tripoli	Mahbub of 20 piasters	Silver	.82.9	
Tunis	Piaster of 16 caroubs	Silver	.11.8	25, 50, 100, 250 and 500 piasters.
Turkey	Piaster	Gold	.04.3	
United States of Colombia	Peso	Silver	.91.8	

B. H. BRISTOW, *Secretary of the Treasury.*

MONTHLY RANGE OF THE GOLD PREMIUM FOR 14 YEARS.

The following table shows the lowest and highest prices of gold at New York, for each month during fourteen years. The left-handed column of each year shows the lowest price, and the right-hand column the highest.

DATE.	1862.		1863.		1864.		1865.		1866.		1867.		1868.	
January	par.	105	134	160¾	151½	160	197½	234½	136⅝	144⅝	132	137⅜	133¼	142¼
February	102⅛	104⅞	153	172¼	157¼	161	196⅝	216⅞	135⅞	140⅝	137⅝	140½	139⅝	144
March	101⅛	102½	139	171¾	159	169⅞	148⅛	201	125	136½	133⅜	140⅞	137⅞	141⅞
April	101½	102¼	146	159	166¼	187	144	160	125	129½	132⅝	141⅞	137⅝	140⅝
May	102⅛	104½	143½	155	168	190	128⅝	145¾	125¼	141⅛	134⅞	138⅞	139⅛	140½
June	103½	109½	140½	148⅞	189	251	135⅝	147⅝	137⅜	167¾	136⅝	138⅝	139⅝	141¼
July	109	120¼	123¼	145	222	285	138	146½	147	155⅝	136⅝	140⅝	140¼	145¼
August	112½	116¼	122⅛	129⅜	231½	262	145⅜	148⅛	146½	152¼	139⅝	142⅝	143½	150
September	116⅛	124	127	143¼	185	255	142⅝	145	143¼	147⅛	141	146⅝	141⅛	145⅛
October	122	137	140⅝	156¾	189	229	144	149	145½	154⅝	140¼	145⅝	133⅞	140½
November	129	133¼	143	154	209	260	145½	148¾	137½	148⅝	137⅝	141¼	132¼	137
December	130	134	147	152⅞	211	244	144⅛	146⅞	131¼	141⅝	133	137⅞	134⅝	136¼

DATE.	1869.		1870.		1871.		1872.		1873.		1874.		1875.	
January	134⅝	136⅞	119⅝	123¼	110½	111¼	108⅛	110⅛	111⅝	114¼	110⅛	112½	111⅞	113⅝
February	130⅞	138⅛	115	121½	110⅝	112¼	109½	111	112⅞	115⅛	111⅝	113	113¼	115⅝
March	130¼	132½	110¼	116⅝	110⅛	111⅝	109⅞	110½	114⅝	118⅛	111¼	113⅝	114⅝	117
April	131⅝	134⅞	111½	115⅝	110⅛	111⅞	109⅞	113¼	116⅝	119⅛	111⅞	114⅝	114	115½
May	134⅛	144⅞	113⅞	115½	111	112¼	112⅛	114⅝	116⅝	118⅝	111⅞	113¼	115	116⅝
June	137	139⅝	110⅞	114⅝	111⅝	113⅛	113	114¾	115	118¼	110½	112¼	116¼	117½
July	134	137⅞	111⅛	122¾	111⅝	113⅝	113½	115¼	115	116⅝	109	110⅞	111⅝	117¼
August	131¼	137⅝	114⅞	122	111⅝	113¼	112⅛	115⅝	114⅝	116¼	109¼	110¼	112⅝	114⅝
September	130⅝	162½	112⅝	116¾	112⅞	115⅝	112¾	115⅛	110⅞	116⅛	109⅝	110½	113¼	117⅝
October	128⅛	131⅞	111⅛	113¼	111⅛	115	112¼	115⅛	107⅝	111¼	109⅝	110⅝	114⅛	117⅝
November	121⅛	128⅝	110	114½	110⅝	112⅝	111⅝	114¼	106⅛	110½	110	112⅝	114⅛	116⅝
December	119¼	124	110¼	111⅝	108⅝	110⅝	111⅝	113½	108⅝	112⅝	110½	112¼	112⅝	115¼

TABLES.   191

AMOUNT OF EACH KIND OF PAPER CURRENCY IN THE UNITED STATES EACH YEAR FOR TWENTY-SIX YEARS.

Year	Demand and 1 and 2 yr. Treasury Notes (Acts March 2, 1861, Dec. 17, 1860, and Dec. 27, '57,) outstanding July 1.	Temporary 10-day loans and one year Certificates of Indebtedness, July 1 each year.	Treasury Notes, payable in 2 yrs. and in 60 days (Act March 3, 1863), July 1 each year.	7.30 Three Year Notes, July 1 each year.	Compound Interest Notes, July 1 each year.	3 per cent. Certificates July 1 each year.	Non-Interest bearing, Demand and Legal Tender Notes (Acts July 17, '61, Feb. 25, '62, July 11, '62, Mar. 3, '63).	Fractional Currency.	Bank Note Circulation January 1 each year. National Banks	Bank Note Circulation January 1 each year. State Banks.	Total of Bank Notes and of Unfunded Government Debt circulating to any extent as money each year.
1854										204,689,000	204,689,000
1855										186,952,000	186,952,000
1856										195,748,000	195,748,000
1857										214,779,000	214,779,000
1858										155,208,000	155,208,000
1859										193,306,000	193,306,000
1860										207,102,000	207,102,000
1861	20,153,455									202,005,000	222,358,455
1862	2,849,112	107,628,956		122,836,550			150,560,000	20,192,456		183,792,000	414,766,298
1863	897,912	259,168,327		139,970,500	15,000,000	50,000,000	381,957,569	20,904,637	39,155	238,671,210	1,043,610,415
1864	278,512	233,089,191	153,471,450	109,356,130	193,756,080	52,120,000	431,959,670	22,894,877	66,768,375	45,419,155	968,050,995
1865	118,992	205,489,061	412,338,710	672,578,850	159,012,140	45,545,000	433,160,569	24,915,829	213,239,530	6,961,499	1,651,275,373
1866	117,512	117,567,196	3,454,300	806,900,250	122,394,480	31,863,000	400,891,936	29,050,676	281,093,894	3,792,013	1,803,762,226
1867	110,712	20,261,670	1,123,930	488,647,140	2,871,410	30,000,000	371,386,723	28,380,723	291,093,294	2,831,729	1,259,414,657
1868	110,512	13,413,029	555,492	37,717,630	2,152,910	50,000,000	356,141,723	32,627,902	294,377,890	2,731,069	817,189,773
1869	108,212	198,310	307,772	1,166,500	768,360	52,120,000	356,121,730	32,114,637	294,476,792	2,351,083	740,025,889
1870	91,835	196,310	230,212	641,000	563,320	45,545,000	356,106,250	39,878,684	292,625,629	2,435,808	740,039,171
1871	91,850	85,370	213,348	475,940	479,400	31,863,000	356,000,064	40,582,874	315,481,611	1,968,528	731,214,774
1872	94,750	83,500	206,811	352,150	115,280	30,000,000	358,188,200	40,855,835	336,283,287	1,511,306	736,349,912
1873	94,676	83,500	142,105	293,450	367,340	5,000	356,078,867	44,799,365	350,820,042	(June 23) 788,291,149
1874	94,575	83,500	57,565	247,650	415,240	5,000	382,076,732	45,961,205	349,402,839	(June 20) 779,031,589
1875	94,575	8,000	113,375	213,375	367,340	5,000	375,811,487	42,129,424	341,889,138	778,476,250
1876	94,525	8,000	104,705	199,250	328,760	5,000	369,832,501	34,446,595	321,598,832	(July 1) 735,558,832
1877							364,681,016		317,048,872	676,813,205
1878									323,514,284	671,495,306
1879							346,681,016		337,181,416	683,962,431

The following table shows the transactions in refunding since March 1, 1877:

Title of Loan.	Rate per ct.	Am't refunded.
Loan of 1858	5	$260,000
Ten-forties of 1864	5	193,890,250
Five-twenties of 1865	6	100,436,050
Consols of 1865	6	202,663,100
Consols of 1867	6	310,622,750
Consols of 1868	6	37,473,800
Total		845,345,950

The following described bonds will mature in 1880 and 1881:

Authorizing Act.	Rate of interest.	Date of Maturity.	Amount.
February 8, 1861	6	Dec. 31, 1880.	$18,415,000
July 17 and Aug. 5, 1861	6	June 30, 1881.	182,605,550
March 3, 1863	6	June 30, 1881.	71,787,000
March 2, 1861	6	July 1, 1881.	823,800
July 14, '70, and Jan. 20, '71	5	May 1, 1881.	508,440,350
Total			782,071,700

The entire transactions in refunding since 1870 have been as follows:

Title of Loan.	Rate per ct.	Am't Refunded.
Loan of 1858	5	$14,217,000
Ten-forties of 1864	5	193,890,250
Five-twenties of 1862	6	401,143,750
Five-twenties of March, 1864	6	1,327,100
Five-twenties of June, 1864	6	59,185,450
Five-twenties of 1865	6	160,144,500
Consols of 1865	6	211,337,050
Consols of 1867	6	316,423,800
Consols of 1868	6	37,677,050
Total		1,395,345,950

Of the $363,802,400 of U. S. bonds held as security for circulation of national banks, there are of

6 per cents	$59,315,450
5 per cents	131,301,600
4½ per cents	34,866,950
4 per cents	138,318,400

Excess of exports over imports in the fiscal year, are as follows:

1876	$97,643,481
1877	151,152,094
1878	257,814,234
1879	264,661,666

The department of agriculture estimates the product for 1879, as follows:

Corn	1,601,000,000	bushels
Wheat	449,000,000	"
Oats	364,000,000	"
Barley	40,000,000	"
Rye	24,000,000	"
Cotton	2,217,000,000	pounds
Tobacco	384,000,000	"

Amount and disposition of money in the country, January 1, 1880, as follows:

Greenbacks and bank notes		$699,634,759
Coin and bullion		398,770,564
In treasury	$221,596,333—	$1,098,405,323
Bank reserves	109,752,489—	331,348,822
		$767,056,501
Estimated loss of currency		130,000,000
Total currency available		$637,056,501
The national banks receive annually upon bonds deposited for the security of their circulation		$17,152,396.75
They return tax upon circulation at 1 per cent		3,009,647.16
Net gain from the Government		$14,142,749.59
Profits on circulation at 8 per cent		24,884,084.00
Total annual profit on circulation		$39,026,833.59

13

DEBTS, REVENUES, EXPENDITURES AND COMMERCE OF NATIONS (1878).

Compiled from the Almanach de Gotha, the Statistical Abstract of the United Kingdom, and from official documents. The figures are for the latest attainable years as to each country:

Countries.	Public debt.	Revenue.	Expenditures.	Imports.	Exports.
Argentine Republic.	$68,416,043	$20,683,537	$20,663,337	$34,910,290	$44,041,131
Austria Proper	1,419,096,072	186,776,170	202,035,039		
Austria-Hungary	205,999,970	60,000,000	58,845,695	258,450,000	204,800,000
Belgium	232,684,553	50,045,972	49,045,128	258,504,000	222,920,400
Bolivia	17,500,000	2,929,574	4,505,504	5,750,000	5,000,000
Brazil	368,351,139	72,548,454	67,789,297	88,045,520	104,232,800
Canada	112,248,378	22,700,000	24,100,000	93,200,000	89,351,328
Chili	50,677,600	21,294,383	22,052,187	39,050,197	37,139,961
China	3,200,000	230,000,000		105,000,000	114,000,000
Colombia	15,399,304	3,114,619	2,779,410	6,949,028	9,994,386
Denmark	52,000,000	13,464,066	13,074,620	50,311,240	33,933,640
Ecuador	17,500,000	20,800,000	21,500,455	7,596,264	3,913,536
Egypt	450,540,000	54,820,818	54,737,670	29,000,000	68,000,000
France	4,695,600,000	514,605,716	519,334,162	4,111,000	9,280,000
Germany	30,000,000	135,584,249	135,000,000	918,850,000	608,200,000
Gt. Britain & Ireland	3,625,286,785	392,825,180	390,626,140	1,869,695,885	1,283,883,010
Greece	40,012,000	7,765,360	7,832,768	794,035,000	713,978,200
Guiana	460,000	1,580,000	4,580,000	1,811,770	2,241,040
Hawaiian Islands	548,022	504,095	460,000	1,682,000	2,090,000
Hungary Proper	274,358,915	106,069,258	116,902,036		
India, British	576,634,330	252,649,885	272,503,145	179,000,000	282,600,000
Italy	1,977,117,845	279,550,000	278,121,440	265,899,000	243,371,000
Japan	148,924,725	63,120,600	62,993,850	24,087,515	27,669,465
Luxembourg	2,400,000	1,438,600	1,409,344		
Mexico	395,500,000	23,807,671	24,891,522	29,062,407	31,659,151
Netherlands	391,242,322	43,973,345	48,785,061	275,416,000	261,750,000
Norway	13,526,128	11,364,220	10,726,500	52,017,280	33,933,640
Paraguay	12,098,417	609,000	750,000	565,595	607,653
Peru	213,482,680	29,801,195	33,755,375		37,500,000
Persia	No debt.	8,240,000	8,750,000	5,625,000	2,813,000
Portugal	428,977,613	29,568,816	29,720,336	38,131,520	26,448,600
Roumania	60,000,000	19,578,885	19,578,885	16,200,000	28,440,000
Russia	1,420,092,043	409,377,280	410,557,403	365,426,400	422,966,400
Servia	5,000,000	2,968,422	2,924,779	6,197,000	5,500,000
Siam		4,000,000	4,000,000	7,100,000	8,300,000
Spain	2,401,612,001	131,500,000	131,824,000	114,000,000	90,000,000
Sweden	39,241,142	23,563,201	21,872,193	85,906,800	62,532,960
Switzerland	6,225,000	8,297,480	8,524,400	Not given.	Not given.
Turkey	1,012,772,200	88,764,050	140,000,000	72,430,000	
United States	2,046,027,066	269,600,587	238,660,009	492,090,406	658,637,457
Uruguay	43,615,000	6,965,683	6,809,000	21,917,800	16,953,000
Venezuela	62,659,687	3,549,000	3,642,500	12,000,000	17,000,000
Total debts	22,987,036,780				

PUBLIC DEBT OF THE UNITED STATES, 1791–1879.

Statement of outstanding principal of the public debt of the United States on the 1st of January of each year from 1791 to 1842, inclusive; and on the 1st of July of each year from 1843 to 1879, inclusive:

(From the Annual Report of the Secretary of the Treasury on the Finances.)

Year	Amount	Year	Amount	Year	Amount
1791..	$75,463,476 52	1821..	$89,987,427 66	1851..	$68,304,796 02
1792..	77,227,924 66	1822..	93,546,676 98	1852..	66,199,341 71
1793..	80,352,634 04	1823..	90,875,877 28	1853..	59,803,117 70
1794..	78,427,404 77	1824..	90,269,777 77	1854..	42,242,222 42
1795..	80,747,587 39	1825..	83,788,432 71	1855..	35,586,858 56
1796..	83,762,172 07	1826..	81,054,059 99	1856..	31,972,537 90
1797..	82,064,479 33	1827..	73,987,357 20	1857..	28,690,831 85
1798..	79,228,529 12	1828..	67,475,043 87	1858..	44,911,881 03
1799..	78,408,669 77	1829..	58,421,413 67	1859..	58,496,837 88
1800..	82,976,294 35	1830..	48,565,406 50	1860..	64,842,287 88
1801..	83,038,050 80	1831..	39,123,191 68	1861..	90,580,873 72
1802..	86,712,632 25	1832..	24,322,235 18	1862..	524,176,412 13
1803..	77,054,686 30	1833..	7,001,698 83	1863..	1,119,772,138 63
1804..	86,427,120 88	1834..	4,760,082 08	1864..	1,815,784,370 57
1805..	82,312,150 50	1835..	37,513 05	1865..	2,680,647,869 74
1806..	75,723,270 66	1836..	336,957 83	1866..	2,773,236,173 69
1807..	69,218,398 64	1837..	3,308,124 07	1867..	2,678,126,103 87
1808..	65,196,317 97	1838..	10,434,221 14	1868..	2,611,687,851 19
1809..	57,023,192 09	1839..	3,573,343 82	1869..	2,588,452,213 94
1810..	53,173,217 52	1840..	5,250,875 54	1870..	2,480,672,427 81
1811..	48,005,587 76	1841..	13,594,480 73	1871..	2,353,211,332 32
1812..	45,209,737 90	1842..	20,601,226 28	1872..	2,253,251,328 78
1813..	55,962,827 57	1843..	32,742,922 00	1873..	2,234,482,993 20
1814..	81,487,846 24	1844..	23,461,652 50	1874..	2,251,690,468 33
1815..	99,833,660 15	1845..	15,925,303 01	1875..	2,232,284,531 95
1816..	127,334,933 74	1846..	15,550,202 97	1876..	2,180,395,067 15
1817..	123,491,965 16	1847..	38,826,534 77	1877..	2,205,301,392 10
1818..	103,466,633 83	1848..	47,034,862 23	1878..	3,256,205,892 53
1819..	95,529,648 28	1849..	63,061,858 69	1879..	2,245,495,072 04
1820..	91,015,566 15	1850..	63,452,773 55		

POPULATION, CAPITALS AND AREAS OF PRINCIPAL NATIONS.

Countries.	Capital.	Last Census.	Population.	Area Square Miles.	Inhabitants to the Square Mile.
Argentine Republic	Buenos Ayres	1875	1,715,681	871,000	1.96
Austria-Hungary	Vienna	1869	35,904,435	226,406	158.58
Belgium	Brussels	1866	4,839,094	11,412	424.03
Bolivia	La Paz	1861	1,742,352	473,300	3.70
Brazil	Rio de Janeiro	1872	10,108,291	3,275,326	3.08
Canada, Dominion of	Ottawa	1871	3,602,321	3,483,952	1.03
Chili	Santiago	1875	2,068,447	130,977	15.79
Chinese Empire	Pekin	Est.	433,500,000	3,924,627	110.45
Colombia	Bogota	1870	2,951,311	432,400	6 07
Egypt	Cairo	Est.	5,252,000	212,500	24.70
Denmark	Copenhagen	1870	1,912,142	14,553	131.32
Ecuador	Quito	1875	866,137	218,984	3.49
France	Paris	1876	36,905,788	201,900	182.79
Germany	Berlin	1875	42,727,360	212,091	201.45
Great Britain and Ireland	London	1871	31,628,338	121,230	268.08
Greece	Athens	1870	1,457,894	19,941	72.96
India, British	Calcutta	1871	190,663,623	950,919	200 50
Italy	Rome	1875	27,482,174	112,677	243.91
Japan	Yeddo	1874	33,625,678	156,604	214.71
Mexico	Mexico	1871	9,276,079	1,030,442	9.00
Morocco	Morocco	Est.	6,000,000	219,000	27.39
Netherlands	Amsterdam	1876	3,865,456	20,527	188.31
Norway	Christiania	1876	1,807,555	122,280	14.78
Paraguay	Asuncion	1873	221,079	57,303	3.85
Persia	Teheran	Est.	6,500,000	648,000	10.03
Peru	Lima	1876	2,673,075	502,760	5.31
Portugal	Lisbon	1872	4,429,382	36,510	121.31
Russian Empire	St. Petersburg	1876	86,952,347	8,404,767	10.34
Roumania	Bucharest	1873	5,073,000	16,817	301.65
Servia	Belgrade	1874	1,352,822	19 721	68.59
Siam	Bangkok	Est.	6,300,000	250,000	25.20
Spain	Madrid	1870	16,835,506	182,758	92.11
Sweden	Stockholm	1876	4,429,713	270,980	25.90
Switzerland	Berne	1876	2,759,854	15,233	181.17
Turkey	Constantinople	Est.	31,930,738	1,812,048	17.62
Uruguay	Montevideo	1876	445,000	70,000	6.35
United States	Washington	1870	38,925,598	3,603,884	10.80
Venezuela	Caracas	1873	1,784,197	368,235	4.92

TABLE OF PRICES FOR FIFTY YEARS.

The following table was prepared by Hon. Jeremiah M. Rusk, of Wisconsin, and used as part of his argument in a speech on the Tariff delivered in Congress August 11, 1876:

Statement of wholesale prices of provisions and other staple goods in the New York market on the 1st day January in each year from 1825 to 1876, inclusive:

(The quotations are for first quality of goods, excepting cotton middlings.)

Year	Wheat per bushel	Flour per barrel	Corn per bushel	Corn meal per barrel	Coal per chaldron	Cotton middlings per pound	Iron, pig, per ton	Lead, pig, per hundred pounds	Leather sole per p'nd	Molasses, New Orleans, per gallon	Molasses, foreign, per gallon	Pork, mess, per barrel	Beef, mess, per barrel	Hams, smoked, per p'd	Lard per pound	Butter per pound	Cheese per pound	Rice per hundred p'ds	Salt per bushel	Sugar, New Orleans, per pound	Sugar, foreign, per p'd	Wool per pound
	$	$	$	$	$	Cts	$	$	Cts	Cts	Cts	$	$	Cts	Cts	Cts	Cts	$	Cts	Cts	Cts	Cts
1825	1 00	5 12	42	2 50	9 00	13	35 00	7 50	22	30	34	13 25	7 75	8	8	20	6	3 00	48	8	8	30
1826	82	5 12	73	3 50	12 00	13	60 00	6 00	21	33	26	11 50	8 00	9	7	15	6	3 00	50	8	8	30
1827	1 00	5 25	67	3 50	11 00	9	50 00	5 00	17	35	27	11 75	8 00	10	9	17	6	3 50	50	7	6	28
1828	88	5 50	56	2 75	11 00	9	50 00	6 00	17	32	30	14 00	8 00	9	9	12	4	3 00	33	7	6	21
1829	1 03	6 00	51	2 75	12 00	9	50 00	5 00	19	28	33	12 50	8 50	9	9	12	5	3 50	45	7	6	17
1830	1 25	5 00	65	2 75	10 50	9	40 00	6 00	17	33	26	13 50	9 00	10	9	15	5	3 25	42	7	5	30
1831	1 25	5 25	65	3 00	10 50	10	40 00	6 00	17	38	25	13 00	8 50	9	9	11	5	3 00	45	7	6	35
1832	1 37	6 00	75	3 00	10 50	10	40 00	5 00	15	36	25	12 50	8 00	9	9	15	6	3 50	38	6	5	55
1833	1 00	5 87	62	3 00	10 50	15	40 00	5 00	14	32	31	14 50	9 50	9	9	11	6	3 25	32	6	5	55
1834	1 03	5 00	65	2 75	9 50	11	35 00	5 00	15	27	25	13 00	9 75	8	7	11	6	3 00	34	6	5	55
1835	1 01	5 25	55	2 75	8 00	15	38 00	6 00	14	37	31	18 00	12 00	9	9	17	8	3 00	40	8	8	40
1836	1 75	10 00	90	4 75	10 00	15	60 00	5 00	15	32	40	23 30	12 00	13	11	20	8	3 00	40	6	8	45
1837	1 85	9 62	85	4 50	8 50	11	50 00	...	16	40	35	21 75	14 00	10	10	18	8	3 50	35	6	6	45

TABLE OF PRICES FOR FIFTY YEARS.—CONTINUED.

Year																						
1839..	1 37	8 75	90	3 87	7 50	14	37 50	......	23	32	26	23 00	15 75	14	13	22	8	4 00	35	6	7	37
1840..	1 00	5 87	57	3 87	6 50	9	37 50	......	17	26	22	14 00	12 00	....	7	14	8	2 75	32	5	5	30
1841..	1 00	4 94	50	2 87	7 00	9	35 00	......	22	27	20	14 00	9 75	....	8	9	6	3 18	30	5	5	25
1842..	1 25	6 00	66	3 00	8 00	8	31 00	4 00	18	25	16	9 00	7 50	....	5	10	6	2 75	....	5	4	18
1843..	87	4 69	57	2 56	5 00	7	27 00	......	16	19	16	8 25	6 00	....	6	9	5	2 50	28	3	4	18
1844..	1 00	4 62	43	2 56	5 00	8	31 00	......	16	29	21	10 00	6 12	....	5	8	4	2 25	....	6	6	25
1845..	1 00	4 68	50	2 50	5 00	5	30 00	8 00	14	24	25	9 25	5 50	5	6	9	5	2 87	24	3	5	28
1846..	1 27	5 87	73	4 00	5 00	6	38 00	4 75	13	23	20	13 25	8 00	10	5	14	6	4 25	28	5	6	26
1847..	1 04	5 50	78	3 87	6 00	10	33 00	4 37	11	34	15	10 25	8 25	6	6	13	6	3 25	25	6	6	22
1848..	1 20	6 37	76	3 25	5 50	7	35 00	4 25	14	28	23	11 00	8 25	9	6	14	6	3 00	26	4	4	28
1849..	1 20	5 87	70	2 93	7 00	6	25 00	4 25	13	24	18	14 12	10 25	9	7	15	6	2 87	21	4	4	25
1850..	1 24	5 37	60	2 93	5 50	11	23 00	4 25	15	26	21	11 75	8 50	10	6	15	5	2 25	23	4	4	30
1851..	1 18	5 06	64	2 93	6 50	13	22 00	4 80	14	29	22	12 12	8 75	8	7	16	5	3 00	22	5	4	33
1852..	1 03	5 00	70	3 00	5 00	8	19 50	4 42	12	27	18	14 62	8 25	....	9	15	6	2 75	20	4	4	30
1853..	1 30	5 75	68	3 81	5 00	9	30 00	6 00	17	29	20	19 50	9 50	....	12	20	8	3 75	27	4	4	38
1854..	2 00	7 87	82	3 75	6 50	10	37 50	6 00	23	27	23	13 37	8 50	....	10	15	8	4 12	45	4	4	38
1855..	2 35	9 12	1 00	4 25	7 00	7	27 50	6 25	19	24	22	12 62	8 25	....	10	20	10	2 50	50	4	4	24
1856..	2 12	8 25	92	4 12	5 90	9	32 00	7 00	24	48	42	17 25	10 50	....	12	23	9	4 25	27	5	7	30
1857..	1 70	6 10	73	3 25	6 50	13	30 00	6 75	31	80	38	19 37	10 50	....	12	20	9	3 27	22	9	5	33
1858..	1 35	4 20	58	3 20	5 00	9	26 00	5 00	22	34	18	15 50	9 00	....	8	14	6	2 75	16	5	5	27
1859..	1 35	4 20	76	3 40	5 25	11	25 00	5 55	25	36	19	17 25	7 75	....	11	16	8	3 00	17	6	5	36
1860..	1 40	5 25	88	3 75	5 50	11	24 00	5 70	21	53	23	16 12	5 00	....	10	15	9	3 50	19	7	6	38
1861..	1 40	5 90	72	3 10	5 50	12	20 00	5 25	20	32	15	16 00	5 75	....	10	11	9	3 25	17	4	4	30
1862..	1 31	5 40	66	3 00	4 25	36	21 00	7 00	20	50	20	12 00	5 00	....	8	13	5	7 37	20	8	6	47
1863..	1 58	5 85	70	3 90	8 50	66	23 00	8 00	29	50	21	14 00	7 00	....	9	18	10	3 75	30	8	8	62
1864..	1 53	8 00	1 27	5 30	8 75	81	42 00	0 50	31	50	38	19 75	5 80	....	12	27	12	8 50	47	----	18	80
1865..	2 55	10 75	1 46	7 75	9 50	1 20	38 00	4 75	38	1 35	53	36 00	20 00	....	20	46	15	12 00	70	...	24	95
1866..	2 30	8 25	90	4 25	13 00	51	50 00	9 75	35	1 00	35	27 75	11 00	....	15	41	17	12 00	45	...	11	70
1867..	3 05	11 40	1 15	5 00	8 00	35	49 00	6 75	32	65	40	20 00	12 00	....	12	38	14	9 00	55	...	9	50
1868..	2 80	10 75	1 38	6 15	6 50	15	38 00	6 45	27	70	37	20 90	12 00	....	12	40	11	8 50	48	...	11	55
1869..	2 00	7 00	1 06	4 25	9 00	26	40 00	6 50	28	60	35	26 50	9 00	....	16	43	15	8 00	48	...	14	60
1870..	1 35	5 60	1 09	4 75	7 50	26	38 00	6 25	30	70	30	29 50	8 00	....	16	39	15	6 75	43	...	10	55
1871..	1 47	6 25	76	4 00	6 50	15	31 00	6 33	29	65	20	20 00	10 00	....	12	23	10	6 75	45	...	9	53
1872..	1 68	8 25	76	3 65	4 50	21	36 00	5 90	24	48	23	14 00	8 00	....	9	25	9	8 25	45	...	9	60
1873..	1 85	9 50	60	3 28	5 00	21	45 00	6 50	28	60	32	14 75	11 00	....	8	25	14	7 50	35	...	8	65
1874..	1 65	6 80	78	4 00	5 25	18	35 00	6 87	27	71	40	11 50	10 00	....	8	24	10	7 50	30	...	8	55
1875..	1 17	5 25	93	4 00	6 00	15	26 00	6 15	28	......	37	20 00	12 00	11	14	40	15	8 00	28	...	8	50
1876..	1 26	5 40	74	3 65	6 50	14	23 00	6 00	27	......	....	21 00	12 50	13	13	36	14	7 00	30	...	...	52

Where the leaders (....) are inserted no quotations were given in the New York markets.

COMPOUND INTEREST.

The Amount of *One Dollar* for Fifty Years.

Years.	3 pr Cent.	4 pr Cent.	5 pr Cent.	6 pr Cent.	8 pr Cent.	10 pr Cent.	Years.
1	1·0300	1·0400	1·0500	1·0600	1·0800	1·1000	1
2	1·0609	1.0816	1·1025	1·1236	1·1664	1·2100	2
3	1·0927	1·1249	1·1576	1·1910	1·2597	1·3310	3
4	1·1255	1·1699	1·2155	1·2625	1·3605	1·4641	4
5	1·1593	1·2167	1·2763	1·3382	1·4693	1·6105	5
6	1·1941	1·2653	1·3401	1·4185	1·5869	1·7716	6
7	1·2299	1·3159	1·4071	1·5036	1·7138	1·9487	7
8	1·2668	1·3686	1·4775	1·5938	1·8509	2·1436	8
9	1·3048	1·4233	1·5513	1·6895	1·9990	2·3579	9
10	1·3439	1·4802	1·6289	1·7908	2·1589	2·5937	10
11	1·3842	1·5395	1·7103	1·8983	2·3316	2·8531	11
12	1·4258	1·6010	1·7959	2·0122	2·5182	3·1384	12
13	1·4685	1·6651	1·8856	2·1329	2·7196	3·4523	13
14	1·5126	1·7317	1·9799	2·2609	2·9372	3·7975	14
*15	1·5580	1·8009	2·0789	2·3966	3·1722	4·1773	*15
16	1·6047	1·8730	2·1829	2·5404	3·4259	4·59 0	16
17	1·6528	1·9479	2·2920	2·6928	3·7000	5·0545	17
18	1·7024	2 0258	2·4066	2·8543	3·9960	5·5599	18
19	1·7535	2·1068	2 5270	3·0256	4·3157	6·1159	19
20	1·8061	2·1911	2 6533	3·2071	4·6610	6·7274	20
21	1·8603	2·2788	2 7860	3·3996	5 0338	7·4002	21
22	1·9161	2·3699	2·9253	3·6035	5·4365	8·1403	22
23	1·9736	2·4647	3·0715	3·8197	5·8715	8 9543	23
24	2 0328	2·5633	3·2251	4·0489	6·3412	9·8497	24
25	2·0938	2·6658	3·3864	4·2919	6·8485	10·8347	25
26	2·1566	2·7725	3·5557	4·5494	7 3964	11·9182	26
27	2·2213	2 8834	3·7335	4·8223	7·9881	13·1100	27
28	2·2879	2·9987	3 9202	5·1117	8·6271	14·4210	28
29	2·3566	3·1187	4·1162	5·4184	9 3173	15·8631	29
30	2·4273	3·2434	4·3219	5 7435	10·0627	17·4494	30
31	2·5001	3·3731	4·5380	6·0881	10·8677	19·1943	31
32	2·5751	3·5081	4·7649	6·4534	11·7371	21·1138	32
33	2·6523	3·6484	5·0032	6·8406	12·6761	23·2252	33
34	2·7319	3 7943	5·2533	7·2511	13·6902	25·5477	34
35	2 8139	3·9461	5·5160	7·6861	14·7853	28·1024	35
36	2·8983	4·1039	5·7918	8·1473	15·9682	30·9127	36
37	2·9852	4·2681	6·0814	8·6368	17 2456	34·0039	37
38	3·0748	4·4388	6·3855	9·1543	18·6253	37·4043	38
39	3·1670	4·6164	6·7048	9·7035	20·1153	41 1448	39
40	3·2620	4·8010	7 0400	10·2857	21 7245	45·2593	40
41	3·3599	4·9931	7·3920	10·9029	23·4625	49·7852	41
42	3·4607	5·1928	7.7616	11·5570	25·3395	54.7637	42
43	3·5645	5·4005	8·1497	12·2505	27·3666	60 2401	43
44	3·6715	5·6165	8·5572	12·9855	29·5560	66·2641	44
45	3·7816	5.8411	8 9850	13·7646	31·9204	72·8905	45
46	3·8950	6·0748	9·4343	14·5905	34·4741	80·1795	46
47	4·0119	6·3178	9·9060	15·4659	37·2320	88·1975	47
48	4·1323	6·5705	10·4013	16·3939	40·2106	97·0172	48
49	4·2562	6·8333	10·9213	17·3775	43·4274	106·7190	49
50	4·3839	7·1067	11·5674	18·4202	46·9016	117·3909	50

*EXAMPLE.—$1 accumulated for fifteen years, at 3 per cent. interest, will amount to $1.56; at 4 per cent., to $1.80; at 5 per cent., to $2.08; at 6 per cent., to $2.40; at 8 per cent., to $3.17; at 10 per cent., to $4.18.

The following tables prepared at the agricultural department from the estimated and reported crop returns, show the amount of the several staples named raised in the United States for the years 1878 and 1879.

PRODUCTS AND VALUE FOR 1879:

Crops.	Products.	Values.
Wheat, bushels	448,755,000	$489,008,000
Corn, bushels	1,544,899,000	580,259,000
Oats, bushels	364,253,000	120,855,000
Rye, bushels	23,646,500	15,505,000
Barley, bushels	40,184,200	23,625,300
Buckwheat, bushels	13,145,650	7,860,480
Cotton, bales	5,020,387	231,000,000
Tobacco, lbs	382,459,659	21,545,591
Hay, tons	35,668,000	325,851,280
Potatoes, bushels	181,469,000	78,971,000
Total		$1,894,480,651

COMPARISON WITH 1878.

The statement for the year 1878 is as follows:

Crops.	Products.	Values.
Wheat, bushels	460,122,400	$326,340,424
Corn, bushels	1,488,218,750	441,153,405
Oats, bushels	414,478,500	101,940,830
Rye, bushels	25,842,790	13,592,726
Barley, bushels	42,245,630	24,483,315
Buckwheat, bushels	12,246,820	6,454,120
Cotton, bales	5,216,603	193,854,641
Tobacco, lbs	392,546,700	22,137,428
Hay, tons	39,608,296	295,543,952
Potatoes, bushels	124,126,650	73,059,125
Total		$1,498,559,966

From this report it will be seen that the value of the crop of 1879 exceeds that of the preceding year by over $400,000,000.

Total amount of specie imported from January 1, 1879, to November 15, was $75,512,092. Production for the fiscal year 1879, $79,711,990, of which $38,899,850 was gold, and $40,812,132 was silver.

Average rate of interest on commercial paper in the City of New York in 1874, 6.4 per cent. In 1879, it averaged 4.4 per cent. Average rate of interest of the Bank of England, January 30, 1878, was 2 per cent. On November 7, 1879, it was 3 per cent. Average interest of the Bank of France, November 7, 1879, was 3 per cent.

The comptroller's office employs ninety-seven men to take charge of the national banking department who are paid by the Government, and their salaries are as follows:

1 Receives	$5,000	a year.
1 "	2,800	"
4 "	2,200	each.
5 "	2,000	"
8 "	1,800	"
11 "	1,400	"
8 "	1,200	"
2 "	1,000	"
1 "	840	"
3 "	720	"
5 "	600	"
40 "	900	"

Annual expenses for dies, plates, printing, etc., are $104,420.

THE POWER OF INTEREST TO ROB.

Money at 2	per cent.,	doubles	in 35	years.
Money at 3	"	"	" 23	"
Money at 4	"	"	" 17	"
Money at 5	"	"	" 14	"
Money at 6	"	"	" 11	"
Money at 7	"	"	" 10	"
Money at 8	"	"	" 9	"
Money at 9	"	"	" 8	"
Money at 10	"	"	" 7	"

Our national, State, municipal, corporate and individual indebtedness, held by the usurer classes, amounts to over *fourteen thousand million dollars:* drawing an average annual interest of six per cent.

The total wealth of the United States at present valuation, does not exceed thirty thousand million dollars. Contraction of the currency to a specie basis will perpetuate and immortalize this indebtedness, so that Shylock will receive the equivalent of the entire country every twenty-two years, for all time to come.

Did the nation ever need a savior more than now? Greenbacks saved it once, and nothing but a plenty of debt-paying greenbacks will save our country now from confiscation, and our people from pauperism and slavery.

THE INCREASING VALUE OF MONEY.

The constitution enjoins upon Congress, among other things, the duty of coining money and regulating the value thereof.

The only way the value of money can be regulated is by regulating its quantity.

This is a prerogative specially delegated to Congress, and as the chief object of Government is to promote the general welfare, it would seem that the time of Congress could be much more profitably spent than in the exhaustive efforts of one party in knocking down the political pins of the other as fast as set up.

There is nothing the commercial and industrial interests of the country so much need as a check on the increasing value of money.

In 1865 a dollar was worth 20 pounds of flour.
In 1867 " " " 22 " "
In 1869 " " " 30 " "
In 1872 " " " 33 " "
In 1874 " " " 35 " "
In 1876 " " " 45 " "
In 1878 " " " 50 " "

Thus, while debt, interest and taxes remain stationary, dollars are becoming so valuable that men can hardly procure enough, with the greatest economy, to meet maturing obligations and defray current expenses.

SALARIES OF PUBLIC OFFICERS.

The following table contains a condensed list of the salaries of some of the principal public officers in the United States:

President of the United States	$50,000
Vice-President of the United States	8,000
Seven Cabinet officers, each	8,000
Ministers to England, France, Germany and Russia, each	17,500
Seven other Foreign Ministers, each	12,000
Three " " " "	10,000
Nine " " " "	7,500
Consuls get from $3,000 to	6,000
Supreme Court Judges, each	10,000
Supreme Court of Claims Judges, each	4,500
District Judges, from 3,500 to	4,000
Governors of New York and Pennsylvania, each	10,000
Governors of California, Colorado and Nevada, each	6,000
Governors of other States, $1,000 to	5,000

PUBLIC DEBT PER CAPITA.

In 1860 the public debt per capita was $1.90, and the interest per capita was 11 cents. In 1879 the public debt per capita was $50, and the interest $2.50 per capita. This seems but a trifle, but when we reflect that this is a steady, ceaseless, never-ending drain of $2.50 per annum for every man, woman and child in America for all time to come, its effects will be like holding out at arm's length a pound weight, which at first requires slight strength, but soon becomes exhausting, and finally unendurable. Ireland has been reduced from affluence to her present condition of misery and abject poverty by a steady rent drain of $1.60 per capita since her soil went into the hands of absent landlords.

SUPREME COURT OF THE UNITED STATES.

Chief Justices.	Associate Justices.	State Whence Appointed	Term of Service.	Yrs. of Service	Born.	Died.
1 John Jay†		New York	1789-1795	6	1745	1829
	1 John Rutledge†	S. Carolina	1789-1791	2	1739	1800
	2 William Cushing	Mass	1789-1810	21	1733	1810
	3 James Wilson	Penn	1789-1798	9	1742	1798
	4 John Blair†	Virginia	1789-1796	7	1732	1800
	5 Rob. H. Harrison†	Maryland	1789-1790	1	1745	1790
	6 James Iredell	N. Carolina	1790-1799	9	1751	1799
	7 Thomas Johnson†	Maryland	1791-1793	2	1732	1819
	8 William Patterson	New Jersey	1793-1806	13	1745	1806
2 John Rutledge‡		S. Carolina	1795-1795		1739	1800
	9 Samuel Chase	Maryland	1796-1811	15	1741	1811
3 Oliver Ellsworth†		Conn	1796-1801	5	1745	1807
	10 Bus'd Washington	Virginia	1798-1829	31	1762	1829
	11 Alfred Moore†	N. Carolina	1799-1804	5	1755	1810
4 John Marshall		Virginia	1801-1835	34	1755	1835
	12 William Johnson	S. Carolina	1804-1834	30	1771	1834
	13 Brock't Livingston	New York	1806-1823	17	1757	1823
	14 Thomas Todd	Kentucky	1807-1826	19	1765	1826
	15 Joseph Story	Mass	1811-1845	34	1779	1845
	16 Gabriel Duval†	Maryland	1811-1836	25	1752	1844
	17 Smith Thompson	New York	1823-1845	22	1767	1845
	18 Robert Trimble	Kentucky	1826-1828	2	1777	1828
	19 John McLean	Ohio	1829-1861	32	1785	1861
	20 Henry Baldwin	Penn	1830-1846	16	1779	1846
	21 James M. Wayne§	Georgia	1835-1867	32	1790	1867
5 Roger B. Taney		Maryland	1836-1864	28	1777	1864
	22 Philip P. Barbour	Virginia	1836-1841	5	1783	1841
	23 John Catron	Tennessee	1837-1865	28	1778	1865
	24 John McKinley	Alabama	1837-1852	15	1780	1852
	25 Peter V. Daniel	Virginia	1841-1860	19	1785	1860
	26 Samuel Nelson	New York	1845-1872	27	1792	1873
	27 Levi Woodbury	New Hamp	1845-1851	6	1789	1851
	28 Robert C. Grier†	Penn	1846-1869	23	1794	1870
	29 Benj. R Curtis†	Mass	1851-1857	6	1809	1874
	30 John A. Campbell†	Alabama	1853-1861	8	1811	....
	31 Nathan Clifford	Maine	1857-	....	1803	....
	32 Noah H. Swayne	Ohio	1861-	....	1805	....
	33 Samuel F. Miller	Iowa	1862-	....	1816	....
	34 David Davis†	Illinois	1862-1877	15	1815	....
	35 Stephen J. Field	California	1866-	....	1816	....
6 Salmon P. Chase		Ohio	1864-1873	9	1808	1873
	36 William Strong	Penn	1870-	....	1808	....
	37 Joseph P. Bradley	New Jersey	1870-	....	1813	....
	38 Ward Hunt	New York	1872-	....	1811	....
7 Morrison R. Waite		Ohio	1874-	....	1816	....
	39 John M. Harlan	Kentucky	1877-	....	1833	....

*The figures before the names of the Associate Justices indicate the order of their appointment. The numbers following refer to the same numbers in the first column, and show the vacancy filled by each appointment.

†Resigned.

‡Presided one term of the court; appointment not confirmed by the Senate.

§The Supreme Court, at its first session in 1790, consisted of a Chief Justice and five Associates. The number of Associate Justices was increased to six in 1807 by the appointment of Thomas Todd; increased to eight in 1837 by the appointments of John Catron and John McKinley; increased to nine in 1863 by the appointment of Stephen J. Field; decreased to eight on the death of John Catron in 1865; decreased to seven on the death of James M. Wayne in 1867; and again increased to eight in 1870.

FAILURES OF BUSINESS MEN.

In the following table we give the number of failures each year from 1857 to 1879, and the amount of liabilities:

Year.	Number.	Amount.
1857	4,932	$201,750,000
1858	4,225	95,749,000
1859	3,913	64,394,000
1860	3,673	79,807,000
1861	6,993	207,210,000
1862	1,652	23,049,309
1863	485	6,864,700
1864	520	8,579,000
1865	530	17,625,000
1866	532	47,333,000
1867	2,386	86,208,000
1868	2,608	63,774,000
1869	2,799	75,954,009
1870	3,551	88,242,000
1871	2,915	86,252,000
1872	4,069	121,056,000
1873	5,183	228,499,000
1874	5,882	155,339,000
1875	7,740	201,070,363
1876	9,092	191,119,786
1877	8,872	190,669,936
1878	10,478	234,383,132
1879	......	....

In May, 1878, Congress passed an act to stop the destruction of greenbacks, since which time the currency has been increasing in volume, times have been getting better, and the number of bankruptcies have been decreasing.

A STARTLING TABLE OF FIGURES—THE GREAT MAELSTROM OF ERROR EXPOSED TO VIEW.

The following table exhibits a statement of the number of State banks, the amount of their circulating notes, and the amount of specie they held at different periods from 1784 to 1861:

Year.	No. B'ks.	Circulation.	Specie.
1784	3	$2,000,000	$10,000,000
1790	4	2,500.000	9,000 000
1796	24	10,500,000	16,500,000
1800	28	10,500,000	17,500,000
1811	89	28,100,000	15,400,000
1815	208	110,000,000	17,000,000
1820	308	44,863 344	19,820,240
1830	330	61,323.898	22,114,917
1834	506	94,839,570	....
1835	704	103,692,495	43,937,625
1836	713	140,301,038	40,019,594
1837	788	149,185,890	37,915,340
1838	829	116,138,910	35,184,112
1839	840	135,170,995	45,132,673
1840	901	106,968,572	33,105,155
1841	784	107,290,214	34,813,958
1842	692	83,734.011	28,440,423
1843	691	58,563,608	33,515,806
1844	696	75,167,646	49,898,269
1845	707	89,680,711	44,241,242
1846	707	105,552,427	42,012,095
1847	715	105,509 766	35,132,516
1848	751	128,506,091	46,369,765
1849	782	114,743,415	43,619,368
1850	824	131,366,526	45,379,345
1851	879	155,165,251	48,671,048
1853	750	146,072,780	47,138,592
1854	1208	204,689,207	59,410,253
1855	1307	186,952,226	53,944,546
1856	1398	195,747,950	59,314,063
1857	1416	214,778,882	58,349,838
1858	1422	155,208,344	74,412,832
1859	1476	193,306,818	104,537,818
1860	1562	207,102,477	83,594,537
1861	1601	202 005 767	87,674,507

If the reader will examine closely the above table they will discover three important facts. 1. That the number of banks in operation at different periods increased and diminished greatly. 2. That the volume of bank notes in circulation was subject to rapid and extensive expansion and contraction. 3. That the amount of specie held by the banks up to 1811 gradually preponderated over the volume of bank notes, and that thereafter it was subject to expansion and contraction to a marked degree, but was always less than half in volume to that of bank notes out any one time.

POPULAR VOTE OF 1856.

	STATES.	James Buchanan Democratic.		John C. Fremont Republican.		M. Fillmore, American.		Total Vote.
		Vote.	Maj.	Vote.	Maj.	Vote.	Maj.	
1	Alabama	46,739	18,187	....	....	28,552	....	75,291
2	Arkansas	21,910	11,123	....	....	10,787	....	32,697
3	California	53,365	*17,200	20,691	....	36,165	....	110,221
4	Connecticut	34,995	....	42,715	5,105	2,615	....	80,325
5	Delaware	8,004	1,521	308	....	6,175	....	14,487
6	Florida	6,358	1,525	....	....	4,833	....	11,191
7	Georgia	56,758	14,350	....	....	42,228	....	98,986
8	Illinois	105,348	†9,159	96,189	....	37,444	....	238,981
9	Indiana	118,670	1,909	94,375	....	22,386	....	235,431
10	Iowa	36,170	....	43,954	‡7,784	9,180	....	89,304
11	Kentucky	74,642	6,912	314	....	67,416	....	142,372
12	Louisiana	22,164	1,455	....	....	20,709	....	42,873
13	Maine	39,080	....	67,379	24,974	3,325	....	109,784
14	Maryland	39,115	....	281	....	47,460	8,064	86,856
15	Massachusetts	39,240	....	108,190	49,324	19,626	....	167,056
16	Michigan	52,136	....	71,762	17,966	1,660	....	125,558
17	Mississippi	35,446	11,251	....	....	24,195	....	59,641
18	Missouri	58,164	9,649	....	....	48,524	....	106,688
19	N. Hampshire	32,789	....	38,345	‡ 5,314	422	....	71,556
20	New Jersey	46,943	*18,605	28,338	....	24,115	....	99,396
21	New York	195,878	....	276,007	‡80,129	124,604	....	596,489
22	North Carolina	48,246	11,360	....	....	36,886	....	85,132
23	Ohio	170,874	....	187,497	‡16,623	*28,126	....	386,497
24	Pennsylvania	230,710	1,025	147,510	....	82,175	....	460,395
25	Rhode Island	6,680	....	11,467	3,112	1,675	....	19,822
26	South Carolina	Electors	chosen	by the	Legis-	lature.	....	....
27	Tennessee	73,638	7,460	....	....	66,178	....	139,816
28	Texas	31,169	15,530	....	....	15,639	....	46,808
29	Vermont	10,569	....	39,561	28,447	515	....	50,675
30	Virginia	89,706	29,105	291	....	60,310	....	150,307
31	Wisconsin	52,843	....	66,090	12,68	579	....	119,512
	Total	1,838,169	142,353	1,341,264	146,730	874,534	8,064	4,053,967
	Buchanan's Plurality		†496,905					

*Plurality over Fillmore. †Plurality over Fremont. ‡Plurality over Buchanan.

POPULAR VOTE OF 1876.

	STATES.	S. J. Tilden, Democratic. Vote.	S. J. Tilden, Democratic. Maj.	R. B. Hayes, Republican. Vote.	R. B. Hayes, Republican. Maj.	Peter Cooper, Greenback.	G. C. Smith, Temperance.	*Scattering.	Total Vote.
1	Alabama......	102,002	33,772	68,230	......	......	......	......	170,232
2	Arkansas.....	58,071	19,113	38,669	......	289	......	......	97,029
3	California....	76,465	......	79,269	2,738	47	......	19	155,800
4	Colorado......	Electors	chosen	by Legis-	lature.	......	......	......	......
5	Connecticut..	61,934	1,712	59,034	......	774	378	36	122,156
6	Delaware.....	13,381	2,629	10,752	......	......	......	......	24,133
7	Florida†......	22,923	......	23,849	926	......	......	......	46,772
8	Georgia......	130,088	79,642	50,446	......	......	......	......	180,534
9	Illinois......	258,601	......	278,232	1,971	17,233	141	286	554,493
10	Indiana......	213,526	§5,515	208,011	......	9,533	......	......	431,070
11	Iowa.........	112,099	......	171,327	50,191	9,001	36	......	292,463
12	Kansas.......	37,902	......	78,322	32,511	7,776	110	23	124,133
13	Kentucky.....	159,690	59,772	97,156	......	1,914	818	......	259,608
14	Louisiana‡....	70,508	......	75,135	4,627	......	......	......	145,643
15	Maine.........	49,823	......	66,300	15,814	663	......	......	116,786
16	Maryland.....	91,780	19,756	71,981	......	33	10	......	163,804
17	Massachusetts	108,777	......	150,063	40,423	779	84	......	259,703
18	Michigan.....	141,095	......	166,534	15,542	9,060	766	71	317,526
19	Minnesota....	48,799	......	72,962	21,780	2,311	72	......	124,144
20	Mississippi...	112,173	59,568	52,605	......	......	......	......	164,778
21	Missouri......	203,077	54,389	145,029	......	3,498	64	97	351,765
22	Nebraska.....	17,554	......	31,916	10,336	2,320	1,599	117	53,506
23	Nevada.......	9,308	......	10,383	1,075	......	......	......	19,691
24	N. Hampshire	38,509	......	41,539	2,954	76	......	......	80,124
25	New Jersey...	115,992	11,690	103,517	......	712	43	......	220,234
26	New York....	521,949	26,568	489,207	......	1,987	2,359	1,828	1,017,330
27	North Carolina	125,427	17,010	108,417	......	......	......	......	233,844
28	Ohio..........	323,182	......	330,698	2,747	8,057	1,636	76	658,649
29	Oregon.......	14,149	......	15,206	547	510	......	......	29,865
30	Pennsylvania	366,158	......	384,122	9,375	7,187	1,319	83	758,849
31	Rhode Island.	10,712	......	15,787	4,947	68	60	......	26,627
32	South Carolina	90,906	......	91,870	964	......	......	......	182,776
33	Tennessee....	133,166	43,600	89,566	......	......	......	......	222,732
34	Texas........	104,755	59,955	44,800	......	......	......	......	149,555
35	Vermont......	20,254	......	44,092	23,838	......	......	......	64,346
36	Virginia.....	139,670	44,112	95,558	......	......	......	......	235,228
37	West Virginia.	56,455	12,384	42,698	......	1,373	......	......	100,526
38	Wisconsin....	123,927	......	130,668	5,205	1,509	27	......	256,131
	Total........	4,284,757	545,672	4,033,950	248,501	81,740	9,522	2,636	8,412,605
	Tilden's Majority		156,909						

*Scattering includes the votes of the anti-Masonic and American Alliance tickets.

†Returning Board's count, Nov. 28, 1876. A majority of 94 to 1,197 was claimed for Tilden by the Democrats, and the opinion of the Supreme Court of Florida gave Tilden 94 majority.

‡Returning Board's count. The figures on the face of the returns, when opened by the Board, are claimed to have been: Tilden, 82,326; Hayes, 77,023. Tilden's majority, 5,303.

§Plurality over Hayes.

PART SECOND.

CHAPTER I.

THE RIGHTS OF MAN.

Every history and traditionary account of creation agree in establishing *the unity* of man, that the whole human race is of one degree, or grade; and consequently that "all men are born free and equal in respect to natural rights, in the same manner as if posterity had been continued by *creation* instead of *generation*."

Paine, in "Natural Rights of Man," says:

"Natural rights are those which always appertain to man in right of his existence. Of this kind are all the intellectual rights, or rights of the mind, and also all those rights of acting as an individual for his own comfort and happiness, which are not injurious to the rights of others.—Civil rights are those which appertain to man in right of his being a member of society. Every civil right has for its foundation some natural right pre-existing in the individual, but to which his individual power is not, in all cases, sufficiently competent. Of this kind are all those which relate to security and protection.

"From this short review, it will be easy to distinguish between that class of natural rights which man retains after entering into society, and those which he throws into common stock as a member of society.

"The natural rights which he retains, are all those in which the power to execute is as perfect in the individual as the right itself. Among this class, as is before mentioned, are all the intellectual rights, or rights of the mind; consequently, religion is one of those rights. The natural rights which are not retained, are all those in which, though the right is perfect in the individual, the power to execute them is defective. They answer not his purposes. A man by natural right, has a right to judge in his own cause; and so far as the right of the mind is concerned, he never surrenders it: but what availeth it him to judge, if he has not power to redress it? He therefore deposits this right in the common stock of society, and takes the arm of society, of which he is a part, in preference and in addition to his own. Society *grants* him nothing. Every man is a proprietor in society, and draws on the capital as a matter of right.

"From these premises, two or three certain conclusions will follow.

"1st, That every civil right grows out of a natural right; or, in other words, is a natural right exchanged.

"2d, That civil power properly considered as such, is made up of the aggregate of that class of the natural rights of man, which becomes defective in the individual in point of power, and answers not his purpose, but when collected to a focus, becomes competent to the purpose of every one.

"3d, That the power produced by the aggregate of natural rights, imperfect in power in the individual, cannot be applied to invade the natural rights which are retained in the individual, and in which the power to execute is as perfect as the right itself."

Deprived of these rights by the arbitrary powers of unjust law, the subjects of despotism and monarchical governments become slaves, and serfs, to the extent that these rights are denied them.

To escape the slavery of despotism, the early settlers of America left the land of their birth and oppression, traversed the wilderness of waves, and made their homes among the wild men, and the wild beasts of the new world. But oppression followed them. Like a beast of prey it smelled their blood afar off, and followed their trail. They cheerfully bore the trials and hardships of the wilderness, but when in addition to these, their oppressors placed upon their necks the yoke they had made themselves exiles to escape, it was more than nature could endure.

Relying upon their own strength, the justice of their cause, and the aid of Divine power, they promulgated to the world the great charter of natural and civil rights upon which our Government is claimed to be established. They took the ground that all power exercised over a people must have some beginning, or origin. It must be either delegated or assumed. There are no other sources. All delegated power is trust, and all assumed power is usurpation. The bill of rights proclaimed by our fathers contained the following:

I. That men are born and should always continue free in respect to their natural rights.

II. That the people is essentially the source of all sovereignty, nor can any individual, or any body of men, be entitled to any authority which is not especially derived from the people.

III. That the just powers of Government are derived from the consent of the governed.

IV. That political liberty consists in the power and right of doing anything that does not injure another.

V. That law should be an expression of the will of the people.

These glorious principles, these inalienable gifts of God to man, were wrenched from the Lion's jaws by our fathers after seven long years of bloody struggle, and they, soon after, made them over, assigned and bequeathed them to their posterity forever as a joint inheritance, in the following words:

"*For the purpose of forming a more perfect Union; to establish justice; to insure domestic tranquility, to promote the general welfare, and to transmit to posterity the blessings of liberty, do ordain and establish this Constitution,*" etc.

Those old patriot heroes believed that men possessed rights, as well as kings. That all men are created equal, and are endowed with certain inalienable rights; that among these rights, are life, liberty and the pursuits of happiness, and that Governments are established among men to secure these rights. Not for personal aggrandizement, not to oppress the people, not to create and foster grinding and robbing monopolies, not to deprive a portion of humanty of their natural rights that a favored few may enjoy a double portion—not to deprive men of their birthrights and blessings bequeathed to them by a benevolent Creator.

They further declared that w..enever any form of Government became destructive to these ends, *it is the right of the people to alter or abolish it!*

The aristocracies of the Old World have robbed the masses of every natural right except the right to toil, suffer, and die.

The poor of Ireland and India suffer and starve, not because there are not fertile lands and abundant harvests, but because the ungodly laws of Britian have robbed the people of their right to the soil, and given to an aristocratic few all the sustenance from the bosom of our common mother earth, and being protected in this robbery by the arbitrary power of the Government, the poor landless tenants are compelled to toil a life time for the crumbs which fall from the table of their lordly robber brothers.

Man inherits from his Creator certain natural rights, among which are:

The control of his own body, labor, skill and genius.

All the powers of his body and mind, and the right to exercise them in any manner he sees fit, provided he does not interfere with the rights of any other individual.

He has an absolute right to his own time, and cannot rightfully be the slave of another. These are his individual rights, which cannot be justly claimed, controlled or usurped by another.

Then man inherits in common with his brother man, the means of Life, Liberty and Happiness, and the facilities to fulfill his destiny, and accomplish his mission on earth.

The air to vitalize the life-currents of his body, is his in common with all animated nature, and its monopoly by any man, or set of men, under cover of law, would be legalized murder, and the masses who had not the means to purchase their breath, would be justified in putting to death the monopolizer, or in abolishing the Government creating it; in self defense.

Light and water are also man's common heritage, and no man has a moral right to deprive another of these life-giving elements. The day for work, and the night for rest—the seasons as they come and go, are the joint inheritance of humanity.

But the most important item, perhaps, in the inventory of man's natural rights, is his inalienable right to occupy, till and enjoy the fruits of his pro-rata of God's green earth, a right which is more fully discussed in the following chapter.

CHAPTER II.

THE LAND QUESTION.

"I see no reason or natural right why a deed upon parchment should convey the domain of land." —BLACKSTONE.

One of the most momentous questions of the day, a question that is destined in the near future to shake civilization from center to circumference, is the Land Question.

What this question is, is well defined by that eminent political economist, John G. Drew, in "Land Labor and Money in History."

"The term Land Reform as it is now currently used, defines a great and rapidly growing demand that—

"*First*, No more land shall be occupied by a person or family than he or they can and will properly cultivate;

"*Second*, That all control of lands shall be vested in the State as trustee for its citizens, thus debarring all and any from proprietorship of land, and confining their ownership to *the products thereof* and the improvements thereon resulting from their enterprise and industry.

"That such conditions were recognized in the Theocracy of the Jews under the Mosaic dispensation is clearly demonstrated by the Fiats of Jehovah that 'the land should not be sold forever,' and the supplementary legislation fixing every fiftieth year, as a sabbath of sabbaths, a jubilee of years when leases should be renewed or cancelled, the bonds of the oppressed should be broken and the enslaved, whether by debt or other bondage, should go free. Every reader of the Bible knows that, and every priest and clergymen can explain the same.

"All eminent historians admit the antiquity of the teaching, and no legalist who values his reputation, Blackstone included, dare deny the entire logic of the position.

"Knowing the utter impotency of efforts honestly and logically directed to successfully combat the arguments of those advocating land reform, the predatory classes have recourse to their only remaining weapon, blackguarding and abuse; exactly as the skunk, not endowed by nature with nobler weapons of offense and defense, hurls his execrable filth at his enemy, which is, by sensitive people and animals, more carefully avoided than the more deadly but less dirty weapons of nobler creatures.

"Contrary to the rules which govern other professional gamblers, they play their best or worst card first, and slap the face of their intended victim with the charge that he is an agrarian.

"In a large majority of instances this is enough to silence the audacious iconoclast, who supposes from the self-satisfied and triumphant tone with which the shot was fired, that it is some newly invented and intensely concentrated missive, containing the sublimated essence of every sin possible to imagine.

"It is possibly more deeply penetrative and devastatively explosive projectile than its old fashioned prototype, "you are an abolitionist," which in the past generation knocked down and kept down many a noble fellow, until, when the time arrived, he sprang to his feet to face the more deadly but less detestable missives of the bomb and bullet in defense of his cherished thoughts.

"Let us pick up and examine that dreadful term and see what it means and what it is made of.

"Niebuhr, the eminent German historian of Rome, antagonizing the great theory that farming was not proper for freemen, says:

"'To what more than her system of colonization, a branch of her agrarian scheme, was she [Rome] indebted for the security and extension of her frontier? A host of warriors were trained up ready to take the field at the call of their country, yet no less ready to exchange the sword for the plowshare.

"'It is not, however, in a military point of view that the value of these institutions is evident. They were of no less domestic importance in providing against the phenomena so frequently met with in great cities of the most squalid indigence by the side of the most profuse extravagance.'

"Or as Victor Hugo would say, monstrous oppulence and monstrous poverty.

"Considering that Niebuhr ranks as amongst the most conservative of historians, his testimony is of peculiar value.

"Dr. Thomas Arnold, very pleasantly known to many as the much-loved principal of the Rugby School when Thomas Hughes was a pupil therein, says of the first land reform known in Roman history:

"'By a strange compensation of fortune the first Roman whose greatness is really historical is the man whose deeds no poet sang and whose memory the early annalists, *repeating the language of the party who destroyed him*, have branded with the charge of Treason and attempted Tyranny. This was Spurius Cassius. He procured, although at the price of his own life [in the fifth century before Christ], the enactment of the first agrarian law.'

"Dr. Arnold notes as reigning not long afterward '*the good King Servius Tullius*,' and quotes him approvingly as an 'agrarian' who divided among the common people the public lands.

"In or about the year 468 before Christ, new consuls were appointed and they were disposed to execute the Agrarian law of Spurius Cassius and settle the people on the unused lands. To this they were strenuously opposed by the patrician classes who, as before noted, had assassinated the author of the law. For two years a violent political conflict raged which was only abated by the ravages of a devastating pestilence perhaps induced and certainly intensified by popular suffering.

"On abatement of the pestilence the Land Question again came up for consideration, and, strange to say, was not supported by the Democratic party. The most charitable historians account for this sudden lethargy by supposing that the people, educated by the prolonged discussion, deemed that simply freedom of the public lands was but too partial a reform and demanded more or nothing.

"No progress was made for nearly seventy years, when in 399, before Christ, a revival of the agrarian law was proposed by the people's tribunes, which was successfully opposed by the aristocracy. The people, by advice of the tribunes, then *refused to pay taxes*, which is, perhaps, the earliest instance of withholding supplies to kill vicious legislation.

"Thirty-one years passed over without progress, but then (before Christ, 368) Licinius was elected Tribune.

"He introduced three laws, which are known as the Licinian code, but although often referred to their texts seem to have been studiously suppressed.

"The first is described as a law to relieve the people from the overwhelming and increasing pressure of debt, and provided that whatever had been paid on a debt in interest, should be deducted from the principal.

"Dr. Arnold, in commenting on this law, says:

"'If the rate of interest had been high, and if a debt had been long standing, the sum paid in interest would not only have equaled, but must in some cases have actually exceeded the amount of the principal, so that the creditor, far from having anything more to receive, would rather have had something to refund.'

"The Second Law was claimed to be necessary to save the people when once out of debt from all need and apology for getting into debt again, and provided that citizens should be granted lands from the public domain (ager publicus) restricting individual occupancy to 500 Jugera—about 300 acres each.

"The Third Law provided that the commons should be placed politically on a level with the patricians.

"As might have been expected, the mere proposal of these laws raised a terrific row among the patrician classes, who by trying to prevent the reading of them to the people (there were no printing presses then) and otherwise obstructing legislation and retarding intelligence, literally and actually performed the same drama in Rome 2,248 years ago that is now acted by Speaker Randall in the American House of Representatives in ignoring the people's representatives, and the subsidized press co-operate in their Conspiracy of Silence for the repression of current history and stifling proposed legislation.

"For five years this struggle continued. Government was suspended, and historians have not yet ceased to wonder that society was not extinguished.

"At length, by Patrician influence, Marcus Furius Camillus was made Dictator, and he instantly summoned all citizens capable of bearing arms to rally around his standard; but his orders were utterly disregarded, and the Senate, to allay the popular fury, called on him to resign his dictatorship, which he did, and died two years later of the pestilence which the miseries of the people had created.

"The Licinian code then became the law of Rome, and in commemoration of so grand an event as the unification of the Roman people, the affirmation of equality and fraternity, a new temple was erected on the Capitoline hill and dedicated to Concord."

For the information of the general reader, as well as to place on the proper page of history a record of the views and arguments of that large and rapidly increasing class who are battling for "Land Reform," or the "emancipation of the soil from the bondage of ownership in man," I append the following:

"The soil is a free gift of God to all His creatures in common; each individual has as valid a right and title to all the soil that is necessary to the subsistance of himself and family as he has to the air, the water, and the light of day.

"They deny the right of Governments to barter away to land monopolists the patrimony of unborn generations. If the three or four millions of people who inhabited this country when the Republic was established held sufficient land for their own use, who gave them the right to convey, or the Government to receive as merchandise the soil which is now demanded for 50,000,000 souls?

"They had the same right to barter away the liberties of posterity as to compel unborn millions to serve landlords ten or fifteen of the best years of their lives to redeem their confiscated patrimony.

"Was the unoccupied soil free as God designed it, *all* the labor of the individual would be his own.

"How is it now? Suppose a young man is compelled to purchase a farm of 160 acres, and to pay some land robber $10 per acre. This would amount to $1,600, and this sum he must earn by the sweat of his brow.

"It will take him ten years, with close economy, to save up this amount.

"Now, this young man has been the land robbers' slave ten years. He has been deprived of ten years of his liberty and pursuit of happiness, to purchase the freedom to enjoy his own rightful heritage. The land robbers might just as well have held him in slavery ten years by a contract with the Government before he was born, and then set him free to go and claim his own, as to make him serve ten years to redeem his own. It may be said that to deprive the land monopolies of their surplus acres, would be interfering with *vested rights*. So the slave owners said when the Government restored to the bondmen their *rights to life, liberty and the pursuits of happiness*. So says every man who is called upon to yield up wrongfully-obtained wealth. *There are no rights in wrongs, vested or otherwise.*

"*The title to stolen goods vests in the real owner, it matters not how many hands they have passed through, or how great a price was paid the thief. Unborn souls cannot rightfully be deprived of their patrimony by the wrongs of their predecessors.*

"Every man should be regarded as equally entitled to all the free gifts of God to His creatures, the soil included. Each man inherits, in common with the universal brotherhood, these blessings. Like every other element of nature, the soil was made for humanity.

"It is proper for the Government to hold it in trust for those of the present and future generations who may need to occupy and till it, but as an article of merchandise it was never intended in the economy of nature, nor is it permitted by the statutes of the Divine law.

"*The merchandise of men should be limited to the productions of their hands and skill. The soil should be free. The improvements a man puts upon land are his own. Those, he can sell, or dispose of,* BUT GOD'S SOIL, NEVER!

"*Man will never be free until the soil from which he derives sustenance is free.*

"Thirty millions of people in America are houseless and homeless. They are trespassers on every sod upon which they place their feet, except in the public highway, while huge monopolies and giant corporations hold by gift from the Government sufficient land to give every family in the nation a farm and the means of subsistance.

"Our homestead law, it is true, gives to every head of a family 160 acres if he will occupy it; but the huge grants of land to railroad and other corporations have pushed individual homesteads so far into the wilderness, that a family is compelled to exile itself from civilization to avail itself of the Government's generosity(?). The earth is the Lord's, and He demands it for His children.

"He has never parted with the title to a foot of it, and He commands the millions of wandering, law made, 'trespassers' TO GO AND CLAIM THEIR INHERITANCE!

"Man's rights to occupy, till, and enjoy the products of any unoccupied soil of earth, is as valid, and as inalienable, as his rights to live and breathe, and no man possesses a natural right, nor have Governments the moral right to confirm in man the ownership, or control of more soil than he can till and is necessary for his and his family's subsistance, while there is one landless soul on earth."

These are the arguments of the land reformers.

From an European stand point, especially England and Ireland, where millions of God's poor have been robbed of their soil, where millions of acres are used as sporting and play grounds for the royal robbers, these arguments have much force.

In America, the condition of the landless is not so bad at present, but no one can deny the fact that the tendency and ultimate results of the specie basis, debt and usury systems which we have adopted is to concentrate landed estates, as well as other capital in the hands of the few.

Pliney says, "The colossal fortunes which ruined Italy and caused the downfall of Rome, were due to the concentration of estates through *usury* or *interest*."

"USURY DID THIS, AND COINED MONEY."

Many suppose that the "Land Question," or Land Reform is a blow aimed at the large agricultural interest of the West—a blow aimed at those enterprising and thrifty farmers who hold titles to several hundred acres of soil, and produce a large surplus of farm crops. This is a mistake. The movement is to protect this very class of men in the enjoyment of their estates.

The policy which the Land Reformers are fighting against, if allowed to prevail, will rob every farmer in the West of his lands, as surely as the lands of a million English farmers passed into the hands of 30,000 of the nobility through a similar policy. This, the money power fully understand, and through their organ, the New York *Times*, have given notice to the farmers of the country to prepare for the event. They first distressed the farmers by depriving the country of money, which reduced values, depressed prices, and made it impossible for them to pay their taxes and defray current expenses from the proceeds of the farm.

"COME INTO MY PARLOR" SAID THE SPIDER TO THE FLY.

On the 12th day of August, 1877, referring to the farmer's hard lot, the New York *Times* said:

"Is there a way of deliverance? There seems to be but one remedy, and that is a slow one, and not immediately effective. To reach it both farmers and capitalists need to be educated to it, but it seems to be inevitable that it must come about in course of time. It is a change of ownership of the soil, and the creation of a class of land-owners on the one hand, and of tenant farmers on the other, something similar in both cases, to what has long existed and now exists, in the older countries of Europe, and similar, also, to a system that is common in our own State of California.

"*Those farmers who are land poor, must sell, and become tenants in place of owners of the soil. The hoarded, idle capital must be invested in these lands and turned over to the poor farmers, who will at once be set upon their feet*—not to go and loaf about towns and villages, spending their money while it may last, but to buy with his money stock, fertilizers, implements and machines, and go to work to cultivate the soil profitably. Instead of their money being sunk and dead in unproductive acres, it will be invested in cows, sheep, swine of improved breeds; in guano and fertilizers, by which the crops will be doubled or trebled. It will then become active and productive, and capable of doubling itself within the year. The farmer will be relieved of the burden of a bad investment on which he now makes no interest, and his money will be placed where it will do the most good. He will at once be lifted from poverty to financial ease, and in place of an unsalable farm he will have to show for his money some property that will realize all that it is worth at a public sale at 24 hours' notice.

"Everything seems ripe for the change. Half the farms in the country are ready to be sold if buyers would only appear, and hundreds that can now be bought for less than their value 20 or 30 years ago, need only some judicious outlay to make them as productive as ever. Few farmers can hope to provide their sons with farms of their own, and there is no place for these young men in the over-crowded cities. But to stock a rented farm is not so difficult a matter for a father intent on starting a son in life. This would be easy to do if the farm could be rented on a long and satisfactory lease. But before this can be done the owner of the land must hold it as a permanent investment, and not as a property to be offered for sale to the first comer. When farm land is so held by the owner, there will be some probability, if not certainty, that it will be permanently improved, and then such property will be largely sought for by tenants who will be able and willing to rent it on long leases and cultivate it in a more productive and profitable manner than farms are now worked. And then will begin a new era in American agriculture, and one that seems to be very desirable."

It is to defeat this deep laid and damnable plot of the money power, and prevent the rich few from gobbling up the soil of America, as it has been gobbled up in England and Ireland—it is to save our farmers from serfdom, and our free soil from the bondage of monopoly, that the Land Reform movement is pushed to the front.

CHAPTER III.

DEBT AND USURY.

"Owe no man anything," was the injunction of a wiser and better man than ancient or modern Shylock. Debt is slavery, which the law should not recognize.

If a man voluntarily bind himself to his neighbor, it is his right—his liberty is his own property; but the right of the neighbor to hold such liberty a moment against the will of the owner, should not be recognized by law.

We would prevent the necessity of debt and usury, by an ample supply of exchange medium to do a cash business. We would abolish the legal relations of debtor and creditor, by repealing all laws for the collection of debt, made after a certain period. It will be said that such a volume of money will render the currency worthless. We deny it, and challenge reasonable proof. There are two great classes in this country who have use for an exchange medium. The producers, of which there are millions, who receive for their products the current money of account. The volume of their products amounts annually to about $6,000,000,000. There is in circulation to pay for this enormous product but about $600,000,000 of currency, or one dollar of currency for ten of products. This deficiency of currency compels products to move slowly, and as our lines of transportation are long, causes trade of all kinds to be sluggish, depresses prices, and compels enormous inflation of credits as a substitute for money. Cities, counties, states, corporations and individuals are obliged to anticipate future incomes, and issue instead, their interest-bearing obligations.

There is another class that handle these $6,000,000,000 of products, or the surplus over the consumption of the producers.

They use a different exchange medium.

They are the bankers, brokers, and great international traders. Their medium of exchange consists of the producers' interest-bearing obligations—bonds and mortgages. Every well secured debt goes to inflate the volume of their currency.

They never go in debt or pay interest.

They have no need of it. The millions upon millions of international transactions are carried on with the use of less than four per cent. of legal tender. The debt system is their main dependence, their chief stock in trade.

This furnishes them an inflated medium of exchange, amounting to many thousands of dollars per capita. The less money the people have, the more they are obliged to go in debt, and the more they go in debt, if debts are well secured, the larger is the interest income of the sharks, and the more their currency is inflated.

Scarcity of money among the people aids the sharks in more ways than one.

It supplies them with a large volume of currency. It prevents the people from contracting it by payment of debts. It yields them a large interest income. It enables them to control the market, and bull and bear prices, to suit their interest. It keeps the people in slavery to them, and enables them through the immense wealth they reap, to control elections, dictate legislation, and thus perpetuate their devilish system of injustice and robbery. We would abolish this system of slavery. We would emancipate humanity from the bondage of debt and usury. It is the mission of the coming revolution.

AUTHORITIES ON USURY—TACITUS ON THE SUBJECT.

"The exaction of interest for the loan of money has been one of the greatest evils of the Roman commonwealth."

A DETESTABLE CUSTOM.

The practice of receiving interest on money is *detestable*, as by it the increase of our fortune arises from the money itself, and not by the employing it to the purpose for which it was intended."—*Aristotle*, Book II, Chap. I.

RECEIVE NO MORE THAN YOU GIVE.

Decretal, Gratian 14--*Quest.* 14, *C.* 1.—"If you lend your money to a man from whom you expect more than you gave, not money alone, but any other thing, whether it be wheat, wine, oil, or any other article; *if you expect to receive any more than you gave you are a usurer*, and, in that respect, reprehensible, not praiseworthy."—*St. Augustine on Psalm xxxvi. An.* 405.

COUNCIL OF TRENT'S CATECHISM.

"Whatever is received above the principal lent, or that capital that was given, whether it be money or anything else that may be purchased or estimated for money, is usury. For it is written in Ezekiel xvi: 'Thou shalt not take usury and increase.' And in Luke vi. 35, our Lord says: 'Lend, hoping for nothing thereby.' *Even among the Gentiles usury was always considered a most grievous and most odious crime.*"

"NOTHING EXCEEDS IN BARBARITY THE MODERN SYSTEM OF USURY."

St. *Chrysostom. Hom. 5, on Matt.*, says: "*Nothing exceeds in barbarity the modern system of usury.* Indeed, these usurers traffic on other people's misfortunes, seeking gain through their adversity; under the pretence of compassion, they dig for the distressed a pit of misery; under the pretence of giving aid, they grind the indigent; extending the hand to receive them into harbor from the storm, they allure him only to be shipwrecked upon shoals and shelves of an unforeseen whirlpool."

"There is nothing really more monstrous in any recorded savagery or absurdity of mankind than that Governments should be able to get money for any folly they may choose to commit by selling to capitalists the right of taxing future generations to the end of time. All the cruelest wars inflicted, all the basest luxuries grasped by the idle classes, are thus paid for by the poor a hundred times over. And yet I am obliged to keep my money in the funds or the bank, because I know of no other mode of keeping it safe; and if I refuse to take the interest, I should only throw it into the hands of the very people who would use it for these evil purposes, or, at all events for less good than I can. Nevertheless, it is daily becoming a more grave question with me what it may presently be right to do. It may be better to diminish private charities, and much more, my own luxury of life, than to comply in any sort with a national sin. But I am not agitated nor anxious in the matter; content to know my principle, and to work steadily towards better fulfillment of it."—JOHN RUSKIN.

BISHOP JEWEL'S TESTIMONY.

In 1560 Bishop Jewel, an eminent Christian divine, wrote as follows on the crime of usury: "Usury is a kind of lending of money, or corne, or oyle, or wine, or of any other thing, wherein, upon covenants and bargaine, we receive again the whole principall which we delivered, *and somewhat more,* for the use and occupying of the same; as if I lend 100 pound, and for it covenant to receive 105 pound, or any other summe, greater than was the summe which I did lend, this is what we call usury; such a kind of bargaining as no good man or godly man ever used. Such a kind of bargaining as all men that ever feared God's judgments have alwaies abhored and condemned. It is filthy gaines and a worke of darkness, it is a monster in nature, the overthrow of mighty kingdoms, the destruction of flourishing States, the decay of wealthy cities, the plagues of the world, and the misery of the people; it is theft, it is the emurthering of our brethren, it's the curse of God and the curse of the people. This is usury. By these signs and tokens you may know it. For wheresoever it raigneth all those mischiefs ensue.

USURY THE WORK OF THE DEVIL.

"Whence springeth usury? Soone shewed. Even thence whence theft, murder, adultery, the plagues, and destruction of the people doe spring. All these are the workes of the divell, and the workes of the flesh. Christ telleth the Pharisees, You are of your father the divell, and the lusts of your father you will doe. Even so may it truely be sayd to the usurer, Thou art of thy father the divell, and the lusts of thy father thou wilt doe, and therefore thou hast pleasure in his workes. The divell entered into the heart of Judas, and put in him this greediness, and covetousness of gaine, for which he was content to sell his Master. Juda's heart was the shop, the divell was the foreman to work in it. They that will be rich fall into tentation and snares, and into many foolish and noysome lusts, which drowne men in perdition and destruction. For the desire of money is the root of all evil. And St. John saith, Whosoever committeth sinne is of the Divell: I. Joh., 3–8. Thus we see that the devill is the planter and father of usury.

WHAT ARE THE FRUITS OF USURY.

"A. 1. It dissolveth the knot and fellowship of mankind. 2. It hardeneth man's heart. 3. It maketh men unnatural, and bereaveth them of charity, and love for their dearest friends. 4. It breedeth misery and provoketh the wrath of God from heaven. 5. It consumeth rich men, it eateth up the poor, it maketh bankrupts and undoeth many householders. 6. The poore occupiers are driven to flee, their wives are left alone, their children are hopeless, and driven to beg their bread, through the unmerciful dealing of the covetous usurer.

"He that is an usurer, wishes that all others may lacke and come to him and borrow of him; that all others may lose, so that he may have gain. Therefore our old forefathers so much abhored this trade, that they thought an usurer unworthy to live in the company of

Christian men. They suffered not a usurer to be witnesse in matters of Law. They suffered him not to make a Testament, and to bestow his goods by will. When an usurer dyed, they would not suffer him to be buried in places appointed for the burial of Christians. So highly did they mislike the unmerciful spoyling and deceiving our brethren.

"But what speak I of the ancient Fathers of the Church? There never was any religion, nor sect, nor state, nor degree, nor profession of men, but they have disliked it. Philosophers, Greeks, Latins, lawyers, divines, Catholice, heretics; all tongues and nations have ever thought an usurer as dangerous as a theefe. The very sense of nature proves it to be so. If the stones could speak, they would say as much."

GOD'S LAW ON USURY.

"And if thy brother be waxen poor, and fallen into decay with thee, *then shalt thou relieve him;* yea though he be a stranger or a sojourner; that he may live with thee. *Thou shalt not give him thy money upon usury, nor lend him thy victuals for increase.*"—*Lev. xxv.* 35, 36.

"If thou lend money to any of my people that is poor that dwelleth with thee, thou shalt not be hard upon him as an extortioner, nor oppress him with usuries."—*Ex. xxii.* 25.

"And I rebuked the nobles and magistrates, and said to them: Do you every one exact usury of your brethren? And I gathered together a great assembly against them." *Nehemiah v.* 7.

"Thou shalt not lend to thy brother money to usury, nor corn, *nor any other thing.* To thy brother thou shalt lend that which he wanteth without usury, that the Lord may bless thee in all thy works."—*Deut. xxiii. 19, 20.*

"Go to now ye rich men, weep and howl for your miseries that shall come upon you. Your riches are corrupted and your garments are moth-eaten; your gold and silver is cankered; and the rust of them shall be a witness against you; and shall eat your flesh as it were fire. * * * * Behold the hire of the laborers who have reaped down your fields which is of you kept back by fraud crieth; and the cries of them which have reaped have entered into the ears of the Lord of Sabaoth. Ye have lived in pleasure on the earth and been wanton; ye have nourished your hearts as in a day of slaughter; ye have condemned and killed the just and he doth not resist you."—*James v. 1-6.*

"Henry VIII was the first monarch who legalized usury in Christendom, Calvin was the first prominent religious teacher who defended it, and Cromwell endorsed it, which so delighted the Jews that they believed him to be the promised Messiah, to give them the dominion of the world, and instituted worship of him in their synagogues, which worship Cromwell promptly suppressed, but permitted their more devastative practices.

"All through these ages to that time, the churches, both Catholic and Protestant, warred upon usury with the same consistency and persistency that they did upon the other deadly sins, but thereafter churchmen became comparatively lukewarm. The term *usury* fell into disuse, and the word *interest* was substituted therefor. Hume, the historian, by no means inclined to liberal ideas, refers very quaintly but pointedly to this substitution as 'a lucky accident in language which has great effect upon men's ideas.' "—*Drew.*

A hundred years before Hume's time, Shakespeare's keen eye had detected the change of terms, and he made Shylock say of Antonio:

> How like a fawning publican he looks!
> I hate him, for he is a Christian;
> But more, for that in low simplicity
> He lends out money gratis, and brings down
> The rate of usance here with us in Venice.
> He rails, where merchants most do congregate,
> On me, my bargains and my well won thrift,
> Which he calls interest.

CHAPTER IV

CONVENTIONS.

BRIEF HISTORY OF NATIONAL POLITICAL CONVENTIONS.

(From Greeley & Cleveland's Political Text-Book, 1860, and other sources.)

National Conventions for the nomination of candidates for President and Vice President are of comparatively recent origin. In the earlier political history of the United States, under the Federal Constitution, candidate for President and Vice President were nominated by congressional and legislative caucuses. Washington was elected as first President under the Constitution, and re-elected for a second term by a unanimous, or nearly unanimous, concurrence of the American people; but an opposition party gradually grew up in Congress, which became formidable during its second term, and which ultimately crystallized into what was then called the Republican Party. John Adams, of Massachusetts, was prominent among the leading Federalists, while Thomas Jefferson, of Virginia, was pre-eminently the author and oracle of the Republican Party, and, by common consent, they were the opposing candidates for the Presidency, on Washington's retirement in 1796-7.

1800.—The first Congressional Caucus to nominate candidates for President and Vice President is said to have been held in Philadelphia, in the year 1800, and to have nominated Mr. Jefferson for the first office, and Aaron Burr for the second. These candidates were elected after a desperate struggle, beating John Adams and Charles C. Pinckney, of South Carolina.

1804.—In 1804 Mr. Jefferson was re-elected President, with George Clinton, of New York, for Vice, encountering but slight opposition; Messrs. Charles C. Pinckney and Rufus King, the opposing candidates, receiving only 14 out of 176 electoral votes. We have been unable to find any record as to the manner of their nomination.

1808.—In January, 1808, when Mr. Jefferson's second term was about to close, a Republican Congressional Caucus was held at Washington, to decide as to the relative claims of Madison and Monroe for the succession, the Legislature of Virginia, which had been said to exert a potent influence over such questions, being, on this occasion, unable to agree as to which of her favored sons should have the preference. Ninety-four out of the 136 Republican members of Congress attended this caucus, and declared their preference of Mr. Madison, who received 83 votes, the remaining 11 being divided between Mr. Monroe and George Clinton. The opposition then supported Mr. Pinckney, but Mr. Madison was elected by a large majority.

1812.—Toward the close of Mr. Madison's earlier term he was nominated for re-election by a Congressional Caucus, held at Washington in May, 1812. In September, of the same year, a convention of the opposition representing eleven States, was held in the City of New York, which nominated DeWitt Clinton, of New York, for President. He was also put in nomination by the Republican Legislature of New York. The ensuing canvass resulted in the re-election of Mr. Madison, who received 128 electoral votes to 89 for DeWitt Clinton.

1816.—In 1816 the Republican Congressional Caucus nominated James Monroe, who received in the caucus 65 votes, to 54 for Wm. H. Crawford, of Georgia. The opposition, or Federalists, named Rufus King, of New York, who received only 34 electoral votes out of 217.

1820.—There was no opposition to the re-election of Mr. Monroe in 1820, a single (Republican) vote being cast against him, and for John Quincy Adams.

1824.—In 1824 the Republican Party could not be induced to abide by the decision of a Congressional Caucus. A large majority of the Republican members formally refused to participate in such a gathering, or be governed by its decision; still, a caucus was called, and attended by the friends of Mr. Crawford alone. Of the 261 Members of Congress at this time, 216 were Democrats or Republicans; yet only 66 responded to their names at roll-call, 64 of whom voted for Mr. Crawford, as the Republican nominee for President. This nomination was very extensively repudiated throughout the country, and three competing Republican candidates were brought into the field through legislative and other machinery, viz.: Andrew Jackson, Henry Clay, and John Quincy Adams. The result of this famous "scrub-race" for the Presidency was, that no one was elected by the people, Gen. Jackson receiving 99 electoral votes, Mr. Adams 84, Mr. Crawford 41, and Mr. Clay 37. The election then devolved on the House of Representatives, when Mr. Adams was chosen, receiving the votes of 13 States, against 7 for Gen. Jackson and 4 for Mr. Crawford. This was the end of "King Caucus."

1828.—Gen. Jackson was immediately thereafter put in nomination for the ensuing term by the Legislature of Tennessee, having only Mr. Adams for an opponent in 1828, when he was elected by a decided majority, receiving 178 electoral votes, to 83 for Mr. Adams.

The first political National Convention in this country of which we have any record was held at Philadelphia in September, 1830, styled the United States Anti-Masonic Convention. It was composed of 96 delegates. Francis Granger, of New York, presided, but no business was transacted.

In compliance with its call, a National Anti-Masonic Convention was held at Baltimore in September, 1831, which nominated William Wirt, of Maryland, for President, and Amos Ellmaker, of Pennsylvania, for Vice President.

The candidates accepted the nomination, and received the electoral vote of Vermont only.

1832.—There was no open opposition in the Democratic Party to the nomination of Gen. Jackson for a second term in 1832, but the party was not so well satisfied with Mr. Calhoun, the Vice-President, so a convention was called to meet at Baltimore, in May, 1832, to nominate a candidate for the second office.

Mr. Van Buren received more than two-thirds of all the votes cast, and was declared nominated.

The National Republicans met in convention at Baltimore, December 12, 1831. Seventeen States and the District of Columbia were represented by 157 delegates, who cast an unanimous vote for Henry Clay, of Kentucky, for President.

1836.—In May, 1835, a Democratic National Convention, representing twenty-one States, assembled at Baltimore. A rule was adopted, that two-thirds of the whole number of votes should be necessary to make a nomination, or to decide any question connected therewith. On the first ballot for President, Mr. Van Buren was nominated unanimously, receiving 265 votes.

In 1835, Gen. William H. Harrison, of Ohio, was nominated for President, with Francis Granger for Vice-President, by a Whig State Convention at Harrisburg, Pa. Gen. Harrison also received nominations in Maryland, New York, Ohio, and other States.

1840.—A Whig National Convention, representing twenty-one States, met at Harrisburg, Pa., December 4, 1839. James Barbour, of Virginia, presided, and the result of the first ballot was the nomination of Gen. William H. Harrison, of Ohio, who received 148 votes, to 90 for Henry Clay, and 16 for Gen. Winfield Scott. John Tyler, of Virginia, was unanimously nominated as the Whig candidate for Vice-President.

A Convention of Abolitionists was held at Warsaw, N. Y., on the 13th of November, 1839, and nominated for President James G. Birney, of New York, and for Vice-President, Francis J. Lemoyne, of Pennsylvania. These gentlemen declined the nomination. Nevertheless, they received a total of 7,609 votes, in various Free States.

A Democratic National Convention met at Baltimore, May 5, 1840, to nominate candidates for President and Vice-President. The Convention then unanimously nominated Mr. Van Buren for re-election as President.

1844.—A Whig National Convention assembled in Baltimore on the 1st of May, 1844, in which every State in the Union was represented, and Mr. Clay was nominated for President by acclamation.

A Democratic National Convention assembled at Baltimore on the 27th of May, 1844, adopted the two-thirds rule, and, after a stormy session of three days, James K. Polk, of Tennessee, was nominated for President, and Silas Wright, of New York, for Vice-President. Mr. Wright declined the nomination, and George M. Dallas, of Pennsylvania, was selected.

The Liberty Party National Convention met at Buffalo on the 30th of August, 1843. James G. Birney, of Michigan, was unanimously nominated for President, with Thomas Morris, of Ohio, for Vice-President.

1848.—A Whig National Convention met at Philadelphia on the 7th of June, 1848. After a rather stormy session of three days, Gen. Zachary Taylor, of Louisiana, was nominated for President, and Millard Fillmore, of New York, for Vice-President.

The Democratic National Convention for 1848 assembled in Baltimore on the 22d of May. The two-thirds rule was adopted, and Gen. Lewis Cass was nominated for President on the fourth ballot.

On the 9th of August, 1848, a Free Democratic or Free Soil Convention was held at Buffalo, which was attended by delegates from seventeen States. Charles Francis Adams, of Massachusetts, presided, and the Convention nominated Messrs. Van Buren and Adams as candidates for President and Vice-President.

1852.—The Whig National Convention of 1852 assembled at Baltimore on the 16th of June, and after an exciting session of six days, nominated Gen. Winfield Scott as President, on the fifty-third ballot.

The Democratic Convention of 1852 assembled at Baltimore on the 1st of June, and the two-thirds rule was adopted. Gen. Franklin Pierce, of New Hampshire, was nominated for President, on the forty-ninth ballot.

The Free Soil Democracy held a National Convention at Pittsburg, on the 11th of August, 1852, Henry Wilson of Mass., presiding. All the Free States were represented, with Delaware, Virginia, Kentucky and Maryland. John P. Hale, of New Hampshire, was nominated for President, with Geo. W. Julian, of Indiana, for Vice-President.

1856.—The Republican National Convention of 1856 met at Philadelphia on the 17th of June. Col. John C. Fremont was unanimously nominated, having received 359 votes on the first ballot against 196 for John McLean.

On February 22, 1856, the American National Nominating Convention organized at Philadelphia, with 227 delegates in attendance. Millard Fillmore was declared to be the nominee, with Andrew Jackson Donelson, of Tennessee, for Vice-President.

The Democratic National Convention of 1856 met at Cincinnati on the 2d of June, and nominated James Buchanan on the seventeenth ballot. John C. Breckinridge, of Kentucky, was unanimously nominated for Vice-President.

A Republican National Convention assembled at Chicago on May 16, 1860, delegates being in attendance from all the Free States, as also from Delaware, Maryland, Virginia, Kentucky, and Missouri. Abraham Lincoln was nominated for the Presidency on the third ballot, receiving 354 out of 466 votes; his principal competitors being William H. Seward, Salmon P. Chase, and Edward Bates.

1860.—A Democratic National Convention assembled at Charleston, S. C., on the 23d of April, 1860, with full delegations present from every State. Dissensions arising, chiefly out of the question of slavery in the Territories, too great to be reconciled, the delegations from seven Southern States withdrew, and the convention adjourned, after fifty-seven ineffectual ballots for a candidate, to meet at Baltimore, June 18. Here Stephen A. Douglas was nominated for President, and B. Fitzpatrick for Vice-President. The latter declined, and H. V. Johnson was substituted by the National Committee. The Convention of Seceders nominated John C. Breckinridge and Joseph Lane.

A "Constitutional Union" Convention from twenty States met at Baltimore, May 9, 1860, and nominated John Bell and Edward Everett for the Presidency and Vice-Presidency.

1864.—The Republican National Convention met at Baltimore, June 7. The re-nomination, for President, of Abraham Lincoln, of Illinois, was made unanimous, he having received the votes of all the States except Missouri, cast for Gen. Grant. For Vice-President, Andrew Johnson, of Tennessee, was nominated on the second ballot, his principal competitors being D. S. Dickinson and H. Hamlin.

The Democratic National Convention met at Chicago, Ill., August 29. Nominations—President, George B. McClellan, of New Jersey; Vice-President, George H. Pendleton, of Ohio.

1868.—The National Republican Convention met at Chicago, Ill., May 20. Nominations—President, Ulysses S. Grant, of Illinois; Vice-President, Schuyler Colfax, of Indiana.

The Democratic National Convention met at New York, July 4. Nominations—President, Horatio Seymour, of New York; Vice-President, Francis P. Blair, Jr., of Missouri.

1872.—The Liberal Republican Convention met at Cincinnati, Ohio, May 1. Nominations—President, Horace Greeley, of New York, on the sixth ballot, by 482 votes, against 187 for David Davis, of Illinois; Vice-President, B. Gratz Brown, of Missouri, on the second ballot.

The Republican National Convention met at Philadelphia, Pa., June 5. Nominations—President, Ulysses S. Grant, on the first ballot, unanimously; Vice-President, Henry Wilson, of Massachusetts, receiving 364½ votes against 321½ for Schuyler Colfax.

The Democratic National Convention met at Baltimore, Md., July 9. Nominations—President, Horace Greeley, on the first ballot, receiving 686 votes to 38 scattering; Vice-President, B. Gratz Brown, who received 713 votes.

The Democratic ("Straight Out") Convention met at Louisville, Ky., September 3. Nominations—President, Charles O'Conor, of New York; Vice-President, John Q. Adams, of Massachusetts. The nominations were declined.

1876.—The Republican National Convention met at Cincinnati, Ohio, June 14. Nominations—President, Rutherford B. Hayes, of Ohio, on the seventh ballot, receiving 384 votes, to 351 for J. G. Blaine, and 21 for B. H. Bristow; Vice-President, William A. Wheeler, of New York.

The Democratic National Convention met at St. Louis, Mo., June 27. Nominations—President, Samuel J. Tilden, of New York, on the second ballot, receiving 535 votes, against 85 for Hendricks, 54 for Wm. Allen, 58 for W. S. Hancock, and six scattering; Vice-President, Thomas A. Hendricks, of Indiana.

A "National Greenback Convention," composed of men opposed to specie resumption and in favor of national paper money to take the place of bank issues, met at Indianapolis, May 17, with nineteen States represented. Peter Cooper, of New York, and Samuel F. Cary, of Ohio, were nominated for President and Vice-President.

A "Prohibition Reform Party" Convention met at Cleveland, May 17, and nominated Green Clay Smith, of Kentucky, and R. T. Stewart, of Ohio.

1880.—The Republican National Convention met at Chicago, June 2, and on the sixth day of the convention nominated James A. Garfield for President, and C. A. Arthur for Vice-President.

The Greenback Labor National Convention met in Chicago, June 9, and nominated Gen. J. B. Weaver for President, and B. J. Chambers, of Texas, for Vice-President.

The Democratic National Convention met in Cincinnati, June 23, and nominated Gen. W. S. Hancock for President, and W. H. English for Vice-President.

CHAPTER V.

PLATFORM

OF THE GREENBACK LABOR PARTY, ADOPTED AT THE NATIONAL CONVENTION, HELD IN CHICAGO, JUNE 9 AND 10, 1880.

Civil Government should guarantee the divine right of every laborer to the results of his toil, thus enabling the producers of wealth to provide themselves with the means for physical comfort, and the facilities for mental, social and moral culture; and we condemn as unworthy of our civilization the barbarism which imposes upon the wealth producers a state of perpetual drudgery as the price of bare animal existence.

Notwithstanding the enormous increase of productive power, the universal introduction of labor-saving machinery, and the discovery of new agents for the increase of wealth, the task of the laborer is scarcely lightened, the hours of toil are but little shortened, and few producers are lifted from poverty into comfort and pecuniary independence.

The associated monopolies, the international syndicates and other income classes demand dear money and cheap labor, a "strong Government," and hence a weak people.

Corporate control of the volume of money has been the means of dividing society into hostile classes; of the unjust distribution of the products of labor, and of building up monopolies of associated capital, endowed with power to confiscate private property. It has kept money scarce, and scarcity of money enforces debt-trade, and public and corporate loans—debt engenders usury, and usury ends in the bankruptcy of the borrower.

Other results are, deranged markets, uncertainty of manufacturing enterprise and agriculture, precarious and intermittent employment for the laborer, industrial war, increasing pauperism and crime and the consequent intimidation and disfranchisement of the producer, and a rapid declension into corporate feudalism.

Therefore we declare—

1. That the right to make and issue money is a sovereign power to be maintained by the people for the common benefit. The delegation of this right to corporations is a surrender of the central attribute of sovereignty, void of constitutional sanction, conferring upon a subordinate irresponsible power, and absolute dominion over industry and commerce. All money, whether metallic or paper, should be issued and its volume controlled by the Government and not by or

through banking corporations, and when so issued should be a full legal tender for all debts, public and private.

2. That the bonds of the United States should not be refunded, but paid as rapidly as it is practicable, according to contract. To enable the Government to meet these obligations, legal tender currency should be substituted for the notes of the national banks, the national banking system abolished, and the unlimited coinage of silver as well as gold established by law.

3. That labor should be so protected by national and state authority as to equalize its burdens and insure a just distribution of its results; the eight-hour law of Congress should be enforced; the sanitary condition of industrial establishments placed under rigid control; the competition of contract convict labor abolished; a bureau of labor statistics established; factories, mines and workshops inspected; the employment of children under fourteen years of age forbidden, and wages paid in cash.

4. Slavery being simply cheap labor, and cheap labor being simply slavery, the importation and presence of Chinese serfs necessarily tends to brutalize and degrade American labor; therefore immediate steps should be taken to abrogate the Burlingame treaty.

5. Railroad land grants forfeited by reason of non-fulfillment of contract should be immediately reclaimed by the Government; and henceforth the public domain reserved exclusively as homes for actual settlers.

6. It is the duty of Congress to regulate inter-state commerce. All lines of communication and transportation should be brought under such legislative control as shall secure moderate, fair and uniform rates for passenger and freight traffic.

7. We denounce, as destructive to prosperity and dangerous to liberty, the action of the old parties in fostering and sustaining gigantic land, railroad and money corporations and monopolies, invested with, and exercising, powers belonging to the Government, and yet not responsible to it for the manner of their use.

8. That the constitution, in giving Congress the power to borrow money, to declare war, to raise and support armies, to provide and maintain a navy, never intended that the men who loaned their money for an interest consideration should be preferred to the soldier and sailor who periled their lives and shed their blood on land and sea in defense of their country, and we condemn the cruel class legislation of the Republican party which, while professing great gratitude to the soldier, has most unjustly discriminated against him, and in favor of the bondholder.

9. All property should bear its just proportion of taxation, and we demand a graduated income tax.

10. We denounce as most dangerous the efforts everywhere manifest to restrict the right of suffrage.

11. We are opposed to an increase of the standing army in time of peace, and the insidious scheme to establish an enormous military power under the guise of militia laws.

12. We demand absolute democratic rules for the Government of Congress, placing all representatives of the people upon an equal footing, and taking away from committees a veto power greater than that of the President.

13. We demand a Government of the people, by the people, and for the people, instead of a Government of the bondholder, by the bondholder, and for the bondholder; and we denounce every attempt to stir up sectional strife as an effort to conceal monstrous crimes against the people.

14. In the furtherance of these ends we ask the co-operation of all fair-minded people. We have no quarrel with individuals, we wage no war upon classes, but only against vicious institutions. We are not content to endure further discipline from our present actual rulers, who, having dominion over money, over transportation, over land and labor, over the machinery of Government, and largely over the press, wield unwarrantable power over our institutions, and over life and property.

JEFFERSON'S POLITICAL MAXIMS.

1. Legal equality of human beings.
2. The people the only source of legitimate power.
3. Absolute and lasting severance of Church and State.
4. Freedom, sovereignty and independence of the respective States.
5. The Union a compact—neither consolidation nor a centralization.
6. Constitution of the Union a special written grant of powers, limited and definite.
7. No hereditary offices, nor order, nor title.
8. No taxation beyond the public want.
9. No National debts if possible.
10. No costly splendor of administration.
11. No proscription of opinion nor of public discussion.
12. No unnecessary interference with individual property or speech.
13. The civil paramount to the military authority.
14. The representative to obey the instructions of his constituents.
15. No favored classes, no monopolies.
16. Elections free, and suffrage universal.
17. No public moneys expended except by warrant of specific appropriation.
18. No mysteries in Government inaccessible to the public eye.
13. Public compensation for public services, moderate salaries, and pervading economy and accountability.

CHAPTER VI.

WHAT CONGRESS HAS DONE FOR SHYLOCK.

In a speech delivered in Congress May 10, 1880, contrasting the Government's generosity toward the money kings with its niggardly treatment of the soldiers, Gen. J. B. Weaver said:

"Now, Mr. Chairman, how has the Government dealt with other classes of public creditors—the bond holding, money-lending classes? Behold the contrast! Soldiers, read, and then avenge yourselves and families at the ballot-box.

"1. When the soldier was absent in the field, when he could not be present in Congress to protect himself and family, the money interest, bankers, and brokers, were permitted to put the sting of death in the back of every greenback bill issued, for the very purpose of depreciating it and rendering it less valuable than gold, and on purpose to make a market for their gold coin.

"2. They were then permitted to buy in the greenbacks at an enormous discount, and in turn to convert them into 5.20 bonds, drawing six per cent. interest in coin.

"3. They procured their bond investments to be exempted from every species of taxation, national, state, and municipal.

"4. Congress then passed an act whereby the bondholder had his interests paid quarterly.

"5. He was allowed by joint resolution of Congress,

approved March 17, 1864, to draw his coin interest in advance for a period not to exceed one year, with or without rebate, at the discretion of the secretary of the treasury, and from 1864 to 1869, when gold was at its highest premium, he was permitted by that law to draw his gold interest in advance without rebate, as appears from an official letter now in my possession signed by H. F. French, acting secretary of the treasury, and dated April, 1880. Under this law the owner of a Government bond for $1,000,000 could draw $60,000 in gold interest in advance; he could then turn around and buy with his $60,000 $150,000 in greenbacks, and then again invest his greenbacks at their face value in 5.20 bonds.

"6. After the money-changer had invested his last dollar in bonds and drawn all the interest possible in advance, and invested that also in Government bonds, he was generously permitted by the national bank act to deposit his securities with the treasury and draw ninety per cent. of their value in national bank notes, which he could use as money, charging him therefor but one per cent. to cover cost of printing.

"7. The 5.20 bonds were payable in the same kind of money that bought them, namely, greenbacks. To prevent this, as will be seen by the following, John Sherman's report to the Senate in 1867, the "credit-strengthening act" of 1869 and the refunding bill of 1870 were passed. After showing by an unanswerable argument that the 5.20 bonds would be paid in currency, Mr. Sherman, in his report, says:

"'It has been proposed that Congress, by resolution, declare that the 5.20 bonds are redeemable only in gold. This, instead of settling the question, will only create divisions and parties, and the resolution when passed will be subject to agitation and repeal. This consideration induces your committee, without deciding the question, to propose the substitution of new bonds, clear and explicit in their terms, for the old bonds, as they become redeemable.'

"This added at least as a mere gift, six hundred millions to the value of the bondholder's investment.

"8. By a clause in the funding bill of 1870, the interest on bonds was also exempted from every species of tax—national, state, or municipal.

"9. In 1873, when the country was suffering from the blight of panic, when the farms of this country went under mortgage, and the bankrupt courts were filled with suitors, the money-changers, to prevent their investments from being interfered with by payment, procured the demonetization of silver, thus making their bonds payable in gold only.

"10. In furtherance of their scheme, through their pliant tool, the present secretary of the treasury, they now, in defiance of law, refuse to pay out the silver coined under the act of 1878, and keep it hoarded in the treasury, and are constantly belaboring Congress for new appropriations to build vaults in which to store it.

"11. They passed the resumption act in 1875, whereby it was provided that every greenback in existence should be taken out of circulation and converted into interest-bearing bonds. They were only prevented from the consummation of this diabolical purpose by the force of public sentiment, which compelled Congress to pass the act of May 30, 1878, forbidding further destruction of the legal tenders.

"12. Notwithstanding the passage of the act last referred to, the National Bankers' association, the capitalists in Boston, New York, Philadelphia, Baltimore, Milwaukee, and Chicago, have petitioned Congress to destroy the legal tenders.

"In obedience to their behest, and utterly regardless of the interests of the industrial classes of the country, the President of the United States, the secretary of the treasury, and the comptroller of the currency have all sent in to Congress their official communication recommending that the greenback shall be taken out of circulation. Mr. Bayard in the Senate and Mr. Lounsberry and Mr. Ballou in the House have introduced bills and joint resolutions to carry out these recommendations.

"13. They now propose by Mr. Fernando Wood's and Garfield's bills, pending before Congress, to refund seven hundred million of these non-taxable bonds and to make them irredeemable for the twenty years.

"14. Since their return from the war, the soldiers, being among the most active and industrious members of society, have been working through sunshine and storm to pay their own and the bondholder's taxes and the interest on the public debt. Wherever a discretion has been lodged with the secretary of the treasury or any other department, it has invariably been exercised in the interest of the bondholder and against the soldier and the common people. (See note C, appendix.

CHAPTER VII.

OUR "FLAT-HEAD" POLICY.

There is a tribe of Indians called "Flat-heads" whose name is derived from having their heads flattened in infancy, while the skull bones are soft and pliable. They are a very low and ignorant people, from the fact that the compressed and distorted skull does not permit a healthy and natural development of the brain; but their mental poverty is in part compensated by their ignorance and lack of appreciation of any higher intelligence.

The female Chinese foot is encased in a shoe prison, and there made to mature without being permitted to expand beyond the dimensions of infancy. Both the head of the Indian and the foot of the Celestial adapt themselves to circumstances, while the body physical seems to suffer little or no inconvenience from the distortion of the extremities. Like a potato grown between two roots, the whole body grows to maturity adapting itself to its conditions, the process being so gradual that no violence is experienced. But suppose the Flat-Heads should capture a prisoner, and should say, "Look here, sir, your head is 'inflated,' it is altogether out of proportion, it is unlike any head in our tribe, it must be 'contracted,' and brought down to the tribal standard."

How long after the process of contraction commenced before suffering would follow? Then the Flat-Head would say, "Grin and bear it; don't suspend the vice-grip, or allow any re-inflation. This comes of your own folly. You have permitted a great over-production of skull; and if we let up now to give you rest, or allow the pain to ease, you will have to travel the terrible road all over again." So by inches the life is squeezed out of the man. The Chinese might cultivate small feet for his daughter, if taken in infancy, without much inconvenience to the child, but if he took a full grown American girl, and should attempt to contract her feet to the standard of a Chinese belle, he would have a cripple for life on his hands.

So it is, we have a nation of financial flat-heads.

The business of a country always corresponds to its money volume. The financiers of Europe and America have cramped the business and enterprise of civilization to the moulds of gold and silver money. For a hundred years the infant brain of American industry was cramped and confined to the narrow walls of this metallic mould. But when the war came, when the life of the Government demanded great power, and a more rapid development of wealth and national life-forces than could be generated in the traditional flat-head system, the pressure was removed. Natural freedom was allowed, labor, skill and enterprise were untrameled, and permitted to come in direct contact with God's bountiful resources, as the leaden anchor of specie was raised, and the light wings of legal tender were spread to the breezes of commerce.

During one decade, untrameled and unoppressed by the vices of specie basis, our business grew into giant proportions. The wealth of the nation doubled, and a degree of prosperity prevailed never before experienced. But after the war closed, when the Government was no longer in danger, when it was safe to hamper and cripple industry, when suicides, privation, idleness, business prostration and general bankruptcy might safely be indulged in for the gratification of the financial flat-head idolators, we were required to enter again upon a life of industrial torture and financial distortion. Our business capacity enlarged to the dimensions of $2,000,000,000 of circulating medium, with an abundance of labor, skill, machinery, and resources to keep it growing for all time to come, was legislated into the flat-head press in 1866, with a view of compressing it to *ante-bellum* dimensions.

CHAPTER VIII.

THE GREAT NATIONAL BEAR.

It is related that in the canton of Berne, in Switzerland, it had been customary from time immemorial, to keep a bear at public expense, and the people had been taught to believe that if they had not a bear on hand, they would be undone, and the country would go to wreck and ruin. So they endured the bear, notwithstanding the expense, and the fatal injury that he inflicted upon pigs and children that happened to step over the line of his jurisdiction. It happened one day that bruin sickened and died too suddenly to have his place immediately supplied with another.

During the interim the people were amazed and delighted to see that the sun continued to shine, the corn to grow and the vintage to flourish, and everything went on the same as before, saving the danger and expense of the bear. So they came to the sensible conclusion not to keep any more bears.

With no more sense, and at much greater expense, the civilized world has been harboring and keeping a bear for the last two thousand years. Every civilized nation has had its bear.

Our revolutionary fathers repulsed the British lion, but accepted the embrace of the English bear, specie basis. It has been an expensive and dangerous beast to keep. In 1809 its depredations occasioned great public distress, and in several instances involved the entire country in bankruptcy and ruin, from which it took years to recover.

In 1814, 1819, 1825, and at other periods, the beast got on his periodical rampage, producing the most terrible and disastrous results.

But the bear must be kept or we, like the peasants of Berne, would be undone.

He was the idol of civilization.

To him society offered up its sacrifices with the same devotion that Hindoo mothers yield up their babes to the crocodiles of the Ganges.

One day he sickened and died. It was on the 25th day of February, 1862.

Devout worshipers from Boston, New York and Philadelphia flocked to Washington to weep and howl over his untimely death.

They were frantic and unconsolable. They feared the sun would cease to shine, the crops to grow, or the tide to ebb and flow.

But time passed on.

The sun kept its course.

The seasons came and went just as of old.

People prospered as they never had before.

Men grew rich.

Labor was fully employed, well paid, and not molested.

Success crowned every effort.

Civilization extended, and the wilderness disappeared.

The rose blossomed where the tangle brush grew.

Railroads spanned the unknown waste.

The march of improvement kept time to the music of machinery and the hum of industry.

There was no bear to molest or make afraid.

Still idolatry, like the old man of the sea, clung to the public mind. Men could not believe that prosperity without gold could be real. They prayed for the return of their idol, and warned society that for all its seeming prosperity and delusive dreams of wealth, corresponding sacrifices must be made to their idol or the country would be a howling bedlam of madmen and fanatics. So on the 12th day of April, 1866, Keeper McCulloch was ordered to commence negotiations for a bear. Immense sacrifices of men and property followed. The first year 2,000 men fell, and over $80,000,000 were lost.

Each succeeding year the number of human sacrifices increased, and the amount of pecuniary loss augmented, until the reinstatement of the beast in 1879, 10,000 men and firms having fallen, and $300,000,000 wealth being sacrificed in the previous year.

Now we have our blood-thirsty god re-installed, and John Sherman as high priest.

Over and above his depredations on society, past and prospective, which is beyond computation, he has cost our treasury direct $230,000,000, for which our bonds are out drawing interest from labor.

Yes, we have on our hands a two hundred and thirty million dollar bear, of no use to society but to eat annually ten or fifteen million dollars' worth of food which society has to furnish, and to be in fashion with the idolatrous nations of Europe, every one of which to-day is a bleeding sacrifice to this brutish god. There he stands watched over and adored by John Sherman, devouring the substance of the people, jeopardizing commerce and trade and menacing labor and enterprise at every step.

These be thy gods, oh, Shylock!

CHAPTER IX.

ENGLAND'S AMERICAN POLICY.

ENGLAND IS PREPARING BY MODERN COMMERCIAL METHODS TO ABSORB THE SUBSTANCE OF AMERICA.

It is officially announced that William H. Vanderbilt has sold 250,000 shares of the New York Central stock to a syndicate of New York capitalists, representing the heaviest banking houses of London, and thus parted with his control over that thoroughfare. This colossal railroad syndicate includes most, or all, of John Sherman's famous bond syndicate, notably August Belmont & Co., Bliss, Morton & Co., J. & W. Seligman & Co., Drexel, Morgan & Co., and J. S. Morgan & Co., of London. Every one of these firms are branches, or agents, of London bankers. To the casual reader, or observer, this huge transaction may look legitimate and innocent enough on its face, as an ordinary business operation, with no more significance than the daily transactions of the stock board. But when viewed in the light of that policy which has governed England for two hundred years, by which she has accumulated a larger amount of capital in proportion to her area and population than was ever before or since scraped together, it looks like an important step in the progress of events long since planned to recover through capital and diplomacy, what she lost a century ago through bullets and American patriotism.

It is England's boast that the sun never sets on her dominions. If she has not conquered all the world, she has at least conquered parts of all the world, and from conquests comes the wealth which she is accumulating. She subdues weak nations not to enlighten, Christianize, and protect, but to enslave and rob. She is to-day the world's great nationalized pirate, with her commercial privateers infesting every sea and navigable stream on the globe. She has picked the bones of poor Ireland dry, and for years the air of India has been fetid with the dead carcases of the victims of her greed and rapacity. Her policy has been "to buy hides of her dependencies for sixpence and sell back to them the tails for a shilling." She conquers to open a market for her manufactured products, to obtain a supply of cheap raw material, and to afford traffic for her means of transportation.

A hundred and fifty years ago one Andrew Gee published in England a work on trade, in which, among other things, he said:

"Manufactures in our American colonies should be discouraged—prohibited. We ought always to keep a watchful eye over our colonies *to restrain them from setting up any of the manufactures which are carried on in England, and any such attempt should be crushed out at the beginning.*

"As they have the providing of rough materials to themselves, so should we have the manufacturing of them. This will turn their industry all to promoting and raising raw material. If we examine into the facts, it will appear that not one-fourth of their product redounds to their own profit, for, out of all that comes here, they only carry back clothing and other necessaries for their families."

During the eighteenth century the American colonies became comparatively independent of the mother country. They had gone somewhat extensively into manufacturing what they needed. By this means they found a ready home market for their surplus raw material, and to supply their monetary wants every colony issued its own paper legal tenders, which, not only made them comparatively independent of England, but contributed vastly to their growth and prosperity. In 1710 a law was enacted in parliament which declared that manufacturing in the colonies tended to lessen their dependence on Great Britain.

In 1750 iron manufacturing in the colonies was prohibited.

In 1765 the emigration of iron artisans to America was prohibited by law.

In 1780 utensils required for the manufacture of wool or silk were prohibited.

In 1781 the exportation of hats from one colony to another was prohibited, and the number of apprentices was limited.

In 1782 no artificer in printing calico, muslins or linens was permitted to emigrate to America.

In 1785 the prohibition was extended to tools used in iron or steel manufacture and to workmen employed.

In 1763 the issue and use of colonial money was suppressed by act of parliament.

Their object was to secure as extensive a market as possible for their manufactured products.

To obtain this, manufacturing in other parts of the world must be discouraged or prohibited.

They also desired cheap raw material and an abundance of it. To obtain this, manufacturing must not only be prevented in other countries, so as to force all labor into the production of raw material, but the money of all nations must be so limited and restricted that prices would remain low, hence the specie standard was established, and gold deified as the God-ordained money of the world. It was only when we discarded this standard, and adopted the legal tender money of the United States, that we were really free and prosperous? But England has again forced us to bow to her idol. Our industries are again in the coils of her deadly embrace. The New York *Tribune* boasts that resumption has driven hundreds of thousands of artisans from unproductive manufacturing into the cultivation of the soil and the raising of a surplus for a foreign market. How did it happen that our manufacturing became unprofitable, and sent 600,000 artisans into the fields to compete with already unprofitable agriculture? A commission appointed by parliament to inquire into the causes of distress and disaffection among English workingmen, reported as follows:

"We believe the laboring classes are very little aware of the extent to which they are often indebted for their being employed at all, to the immense losses which their employers voluntarily incur in order to destroy foreign competition, and to gain and keep possession of foreign markets.

"The large capitalists of this country are the great instruments of warfare against the competing capitalists of foreign countries, and are the most essential instruments now remaining by which British manufactures can maintain the supremacy. The elements, cheap labor, cheap and abundant raw material, and means of transportation, are rapidly in process of being realized."

This report says that English manufacturers have sold their goods at an annual aggregate loss of $100,000,000, in order to undersell and break down foreign competition. This is why manufacturing has become unprofitable in America, and 600,000 artisans were driven into the western lands to raise cheap raw material for English factories. Foreign capital already controls our banking institutions, regulates our monetary affairs, dictates our financial legislation, and successfully opposes all measures inimical to its interests. It has come to pass that but few men can be elected to our national legislature, and none to the position of chief executive, who are not identified with, or pledged to the support of the banking interest. This was the most important step in the plot. The control over our financial affairs, so as to depress industry and discourage enterprise, with the cutting of prices in England, was the step necessary to kill competition. This they have well-nigh accomplished.

They have regained their manufacturing supremacy. They have procured cheap labor and an abundance of cheap raw material in America. They have already a monopoly of transportation by sea; the great carrying trade between the two continents being borne under the British flag.

Her next step will be to get possession and control of our trunk railroad lines from the seaboard to the centers of production; nor will she cease until she succeeds in monopolizing our inland, as well as our ocean commerce. This monopoly of our transportation lines, can not only make their own terms with producers, but control the votes of the nation as the Pennsylvania railroad has for years commanded the vote and dictated the legislation of that State. It may be possible that our inland transportation, as well as our medium of exchange, will yet require the protecting arm of the Government.

Powers as great and dangerous as those wielded by banking and railroad monopolies, should not be exercised by individuals or corporations, much less by foreigners and aliens. These have already become too formidable for legislatures and officials to contend with, and unless the people put forth a united effort to save themselves, their boasted independence will become a phantom, and their temple will fall when grappled by these giant pirates of the land and sea.

CHAPTER X.

THE ARROGANCE OF CAPITAL.

IT DEMANDS A STRONG GOVERNMENT—A STRONGER GOVERNMENT MEANS A WEAKER PEOPLE—SHARON'S VIEWS—WEALTH MUST RULE THE COUNTRY, OR RIVERS OF BLOOD WILL FLOW.

There are many honest and patriotic Republicans who sincerely believe that their party is as loyal to popular liberty, and to the great industrial interests of the country, to-day as it was fifteen or twenty years ago when it was struggling to wrest liberty and labor from the despotism of slavery. They refuse to believe that the machinery of the Republican party, like *The Tribune* of Horace Greeley, has been usurped by despots, and seized upon by the enemies of justice, equality and popular liberty, who are using it for baser purposes than ever the Democratic party was made to serve after it prostituted itself at the feet of the Slave Power. When it is charged by the advocates of the people's rights that the tendency and aims of the Republican party are to destroy constitutional liberty and to build up and protect a plutocracy of organized capital, to grind the poor, and to oppress and rob the producing classes, it is not believed by the Republican masses who are being led blindly to their own slaughter. But if they will not believe Moses and the prophets, will they believe one of their own chosen oracles? The following from the pen of Senator Sharon, published in his own organ, *The Nevada Chronicle*, is testimony that no Republican can impeach or deny. He says:

"We need a stronger Government. The wealth of the country demands it. Without capital and the capitalists, our Government would not be worth a fig. The capital of the country demands protection; its rights are as sacred as the rights of the paupers, who are continually prating about the encroachment of capital and against centralization. *We have tried Grant and we know him to be the man for the place above all others.* He has nerve. As President he would be Commander-in-Chief of the army and navy, and when the communistic tramps of the country raised mobs to tear up railroad tracks and to sack cities on the sham cry of 'bread or blood,' he would not hesitate to turn loose upon them canister and grape. *The wealth of the country has to bear the burdens of the Government, and it shall control it.* The people are becoming educated up to this theory rapidly, and the sooner this theory is recognized in the constitution and laws the better it will be for the people.

"*Without bloodshed, and rivers of it, there will be no political change of administration.* The monied interests of the country for self-preservation *must sustain the Republican party.* The railroads, the banks, the manufacturers, the heavy importers, and all classes of business in which millions are invested, will maintain the supremacy of the Republican party. Democratic success would be bankruptcy to them. *To avert fearful bloodshed a strong central Government should be established as soon as possible.*"

A little more frank than his co-conspirators, Senator

Sharon, no doubt, reflects the sentiments of the leaders of his party.

The wealth of the nation demands a stronger Government, for the capital of the country requires protection.

What is this Republican idea of a "stronger Government," and what capital of the country is in danger, that it cannot be protected by our present form of popular Government?

Is there a crime against person or property known to society that is not amply guarded against by statutes and penalties? Have we not an ample judiciary and constabulary in every city, town, and hamlet to protect the innocent and to punish the guilty? Does not capital collect its interest, its rents, and its exorbitant rates of transportation? Does it not foreclose its mortgages and confiscate its collaterals?

Where, and what, is the danger that threatens the money kings, demanding a Government stronger than that which has served us for a century and proved itself the "strongest" on the globe?

On the frontiers, in the mining districts, where the prospects of immediate gain attract large numbers of the worst desperadoes in the country, extraordinary measures are sometimes resorted to. The law may be deemed too tardy to meet the demands of justice, and the vigilance committee is substituted as a necessity of the emergency. But does the Republican party propose to transform the Government into a great national vigilance committee to arrest and execute, without the form of law, all such restless spirits as squirm under the iron heel of capital, or rebel at the robbery and extortion of oppressive monopolies?

No, it is not the fear that the masses will violate law

that demands a stronger Government, *but that they will repeal unjust statutes, and restrain by wholesome legislation over-reaching and oppressive combinations of capital from robbing the industrial masses,* and enact those more in accordance with the spirit of the Declaration of Independence and the rights of man.

Fifteen thousand million dollars of interest-bearing obligations have been filched and forced from the people through the Republican legislation of the last eighteen years. This is the capital that demands protection at the hands of a stronger, centralized power. Resumption of specie payment has doubled its value, and the object and aim of its owners are to perpetuate it, and to add still more to its value by the establishment of the single gold standard.

After the Saxon brigands and freebooters had robbed the Britons of their soil and their subsistence, they levied annual pensions and annuities upon their victims in amount sufficient to subsist the robbers and their posterity for all time to come in affluence and royal splendor, and in order to perpetuate this scheme of rapine and plunder, they saw that it was necessary to debar their victims for all time to come from any voice in the political affairs of the nation, and to centralize and perpetuate the sovereign power of the realm in the hands of the beneficiaries of their scheme of spoliation, and their hereditary representatives.

A few thousand men in this republic have combined, and through the aid of deception and false pretences, secured legislation which has put them in a position to levy contributions upon American industry as unjust and burdensome as those laid by the Norman robbers upon the labor of Britain. This combination of men consists of the bankers and railroad companies. They have consolidated their interests and are now prepared to enter upon their gigantic work of pillage.

The former, controlling the medium of exchange, and holding interest-bearing obligations against the people which draw annually $1,000,000,000 of their substance, can control prices, while the latter, by monopolizing the routes and medium of transportation, together form a combination with ample power, if unmolested, to reap the harvest of every field of industry, and every department of enterprise and production in the country. But to do this they need protection—they need a stronger Government. Power must be taken from the working people to defend themselves. Those who are robbed must be denied the means of defense and self-protection. Power in America, as in Europe, must be centralized in the hands of the robbers.

It is not the vandalism of the pauper and the tramp that calls for a stronger Government, but the freedom of the press and the suffrages of the outraged millions need to be suppressed; for when the millions of freemen become aroused to the dangers which threaten their liberty and their prosperity, they will repeal statutes which sustain robbing monopolies. The "rights of capital," in the sense in which it is used by Senator Sharon, are not as sacred as the rights of the pauper. Every fortune of a million dollars possessed by one man, is made up of the substance wrongfully filched from other men, forcing them into pauperism. The pauper is the inevitable result of the millionaire. To be a millionaire necessitates the existence of a thousand paupers. If 30,000 men in America were millionaires they would possess all the wealth of the nation, leaving 45,000,000 paupers. The tendency of monopoly and consolidated capital is to bring about this result.

It can be averted only by the immediate and determined action of the people restraining this tendency, and limiting and controlling monopoly by such legislation as will permit a more just and equitable distribution of the products of wealth, and give to every producer the full earnings of his labor.

The people need not be deceived.

The edict has gone forth.

Capital has declared war upon labor and threatens to shed rivers of blood if the latter does not consent to be robbed and enslaved by the former.

A stronger Government means a weaker people. To centralize power, means to strip the people of their liberties, their franchises, and their sovereignty, to confer them upon a despot.

Are the people ready for their chains?

Their clank may be heard in the halls of Congress. Don't mistake it for the jingle of resumption.

CHAPTER XI.

A FARMERS' REPUBLIC.

TO THE FARMERS OF AMERICA.

The last report of the commissioner of agriculture estimates the number of males of all occupations in the United States at 15,000,000, and that more than half of this number, to-wit, 7,600,000, are engaged in agricultural pursuits.

That the total value of farms, farm animals and farm implements is $13,461,200,433, or two-thirds of the total productive wealth of the nation.

That the value of farm products and animals for 1878 was $3,000,000,000, against $2,800,000,000 of mining and manufacturing products.

Thus it appears that not only a majority of the people of the United States are engaged in agriculture, but a majority of the wealth is invested in it, and a majority of the products of the nation is derived from that source. So far, the farmers are the predominating class in society. They can have things pretty much their own way, if they act in harmony. There are also 2,900,000 men engaged in mining and manufacturing, whose interests are identical with the interests of the farmer. These two classes constitute two-thirds of the voting population of the country. These two classes produce all the wealth and pay all the taxes, but exercise little or no influence in shaping the policies of the Government, or in disbursing the vast sums they annually contribute. These privileges have been usurped, and are exercised by a class of non-taxed and non-producers, who make politics a profession, and office an occupation to be exercised in the interest of clients who will pay the largest fees.

Nearly every lawyer who chooses that profession for a livelihood, regards it as the only path to political promotion. Men enter the legal profession as a stepping-stone to official position. The first lesson that a lawyer is taught is to ignore right and justice, and labor with all his zeal and powers for a client, regardless of the merits or justice of his case. If a murderer is brought into court with his hands red with the blood of innocence, the lawyer, who for a fee undertakes his defense, labors as zealously for his acquittal as though he were as innocent as a babe.

The Congress of the United States, and the legislatures of the several States, have become political bars, supported at the expense of the people, to engineer and pettifog measures through to final legislative judgment in the interest of capitalistic stock jobbers and financial gamblers. If a clan of Wall Street gold gamblers desire the money of the country to be depreciated so they may gamble and wrench from society vast sums by gold speculations, they have simply to employ the ablest attorneys in Congress, have a bill passed to make all duties on imports and interest on the bonds payable in gold, and then take from the greenback the legal tender quality of money so as to depreciate it and furnish a market for their gold. The people are thus defrauded because they have no representation in that body. It is composed of an army of lawyers. If one or a dozen get a big job from Vanderbilt, Scott, Belmont, the Rothschilds or the national banks, it goes through by courtesy, those not directly employed and paid not knowing how soon they may have a paying case, and need a similar courtesy.

Look at the legislation for the past sixteen years. It has been a series of jobs for the benefit of capitalistic monopolies, and not one act for the benefit of the farmer and the manufacturer.

On the other hand, the legislation of the past few years, made in the interest of banks, bondholders, capital and railroad monopolies, has had the intended effect of adding billions to the wealth of these congressional clients, every dollar of which has been filched from the tax-paying, producing, misrepresented farmers and manufacturers.

Congress and legislatures have ceased to represent the people; the lobby alone constitutes their clientage. This is not to be wondered at. They are not only encouraged in it by re-elections, but are paid for it by the beneficiaries of their venality.

The producing classes have the power of protection and redress in their own hands, but notwithstanding they have been robbed, stripped and flayed by inferior numbers, they march to the polls like lambs to the slaughter, and under the lash of party discipline vote for the same men and measures which have ruined them, and thus license them to continue their nefarious schemes of plunder.

During the years of our greatest industrial and commercial prosperity, eleven millions of laborers, artisans, agriculturists, mechanics and manufacturers, wrought annually from the raw material, the earth and its resources, the following products and values (as gathered from reliable statistics), for use and general distribution, to add to the already accumulated wealth of the nation:

Products of artisans, machinists, carpenters, blacksmiths, masons and the like	$1,000,000,000
Leather manufactures	226,000,000
Iron and steel manufactures	120,000,000
Cotton manufactures	71,500,000
Woolen manufacturing	66,000,000
Unskilled labor and distributors	1,600,000,000
Fisheries	100,000,000
Railway service	360,000,000
Agriculture	3,300,000,000
Making the gross product of the country	$7,000,000,000

This wealth was produced by the heads of families and other persons representing 98 per cent. of the entire population of the United States.

It was at a time when gold and silver were entirely out of use as a medium of exchange, and a large and generous supply of greenbacks constituted the money of the realm. The volume of the circulating medium approximated $2,000,000,000. The only real uses the country had for this money was to purchase the raw material, pay for the labor, and to distribute the above products. The eleven millions of wealth-producers were alone interested in the *quality* and *quantity* of this important tool of trade.

No man or set of men, who were not engaged in actual production, had a right to a voice in determining what kind or quantity of tools the producers should be supplied with. For the first time in the history of the nation, the wealth-producers were accidentally, through the emergencies of the war, provided with anything like an adequate supply of money. Even this supply was met with bitter and powerful opposition by parties both in this and foreign countries, not by producers of wealth, but by gamblers in the product of others' toil. Not one of the ninety-eight per cent. of the people objected to the increase of the money volume, or complained that greenbacks had been substituted for gold. After the war, when the nation's existence, and the perpetuity of the union were no longer in jeopardy, a system of contraction was inaugurated, to squeeze out of use and circulation the excess of money which the war had forced into the channels of trade and production. So in his report of December 4, 1865, Hugh McCulloch said to Congress:

"The issue of United States notes as lawful money was a measure of expediency, doubtless, and necessary in the great emergency in which it was adopted, but this emergency no longer exists, *and however satisfactory these notes may be as a circulating medium, and however desirable may be the saving of interest*, these considerations will not satisfy a departure from that *construction* of the constitution which is essential to the equal and harmonious working of our *peculiar institutions*."

The "peculiar institutions" which Mr. McCulloch referred to as being unbalanced by the excess of war money, were not those of labor, enterprise and production, for which alone money is required, but the banking institutions, the gambling dens of the Money Power, whose nefarious occupation was gone, and whose sources of robbery were cut off, while the Government stood between them and the producer, and supplied the latter with ample means of production. These were the "peculiar institutions," from one of which in Indiana Mr. McCulloch was called to Washington to place in "equal and harmonious working order again." He adds:

"The rapidity with which the Government notes can be withdrawn will depend upon the ability of the secretaries to dispose of securities. The secretary therefore respectfully *but most earnestly recommends*,
'First, That Congress declare that the compound interest notes, shall cease to be a legal tender. Second, That the secretary be author

ized to sell bonds of the United States bearing interest at a rate not exceeding 6 per cent. *for the purpose of retiring not only compound interest notes, but the United States notes.*

"*The first thing to be done is to establish a policy of contraction.*"

This, Congress established by resolution on the 18th of December, 1865.

How many of the eleven millions of producers, toiling in their shops and factories, delving in the subterranean store houses of the earth, or bending their backs to the harvest sun, petitioned Mr. McCulloch to make these suggestions to Congress on its meeting?

How many of these millions asked that the thing for which they were all toiling might be made more scarce and difficult to obtain?

How many of them prayed that instead of receiving greenbacks for their products, they might be made to pay a semi-annual gold bonus to have them destroyed?

How many of them voluntarily consented to have the value of their property depreciated one-half and the value of their products reduced? How many of them consented to be turned into the streets, their families into the poor house, a hundred thousand bankrupted—and the most fortunate among them to be taxed beyond their ability to pay—simply to conform to a system of contraction, for the benefit of whom?

Reader, do you believe a single laborer or producer, or manufacturer or a miner, a merchant or a transporter of merchandise, a farmer or a mechanic, would have voted for this measure if he had been called upon, and had known the result? Not one. Not one of the eleven millions asked for it or was even consulted in regard to it.

Outside of the eleven millions of producers is a class —two per cent. of the population—who live off of labor, controlling and gambling in its necessities. A class who "weave not neither do they spin, yet Solomon in all his glory was not arrayed like one of these."

A class who never added one farthing to the wealth of the world, who are not entitled to handle a dollar of money, never having produced its equivalent, as exempt from taxation as infants, and having to bear no more risks, burdens, or responsibilities in the affairs of the Government than the inmates of the poor house, arrogate to themselves not only the governing and law-making power, but the right to control and monopolize the most important instrument of production, with which they may gamble and win the product. During all the dark days of contraction, while the wealth products of labor were shrinking in a direct ratio with the shrinkage of the money volume, the usurer's lamps burned brighter and brigter as the purchasing capacity of his interest dollars expanded to absorb the shrinking value of labor products. As men of enterprise and production fell, the gambler rose higher and higher on the prostrate forms of his victims.

As the wrecks of productive enterprises increased, the foundations of banking institutions multiplied. As the wages of labor and prices of products diminished, the value of interest and interest obligations augmented.

As the garments of the laborer and his wife and little ones faded and fringed, those of the gambler and his household changed to purple and fine linen.

As the wolves of want and starvation gathered at the doors of enforced idleness, pomp and luxury abounded in the temples of Mammon.

Here is the proof. A prominent Iowa farmer, Hon. Samuel Sinnett, wrote, in 1878:

"The prices of some articles are eighteen per cent. lower than they were before the war. Corn has not been so low since 1845, except in 1861. Cotton not so low in twenty-three years, and mess pork, not since 1844. These prices render the farmer hopeless, destroy his energy, and dwarf his manhood until he only seeks to struggle along from year to year without trying to keep up his improvements, from the fact that all the enterprising of this class are becoming bankrupts, and his real estate is shrinking in value while he finds himself actually burdened with products that will not net him *the price of production.* At Des Moines the average price of pork (live hogs) is two dollars per hundred, corn from twelve to fifteen cents, hay from two to four dollars per ton, and other products in proportion.

"Now, I assert that none of these articles can be produced for less than fifty per cent. in advance of these prices. No farmer in the West expects to receive any interest on the capital he has invested in his farm under present prices, and as many of them are in debt, and their farms mortgaged, it is easy to perceive that ultimate ruin must soon come.

The New York *Journal of Commerce,* January 1, makes a comparison of prices in that city for a decade, with the following showing:

PRODUCTS.	1868.	1878.
Flour	$8 75 to $9 50	$3 10 to $3 50
Oats	$1 40	.34 cts.
Cotton, per lb	.16 cts.	.07 cts.
Hay, per ton	$24 00	$9 00
Mess Pork	$21 00	$7 05
Mess Beef	$32 00	$14 50
Butter	.45 cts.	.10 cts.
Cheese	.19 cts.	.8 3 7 cts.

The *Boston Advertiser* published a table of prices in that city on January 1, 1879, as compared with those of 1860, as follows:

PRODUCTS.	1860.	1879.
Mess Pork	$17 to $18	$8.50 to $9
Mess Beef	$11 05	$10 06
Lard	.13 cts.	.06 to .07 cts.
Hams	.13 cts.	7½ cts.
Corn	.70 cts.	.35 to 48 cts.

While these products have declined in value nearly one-half since the specie payment period of 1860, and their producers are the bearers of the great bulk of the tax burden, the national tax has increased from $56,054,599 in 1860, to $237,446,776 in 1878, while state, county, town and municipal taxation has at least doubled.

Under the finance system which has produced this condition of things, and which both the old political parties are pledged to perpetuate and aggravate by still more stringent legislation, what hope is there for the farmer? As low as prices are and daily shrinking, the policy of the Money Power is forcing upon the farmer competition more destructive to his interests than Chinese immigration is to the labor of the Pacific coast.

But England's policy is "cheap labor, cheap bread," and she is carrying it out in the United States through the agency of her capital in the hands of leading politicians, with as much ease as she does in India and Ireland. The policy of contraction as expressed by that eminent member and representative of the English Cobden Club, David A. Wells, in the following words, has done the work:

"Discarding all indirect methods, I would adopt what may be called the 'cremation' process, or I would have it enjoined on the secretary of the treasury to destroy by burning on a given day of every week, commencing at the earliest practicable moment, a certain amount of legal tender notes, fixing the minimum at not less than $500,000 per week."

Having portrayed the present and prospective condition of the American farmer under the Demo-Republican finance policy, and the causes which have produced, and must inevitably perpetuate if not aggravate it, let us see what effect this same policy has had upon the prosperity of that other class who reap not, neither do they spin.

During the long tedious years of ruin and bankruptcy among farmers and producers, from 1866 to 1878, William H. English, the Democratic nominee for Vice President, was President of the First National Bank of Indianapolis. Upon retiring from that trust, in 1877, he made a report to the stockholders, from which the following is an extract:

"I congratulate the officers and stockholders of our enterprise. The bank has been in operation fourteen years under my control, with a capital stock of $500,000. In the meantime, it has voluntarily returned $500,000 of capital stock back to its stockholders, besides paying them in dividends $1,496,250, part of which was in gold; and I now turn it over to you with a capital unimpaired and $327,000 of the undivided earnings on hand. To this may be added the premiums of United States bonds at present prices, amounting to $36,000, besides quite a large amount for lost or destroyed bills."

The items of profits are as follows:

Returned to stockholders, capital	$500,000
Dividends to stockholders	1,496,250
Undivided earnings	327,000
Premiums on bonds	36,000
Lost or destroyed bills	24,000
Total	$2,383,250

The New York *Commercial Advertiser* gives the accumulation of ten men and firms of that city for the year of 1879, as follows:

The Vanderbilt estate	$30,000,000
Jay Gould	15,000,000
Russel Sage	10,000,000
Sidney Dillon	10,000,000
James R. Keene	8,000,000
The First National Bank	2,000,000
Dexter, Morgan & Co	2,000,000
Three or four others, each	3,000,000
Total	$80,000,000

Not a dollar of this vast sum was produced or created by the men who accumulated it, but every penny was taken from wealth producers without a farthing's consideration. It required the labor of 400,000 men daily, for a year, to earn this amount over and above the means of their daily subsistence. Without any increase in the aggregate wealth of the country, these ten men and firms were able to rake into their coffers eighty million dollars that was produced by, and justly belonged to, other men. Through cunningly contrived schemes and systems, backed up and sustained by special legislation, a few hundred of these vampires absorb annually from production $1,000,000,000, and with each year their powers of absorption increase in a compound ratio. It is only a question of time, if their machinery is not broken up and their schemes of plunder checked, when they will possess the entire wealth of the nation, with a mortgage on society for all future increase, save a bare subsistence for the millions of toilers. The condition of Ireland and the laboring masses of England is sufficient to stimulate American toilers to throw off the yoke that is oppressing them, to break the fetters that are being riveted upon them, while they have strength to emancipate and save themselves, and before they find themselves in the helpless condition of their fellows across the sea.

All this from the neglect of farmers to see that they are honestly represented in Congress and State Legislatures.

They alone are responsible for filling Congress with lawyers and bankers.

The Congress which inaugurated the present financial policy of the Government, was made up of 250 bankers and lawyers and 22 farmers.

The Congress previous to the present, was made up of 189 bankers, 99 lawyers, 14 merchants, 13 manufacturers, 7 doctors, 1 mechanic. Farmers, *not one!* the money power having 76 majority over all others.

Who wonders that the people's interests are neglected?

What can *one mechanic* do for 40,000,000 laborers against *two hundred* non-producers whose interests are to *rob* industry?

The Government to-day represents a Money Power which occupies the Executive chair, fills all important positions in subordinate departments, and enacts all the laws.

It laughs at our boasted sovereignty, and snaps its fingers at our ballot-boxes.

It selects and puts in nomination its own tools, and deceives the people with the idea that an election is an expression of their will.

It has protected itself against the possibility of taxation by a contract with the Government before it became its creditor.

It has obligated the Government to contribute to it all the surplus increase of wealth and then destroyed the currency of the country to prevent the people from liquidating the obligations.

It has added millions of dollars to its own strength

and in a corresponding ratio weakened the people and deprived them of the means of defense.

Partisan follies have gone to seed, and labor and enterprise are reaping the harvest.

The people have loaned to their enemy the weapons of their defense. They have unlocked their doors and set thieves to guard their treasures, and now as soon as the nominations of 1880 are flashed across the continent, every cringing partisan slave rushes to lick the hand still raised to shed the remaining blood in labor's veins.

And this in a land where the majority inherit absolute sovereignty, but basely submits to be led or driven as beasts of burden under the Democratic or Republican lash in the hands of gamblers and political slave masters.

CHAPTER XII.

CONCLUSION.

THE LESSONS OF HISTORY.

Rome rose to the zenith of her glory on the wings of two thousand million dollars of fiat money, possessing little or no intrinsic value, and remained there so long as she maintained this tool of exchange, based on a per capita ratio.

It was only after her rulers, coming in possession of gold and silver, plundered from the victims of conquest; established the system of intrinsic value money on a volume of the precious metals less than $200,000,000, did her glory wane, and finally disappear in the night of the Dark Ages.

Why did she make this change? Because the owners of the precious metals saw that by limiting the money to gold and silver, they could convert their stolen trophies into an engine to rob their own people. The process of contraction was set in motion. A day was set when the public revenues were to be collected in gold and silver. The money which had made Rome what she was, was degraded by the very hand it had made strong. It began to depreciate in value. As gold and silver were scarce, prices declined. Labor was thrown out of employment. The land was filled with bankrupts, and soon became overrun with tramps and bandits. The historian says of the times:

"The people gave themselves up in despair in the fields, as beasts of burden lie down beneath their load and refuse to rise. The disintegration of society was almost complete. All public spirit, all generous emotions, all noble aspirations of man shriveled and disappeared as the volume of money shrunk, and prices fell. As men decayed wealth accumulated in the hands of the few. Not only did whole provinces become the property of one man, but usury existed in so frightful a form that even the virtuous Brutus received sixty per cent. for the use of money."

Pliney says: "These colossal fortunes which ruined Italy, were *due to the concentration of estates* through USURY, so scarce was money."

But Italy revived, and by what means? She discarded her gold and silver basis and expanded her paper currency. She arose from her sleep of a thousand years, and on the wings of her fiat credit tokens, has well nigh regained her lost glory.

She has multiplied her commerce four fold, and her railways seven fold, tunneling the Alps and the Appenines and building hundreds of miles through and over the adamantine rock of her mountains. She has set her millions of beggars and tramps to work in productive enterprise, and added hundreds of millions to the wealth of the kingdom, which is as real and permanent as though it had been produced by the aid of gold, instead of paper.

In 1797, the wars in which England was engaged, forced her to haul in her gold and silver anchors, and spread her fiat sails to the breeze. The result was her revenues rose from $115,000,000 in 1797 to $360,000,000 in 1815. At the time England suspended, her currency volume all told, including coin and paper, aggregated about $45,000,000. Under suspension, it gradually increased to $127,000,000. The effects of this expansion is expressed by Sir Archibald Allison in the following words:

"Ushered in by a combination of circumstances the most calamitous, both with reference to external security and internal industry, *it terminated in* A BLAZE OF GLORY *and flood of prosperity* which have never, since the beginning of the world, descended upon any nation."

A writer in the *North American Review*, speaking of this period, says:

"The conquests in arts and arms during the eighteen years of expansion of pure fiat credit, were without example in the history of England, and her progress in wealth and power was without a parallel in the history of the world. She won the sovereignty of the seas at Trafalgar, and the first military place in history at Waterloo. She became, during this period matchless in the possession of every incident of greatness, wealth and power."

During this period of fiat paper money, England conquered the world of commerce and expanded four fold her diversified industries. But her dangers having passed, she relapsed again into the death-damps of specie basis, cast her gold anchor, and furled her fiat sails which had wafted her to glory.

A day of resumption was set.

Contraction commenced in 1815, and wrecked fortunes marked its pathway. Money became scarce, enterprises became crippled, credits were drawn upon, debts multiplied, factories were compelled to suspend operation, men were thrown out of employment, starvation overtook the poor, bread riots ensued, and the army was increased to shoot down the famishing thousands who sought bread at the risk of their lives and liberties. Allison says:

"In hundreds of cases, from the tremendous reduction which now took place, landed estates barely sold for as much as would pay off the mortgages, and hence the owners were stripped of all, and left beggars.

"In August, 1820, *sixty thousand* starving 'rioters' assembled in Manchester, demanding bread, when they were dispersed by the troops, many of whom were shot dead."

Why did England abandon the policy which had wrought such wonderful prosperity, for the old, which brought ruin and desolation?

Because she was ruled by a fixed income class, whose annuities would bring them but half as much when prices were high, as they would when prices were low. To double the value of their incomes, they had to depress the values of everything else, and to do this, the volume of money must be diminished, and to secure such diminution, and make it permanent, the single gold standard was established in 1816, and now 30,000 men who fatten upon usury have come into possession of the soil which was then owned by 1,750,000 farmers.

After the Franco-German War, France in order to pay her $1,000,000,000 indemnity to Germany, abandoned her coin basis, and expanded her irredeemable paper to the extent of $640,000,000, which was kept at par by being honored and received by a prostrate nation, which is to-day the most prosperous in Europe.

Germany on the other hand, free from debt, and having received her indemnity from France, adopted the English system of gold basis, and is as thoroughly conquered and subjugated thereby, as was France by the victorious arms of the Prussians.

The United States presents the next lesson to the thoughtful student. From a height of prosperity, in 1866, under the same system that raised Rome and England to their most exalted positions, and that which to-day places France and Italy foremost in the rank of European prosperity, this country has fallen, and is gradually sinking to the level of those that have gone before her from the same cause. Our mines neglected, and filling with water and damps. Our shipyards silent. Our furnace fires smouldering. Our land covered with tramps, burglars and mortgages. Our prisons and alms houses filled to overflowing.

Our tax burdens increasing as values shrink and fade away.

As we had more than doubled the accumulations of two centuries during the decade from 1865 to 1875, we required double the currency the latter year that we did the former, but, instead of receiving it, we were deprived of the larger proportion of what we had in 1865.

We contracted our currency at the very time when an opposite policy was necessary to retain the equilibrium of prices, with the increasing demand for labor and products. Why did we abandon a policy that had proved so beneficial, without an evil result to detract from its merits? For the same reason that Rome, England and Germany adopted the gold basis, viz.: to depress general prices and values, that the value and purchasing power of the usurer's harvest might be enhanced and augmented so as to rob the people of the accumulations of fifteen years of unparalleled production and prosperity, and to reap the annual harvest of labor for all time to come.

THE DEMON TASK MASTER.

LUCIUS GOSS.

Why this universal wailing,
Over all this land prevailing,
This entreaty unavailing? Why this gloom and dark despair?
See the sun of hope is setting!
Man his brother is forgetting,
And a curse is slowly falling
On this land of promise rare;
And the faces are appalling,
That were once so bright and fair—
Want and misery everywhere!

Mark the toiler, sowing, reaping,
And the golden sheaves upheaping,
What a hidden monster, sweeping for his own insatiate maw,
Gathers fast and faster, faster,
Though privations and disaster
Smite the weary, sweating toiler
Till the pangs of hunger gnaw;
Never does the fierce despoiler
His rapacious grasp withdraw;
Greed so cruel knows no law.

Hear the workshop's ceaseless clatter,
Hear the workmen's footsteps patter,
When they join or quickly scatter, when to each a task is shown;
Each a burden carries, double,
Load of toil, and load of trouble;
For an iron master watches
From a secret door unknown;
From each mouth he quickly snatches
Every word and meaning tone—
He is master, here, alone.

How the pistons heave and tumble,
How the wheels do drum and rumble?
How obedient—not a grumble when those brawny arms control.
Strange, that while such puny muscle
Rules so surely all this bustle,
A more potent power, uncanny,
Rules still surer brain and soul;
Strange, indeed, the brawny many
Let a baleful power control
Wealth of brawn and brain and soul.

In the gloomy mine descending,
  Where the flickering lights are blending;
Note how close is death impending—foul his breath upon the air.
  Careless is the warning spoken,
  Scarce the delvers heed the token.

For a monster, darker, grimmer,
  Makes them madly, rashly dare,
And, through lamplight's glare and glimmer,
  Holds them fiercely, surely, there,
    With the bravery of despair.

    Go to yonder lonely garret,
    If your heart is strong to bear it,
Mark the half-bent shadow where it darks the black wall scarcely more;
    There a famished woman sitting,
    Works with patience unremitting,
With her weary, ceaseless stitching,
  Keeps the wolf just out the door;
While a demon still enriching
  Self with stealing from her store,
    Robs her pittance lower and lower.

    Is this the land where hands of labor
    Clasp the hands of toiling neighbor,
And the plowshare—not the saber—is the scepter held supreme?
    Is it here where honest toilers
    Need not fear of strong despoilers,
Since all men are free and equal?
  Ah! If things are what they seem,
This is but the bitter sequel,
  Waking of a century's dream,—
    A turning back of progress' stream.

    Shall this demon reign eternal
    O'er this blessed land fraternal?
Shall enchantment so infernal hold us ever 'neath its spell?
    No! By all the powers of heaven
    From this land he shall be driven,
Usury be hurled, unshriven,
  To the lowest depths of hell;
Then a mighty shout be given,
  Hear the hosts their voices swell,
    "LABOR CONQUERS—ALL IS WELL!"

THE END.

APPENDIX.

NOTE A. TO PAGE 133.

NATIONAL BANKS—REGULATIONS OF THE BANKING BUSINESS.

The original act required the national banks to keep on hand a certain amount of legal tender with which to redeem their notes when presented for that purpose.

SEC. 5191. Every national banking association in either of the following cities: Albany, Baltimore, Boston, Cincinnati, Chicago, Cleveland, Detroit, Louisville, Milwaukee, New Orleans, New York, Philadelphia, Pittsburgh, Saint Louis, San Francisco, and Washington, shall at all times have on hand, in lawful money of the United States, an amount equal to at least twenty-five per centum of the aggregate amount of its notes in circulation and its deposits; and every other association shall at all times have on hand an amount equal to at least fifteen per cent. of its notes in circulation and its deposits.

Act of June 20, 1874, repealed the above clauses, as follows:

SEC. 2. That section thirty-one of the "national bank act" be so amended that the several associations therein provided for *shall not hereafter be required to keep on hand any amount of money whatever by reason of the amount of their respective circulations;* but the monies required by said section to be kept at all times on hand shall be determined by the amount of deposits in all respects, as provided for in the said section.

NOTE B, TO PAGE 139.

BANK NOTES EXEMPT FROM TAXATION.

Act June 30, 1864. And all bonds, treasury notes and other obligations of the United States shall be exempt from taxation by or under State or municipal authority.

The exemption referred to in the foregoing extends to national bank currency.

Revised statutes.

SEC. 5413. The words "obligation or other security of the United States" shall be held to mean all bonds, certificates of indebtedness, national [bank] currency, coupons, United States notes, treasury notes, fractional notes, certificates of deposit, bills, checks, or drafts for money, drawn by or upon authorized officers of the United States, stamps and other representatives of value, of whatever denomination, which have been or may [be] issued under any act of Congress.

The foregoing section was amended February 18, 1875, by inserting after the word "national" in third line, the word "bank."

NOTE C, TO PAGE 245.

THE SOLDIER AND THE BONDHOLDER.

We give below, in tabulated form, the statement from Secretary Sherman of the expenses of the Government on account of the late civil war, from July 1, 1861, to June 30, 1879, inclusive:

Ordinary expenditures	$609,549,124
Expenditures growing out of the war	$6,187,243,385
Total	$6,796,792,509

The principal items of the war expenses are the following, the last six being given in round numbers:

Interest on the public debt	$1,764,256,198
Pay of two and three years volunteers	1,040,102,702
Subsistence of the army	381,417,548
Clothing of the army	345,543,880
Army transportation	336,793,885
Purchase of horses	126,672,423
Other quartermaster expenditures (in round numbers)	320,000,000
Army pensions	407,429,193
Bounties (including additional bounties under the act of 1866)	140,281,178
Refunding to states for war expenses	41,000,000
Purchase of arms for volunteers and regulars	76,000,000
Ordnance supplies	56,000,000
Expenses of assessing and collecting internal revenue	113,000,000
Expenses of national loans and currency	51,523,000
Premiums	59,738,000

According to this statement, the pay, cost of food and clothing of the volunteers amounted to $1,767,064,130, while the bondholders' interest to the date of June 30, 1879, was $1,764,256,198, and another year's interest must be added to find the amount paid to the present date.

Thus we find that the bondholders have been paid over fifty millions more for their services than the soldiers were paid for theirs.

Not only this, but the bondholders are to receive back double their principal invested—a principal which was loaned in depreciated currency to be paid back in gold or its equivalent. The soldiers' principal of health, of strength, of vigorous constitution is gone forever, and can never be repaid.—*Chicago Express*.

NOTE D, TO PAGE 50.

The following comprise all the treasury notes, legal tenders and other species of money issued by the United States during the war, from 1861 to 1865:

TREASURY NOTES OF 1861.

The act of March 2, 1861, (12 Stat. 178) authorized the issue of $35,000,000 of treasury notes, to be received in payment of all debts due the United States, including custom duties, and were redeemable at any time within ten years. Amount issued......... $35,364,450

DEMAND NOTES.

The act of July 17, 1861, (12 Stat. 259) authorized the issue of $50,000,000 of treasury notes, not bearing interest, payable on demand. The act of February 12, 1862, increased the amount authorized $10,000,000, all of which were made legal tenders by act of March, 1862. Amount issued......... $60,000,000

SEVEN THIRTIES OF 1861.

The act of July 17, 1861, (12 Stat. 259) authorized a loan of $250,000,000, part of which was to be in treasury notes, with interest at seven and three-tenths per centum per annum, payable three years after date. Amount issued......................$140,094,750

LEGAL TENDER NOTES.

The act of February 25, 1862, (12 Stat 345) authorized the issue of $150,000,000 United States notes, not bearing interest, payable to bearer. Those notes to be a legal tender, except for *interest* on the public debt and duties on imports. Act of July 11, 1862, authorized an additional $150,000,000 of these notes. Act of March 3, 1863, (12 Stat. 710) an additional $150,000,000. Of this class of notes there were issued...$915,420,031

(See report Secretary of Treasury.)

CERTIFICATES OF INDEBTEDNESS.

The act of March 1, 1862, (12 Stat. 352) authorized the issue of certificates of indebtedness (got up in the form of money) to public creditors, who might elect to receive them, to bear interest at the rate of six per cent. per annum. The act of May 17, 1862, (12 Stat. 370) authorizing the issue of these certificates in payment of disbursing officer's checks. Interest and principal payable in lawful money. Amount issued..................................$561,753,241

FRACTIONAL CURRENCY.

Total amount authorized.............. $50,000,000

ONE YEAR NOTES.

Act of March 3, 1863, (12 Stat. 710) authorized the issue of $400,000,000 treasury notes, with interest not to exceed six per cent., redeemable in three years, principal and interest payable in greenbacks, and to be *legal tender to the extent that greenbacks were.* Amount issued.................. $44,520,000

TWO YEAR NOTES.

The act of March 3, (12 Stat. 710) authorized the issue of $400,000,000 treasury notes, interest six per cent., principal and interest payable in greenbacks, after ten years, and to be legal tender at their face. Amount issued..$166,400,000

COIN CERTIFICATES.

The Fifth Section of the act of March 3, 1863, (12 Stat. 711) authorized the deposit of gold coin and bullion with the treasurer, and the issue of certificates therefor, in denominations the same as United States notes; *also authorized the issue of these certificates in payment of interest on the public debt* and directs their *receipt in payment of duties on imports.* Amount issued....$562,776,400

COMPOUND INTEREST NOTES.

The act of March 3, 1863, (12 Stat. 709) authorized the issue of $400,000,000 treasury notes, with six per cent. compound interest, payable in lawful money, after three years, *and to be a legal tender at their face value.* Amount issued.................$263,595,440

SEVEN THIRTIES OF 1864 AND 1865.

The act of June 30, 1864, (13 Stat. 218) authorized the issue of $200,000,000 *treasury notes* of not less than $10 each, payable at not more than three years from date, or redeemable at any time after three years, with interest at not exceeding seven and three-tenths per cent. per annum.

The act of March 3, 1865, (13 Stat. 408) authorized a loan of $600,000,000, and the issue therefor of bonds, *or treasury notes*, bearing seven and three-tenths per cent. interest per annum.

These were all issued in the form of treasury notes, to be paid out as money to soldiers and other creditors of the Government. Amount issued......................$829,992,500

The act declares that such of the seven-thirties as shall be made payable, principal and interest at maturity, shall be a legal tender to the same extent as United States notes. This was the last legal-tender act of Congress.

QUESTIONS AND ANSWERS.

During the preparation of this volume the following questions have been asked, which I insert with their appropriate answers:

1. What is the difference between the old United States bank and its branches, and the National banks and branches?
2. Is the Government bound for the redemption of national bank currency?
3. How old are our national banks?
4. Were the bonds by express terms of the law payable in coin prior to the credit strengthening act?

5. What amount of gold and silver is there in the United States available for redemption?
6. Did the credit strengthening act specially bind the Government to pay the bonds in coin?
7. What proportion of the bonds are held by foreigners?
8. What is the sum of the bonded debt?
9. What are the Government's resources, or available means, to pay the bonds?
10. What is the amount of coin and bullion in the world available for money?
11. Can the bonded debt be paid before maturity?
12. If the bonds remain unpaid, how long will it take for the interest to absorb the wealth of the nation?

1. The old United States bank and twenty-six branches had a capital of but $35,000,000, and its notes were redeemable in coin. President Jackson vetoed the bill to re-charter it on the grounds that it was a dangerous money power, controlling both Congress and the executive, and even local elections and State legislatures. Not only this, Jackson held to the greenback doctrine that the paper money of the country, as well as coin, should be issued by the Government, and instead of being based on coin, "the paper money should be based upon *the faith and revenues of the nation.*"

The national banks have an aggregate capital of about $500,000,000, and there are 2,060 of them. Their power for evil is as much greater than the old banks as are their numbers and combined capital. We have no one Jackson able to crush the monster, but we have a Greenback army of Jacksons who will try to do it.

2. The Government holds United States bonds to indemnify holders of national currency against loss. If these bonds sell for enough to redeem the notes of broken national banks, the Government will redeem them, and not otherwise.

3. The first national bank chartered was Jay Cooke & Co.'s in the City of Washington, about the beginning of 1864.

4. No war bonds except about $270,000,000 of 10–40s were by the terms of the law expressly payable in coin —the balance in lawful money except the interest, which was payable in coin.

5. Not to exceed $150,000,000 of coin is held by the banks and United States treasury for redemption purposes.

6. The credit strengthening act declared all the bonds payable "*in coin or its equivalent.*"

7. The bonds are used as an international currency by the large American and European traders. Most of them, however, are held by John Sherman's syndicate, who are New York partners of London and German bankers and capitalists.

8. The sum of the bonded debt, August 1, was $1,901,716,110.

9. The Government's only resources or means to pay the public debt, are its revenues from taxation, and the issue of its own legal tenders. Heretofore it has paid one debt by making another. It paid off the 5.20 bonds in 4 per cents., worth a trifle more than gold.

10. The amount of coin and bullion in the world is estimated by Fawcett, as follows:

Gold	$1,975,550,000
Silver	1,800,000,000
Total	$3,775,550,000

11. It can be paid any time the Government has the legal tender to liquidate it, and if such legal tender is refused, interest may legally cease.

12. The wealth of the nation is estimated at $27,000,000,000. Calling the public debt $2,000,000,000 at 4 per cent. compounded according to bank custom and calculation, it would amount in forty-eight years to $27,-

$600,000,000, or $800,000,000 more than the entire wealth of the nation.

 1. When did the destruction of greenbacks (by burning) commence?
 2. When did it cease; from what cause, and how much was destroyed?
 3. Were bonds ever bought from the Government for greenbacks other than giving dollar for dollar? Hard money men tell us that when gold was 2.85 it took $2.85 of greenbacks to buy $1 of bonds.
 4. Could the bonds be called in immediately and paid off without breaking faith with the holders as to the time they were to run?
 5. Were the 10.40 bonds sold for greenbacks, or exchanged for other bonds?
 6. How much gold has been paid out of the treasury for redemption purposes?

1. The law authorizing the contraction and destruction of the greenbacks was passed April 12, 1866, and the process commenced immediately thereafter.

2. The act of contraction, as far as greenbacks were concerned, was repealed in January, 1868, after $70,736,630 of legal tenders had been destroyed. It was brought about by the force of public sentiment. Aside from the legal tenders, over $1,500,000,000 of treasury notes used as currency were destroyed.

3. When gold was 2.85 and greenbacks worth less than 40 cents in gold on the dollar, greenbacks were convertible into bonds at par.

4. If the public good required the immediate payment of the bonds in greenbacks, or any other kind of money at the disposal of the Government, it would not be so great a breach of faith as it was for the Government to unconditionally abolish slavery, without consideration to the owners, after the institution had been supported for years by the laws and the constitution of the country. That institution became a public evil, threatening the life of the nation and the liberties of the people. But the slaves were the private property of individuals, ac-

quired according to the laws of the land. Should our public debt, the bonds and bondholders, become a source of danger to American liberty, and sorely oppressive to American industry, the Government has the same right even to repudiate the debt, absolutely, that it had to confiscate the slaves and repudiate the institution of slavery.

5. The 10.40 bonds were authorized to be, and were sold for lawful money (greenbacks) of the United States, or for any of the certificates of indebtedness or treasury notes outstanding.

6. A little more than $5,000,000 of gold has been paid out for the redemption of greenbacks, according to the last treasury report, since January, 1879, while the interest we are paying on the borrowed gold held for redemption purposes, costs about $5,200,000 a year.

THE CREDIT STRENGTHENING ACT.

Congressman Van H. Manning, of Mississippi, in a recent speech, stated that the credit strengthening act, changing the currency bonds to coin bonds, was a contract between the Government on the one hand, and the bondholders on the other; that the bondholders agreed to make a reduction of 2 per cent. in the interest if the Government would change their currency bonds to coin bonds, and make them payable thirty years after date; that the 2 per cent. reduction was the consideration given by the bondholders in the transaction, and that this consideration made the act binding in law, and that there was no alternative by which we could relieve ourselves of the bonds under thirty years without amending the constitution, and no power in this Government that could force the payment of the bonds sooner, not even in gold, without changing the constitution. Will you give an opinion on this subject?

The credit strengthening act was passed in March, 1869. An attempt was made to pass it during the session of 1867-8, but failed. During its pending, a presidential nomination and election took place. The Democratic party nominated Horatio Seymour on a platform that opposed the payment of currency obligations in coin. The Republican party nominated U. S. Grant on the urgent solicitation and petition of forty capitalists of New York City, who represented in the aggregate about $500,000,000. In regard to the political fugling at this time, and the "contract" which Mr. Van H. Manning claims was entered into between the Government and the bondholders, a cotemporaneous writer says:

"The Rothschilds were in possession of several hundred millions of 5.20 bonds, purchased at about 60 cents on the dollar, or less, and were particularly interested. Their agent, August Belmont, who secured the position of chairman of the Democratic National Committee, was instructed by Baron James Rothschilds as early as March 13, 1868, that unless the Democratic party went in for paying the 5 20 bonds in gold, *it must be defeated*. The first step was to have the National Convention held in New York City. It accordingly convened there on the 4th of July, 1868. Belmont and his satalites were unable to control the convention, at least in the matter of the platform, and it declared that all obligations against the Government not expressly payable in coin should be paid in lawful money of the United States. Belmont owned a large interest in The New York *World*, the leading Democratic paper of the country, which, on the 15th of October, came out in a double-leaded editorial denouncing Seymour as unavailable and unfit, and advised his withdrawal. This so demoralized the Democracy that Grant had an easy walk over the course."

Before this time, John Sherman, O. P. Morton, and other leading Republican Senators had opposed coin payment of the bonds. After Grant's election they advocated it, or were silent on the subject. In his inaugural speech Grant warned his party *that no repudiator of one farthing of the public debt would be trusted in public place.*" He immediately called an extra session of Congress. The first bill presented, the first bill passed, and the first act approved, was the credit strengthening act. Not a word was uttered in Congress or out, about a reduction of interest and refunding of the 6 per cent. bonds into 4 per cents. for nearly two years afterwards. If there was such a contract there must be a record of it. It was never made public, never acted upon in Congress, never made known to the people. The only contract ever made with the bondholders was that political contract of 1868, between Grant and the Republican leaders on the one side, and Belmont and other Democratic bondholders on the other, that if the former would pledge themselves to pass and carry out the credit strengthening act if elected, the other would defeat their own party, and secure the election of the former. That was the only contract. Grant's two terms, and John Sherman's continuation at the head of the finance department, was the Republican consideration, and gold payment of the 5.20 bonds was the consideration on the part of the bondholding Democracy. The contract was a fraud in its conception, its execution a violation of the constitution, and constitutes one of the most damnable acts of political corruption, and the most villainous betrayal of public trust, ever practiced upon an unsuspecting and confiding constituency; and, when fully understood, it will brand with eternal infamy every name in connection with the disreputable transaction.

THE $400,000,000 RESTRICTION.

Will you give an opinion on the following Chicago *Tribune* editorial?

"Under our constitution the power to make paper money in time of peace a legal tender does not exist. A majority of the Supreme Court sanctioned the issue of such paper during the war as an act of imperious national necessity. It was also decided that, the necessity having passed, the amount of such paper was limited to the sum originally designated, $400,000,000.

"There is no constitutional power on the part of the Government to increase the legal tender paper beyond this limit, and, if this 'war-money' be withdrawn, there is no power to make a new issue of paper of that kind. Herein is the wide difference between our Government and all others. In France, England and Germany, and all other nations, the power to make paper a legal tender is ample, and can be exercised at any time, as it is now in England."

The *Tribune's* assumption that no power exists under our constitution to make paper money, in time of peace, a legal tender is without warrant in law, logic or common sense. It admits that all other nations possess this power, and that herein is the wide difference between our Government and all others. If all other nations possess this power, where did they get it? Did the monarchies of the old world absorb all of this power, leaving none for the republics of the new?

The monetary prerogative is a sovereign attribute. In this country the power to make anything legal tender rested with the people at large, in common with all other powers of sovereignty. By the constitution the people delegated to Congress all the power they possessed over the money question. The Supreme Court decided that if Congress had not the power to decide what should be legal tender in this country, the power was annihilated. The court further decided that Congress was not only authorized, but required to issue paper legal tenders when any emergency should require it, whether that emergency be war, famine, financial depression, or any exportation, or destruction of the money volume, and that Congress, and not the court was the proper judge of the necessity or emergency. The court also decided that Congress had a clear right to adopt *any measure* necessary to carry out any of the objects of the Government, and not specifically denied or forbidden by the constitution.

The limit of $400,000,000 was not passed upon by the court. It made no reference to the volume. The first legal tender act limited the volume to $150,000,000.

The second extended it to $300,000,000. The volume was afterwards increased to $432,000,000 greenbacks proper, and over $1,000,000,000 interest-bearing legal tender treasury notes.

The $400,000,000 limit was an act of Congress passed June 30, 1864, near the close of the war. It provided for the issue of $400,000,000 legal tender 7.30 treasury notes to be redeemed in three years, and also provided that the permanent volume of United States notes should never exceed $400,000,000. Congress had the same authority to limit the volume to four thousand millions, that it had to fix the sum at four hundred millions. And it has the same authority to change or enlarge the volume that it has to contract or extinguish it. The Constitution confers upon Congress all the power over the money question that exists in sovereignty. The people yielded up to that body all the power they possessed over that element in regard to legal tender. Whatever any power below heaven can do, in regard to legal tender, Congress can perform under the constitution. It is false, and a national libel, to say that our Government does not possess as much power to protect its citizens as the monarchies of the old world. It is absurd to claim that Congress has power to issue paper legal tender to protect itself, while it is denied the right to make such issues to protect the people. "Congress shall have power to coin money"—it matters not whether it is demanded for war or for commerce. The constitution does not specify the emergencies which shall warrant the making of paper legal tenders. Congress is the sole judge of the necessity. The court has so decided; if the emergency should come in time of peace, the Government has the same right to issue them as if the emergency was war. If Congress can make paper legal tender for war, it can for peace. If it can make $400,000,000, it can make $4,000,000,000. If it has any power over the quantity or quality of legal tender, it has all power, and it is its own judge of the necessity and extent of its exercise.

THE GREENBACK.

"What constitutes the value of the greenback?"

Its value consists in the service it is capable of performing.

"Suppose a man receives a hundred dollar greenback from the Government for a mule, the Government has received a hundred dollars of intrinsic value, but where does the man get his value?"

By doing as the Government did, give it in exchange for a hundred dollars' worth of other property that he may need, that some other man has to spare.

"Where will No. 2 get his value?"

By repeating the operation with some other man.

"In the end, will not the last man who receives it be short a hundred dollars?"

No; for the last man who receives it is the Government's tax-gatherer. It returns to the party who first issued it, and received full value of it. It has made the financial circuit, and every man who received it in exchange for a hundred dollars of intrinsic value he did not need, has received for it a hundred dollars of intrinsic value he did need. Every hand it has passed through has been accommodated, no loss has been sustained, no expense has been incurred by the Government or the people in interest to detract from the value of the property exchanged, in short it has performed all the service without cost that ten gold eagles could have performed at an expense of a hundred dollars and interest.

"I see that so long as it can be made to keep up the circuit, it is superior to coin, or money of intrinsic value, but may not loss of confidence stop it in its course, and prevent it from making the circuit, and thereby subject the man who last receives it to loss?"

Its legal tender qualities will perpetuate confidence and keep it moving on its course homeward.

"What constitutes that quality called legal tender?"

It is a solemn compact by all the people of the nation; expressed by their chosen representatives, and approved by their executive, that to enable it to keep in motion on its circuit, so as not to stop on the hands of any member of society, each shall receive of the other for all debts dues and taxes of every nature and description, at its full face value, and unless a law be passed invalidating this contract, confidence is perpetuated by thus perpetuating its services and offices.

"What are the advantages of this currency over bank notes?"

1. It is within the control of our own people, while bank currency may be entirely in the control of aliens, foreigners and enemies.

2. It costs nothing but the printing of it, while bank currency costs its face at the start, and from 4 to 6 per cent. per annum to maintain it.

3. It is legal tender between man and man, which bank notes are not.

4. Its redemption is always sure under the compact of legal tender, both between the members of society and between them and their Government, while bank note redemption may be only in greenbacks, and even for this the banks are not required to keep on hand a dollar of reserve for that purpose.

Should they fail, the Government has promised to redeem them in time, which might cause much delay, inconvenience, and even a heavy loss if the money were necessary to make legal tender payment.

"Has coin any advantages over greenbacks as a domestic currency?"

Not any, but many disadvantages.

In fact it should never be used as a medium of exchange except in the form of bullion to pay foreign balances.

It is both expensive and inconvenient, and performs the service of money no better than greenbacks, and is liable to be exported in large quantities, at a time our own industries need it most, thereby endangering money amines, panics and ruinous financial disturbances.

THE INCREASE OF DEBT.

"Have the vast debts of the world more than doubled during the last twenty-five years in consequence of extravagance and over-production of the laboring class, as is charged?"

The increase of debt has grown out of the extravagance of despots, and the over-production of fools to submit to it.

As men are but children of a larger growth, so kings and rulers are but men of larger powers. Each class has its sports. The child chases the butterfly and robs the bird's nest. The man delights in the fox and rabbit chase, the horse race and cock fight, while kings and rulers stake their realms on games and ten pins in which the balls used are made of cast iron, and pins of men.

In these sports, those pins that are knocked down are buried, while those that remain are compelled to pay the expenses and foot the bills on both sides.

Let us for a moment consider the costs of these extravagant sports for the last twenty-five years.

From carefully compiled official statistics of the various nations, we gather the following facts which include in addition to troops slain in battle, a portion of the deaths occasioned by the ravages of war:

1. Lives lost:

Crimean war (1852 to 1857)	750,000
Italian war (1859)	45,000
Schleswig-Holstein	3,000
American civil war	500,000
Prussia, Austria and Italy (1866)	45,000
Mexico, China, Morocco, Paraguay	65,000
Franco-German (1870-75)	215,000
Bulgaria and Armenia (1876-77)	25,000
Total	1,648,000

2. Cost:

Crimean war	£340,000,000
Italian war (1859)	60,000,000
American civil war (north)	940,000,000
American civil war (south)	460,000,000
Schleswig-Holstein	7,000,000
Austria and Prussia (1866)	66,000,000
Mexico, Morocco and Paraguay	40,000,000
Franco-German	500,000,000
Total	£3,813,000,000

This reduced to dollars is $19,065,000,000.

This vast sum of over nineteen thousand million dollars added to the people's burdens within the last twenty-five years is enough to stagger the enterprise of the world for the next century. To bear it, and to meet its annual interest, requires the co-operation of every hand of labor and resource of wealth.

To pay off these enormous debts and to meet the annual interest with no other medium of exchange but that based upon the limited and diminishing quantity of gold and silver in the world, will enslave and impoverish every soul on earth except the holders of these debts, who, through them, will be made the owners of the globe and the perpetual rulers of men.

www.ingramcontent.com/pod-product-compliance
Lightning Source LLC
Chambersburg PA
CBHW030819230426
43667CB00008B/1289